THE HOLY SPIRIT IN THE LIFE OF THE CHURCH

THE HOLY SPIRIT IN THE LIFE OF THE CHURCH

FROM BIBLICAL TIMES TO THE PRESENT

Edited by
Paul D. Opsahl

AUGSBURG Publishing House • Minneapolis

THE HOLY SPIRIT IN THE LIFE OF THE CHURCH

MANUFACTURED IN THE UNITED STATES OF AMERICA

Contents

Appendix A

Appendix B

Preface

The essays and Appendix A of this volume represent the first phase of a major study project conducted by the Division of Theological Studies of the Lutheran Council in the USA and dealing with the Holy Spirit and his manifestations in the world today. This first phase, a reexamination of the doctrine of the Holy Spirit and its relevance for contemporary theology, consisted of four national conferences, each involving 20-25 pastors and theological professors: November 22-25, 1974, at Wartburg Seminary, Dubuque, Iowa; April 25-27, 1975, at Lutheran Theological Seminary, Columbus, Ohio; October 24-26, 1975, near Chicago; and April 30-May 2, 1976, at Wartburg Seminary.[1] Most of the papers commissioned for this study are revised and printed in this volume.

In authorizing publication of this material, the Standing Committee of the Division of Theological Studies was not offering an official statement on the subject. Their hope is that these materials may be of help to Lutherans in the United States in rethinking the place and importance of the Holy Spirit in Lutheran theology and that they may help Christians give attention to crucial issues in the faith and life of today's church.[2]

The study opened with a presentation by Gerhard Krodel, formerly professor of New Testament at Lutheran Theological Seminary at Philadelphia and now dean at the Lutheran Theological Seminary at Gettysburg, on biblical foundations for the doctrine of the Spirit, notably as set forth in the Old Testament, the Synoptic Gospels, and Acts.

7

Edgar Krentz, professor of New Testament formerly at Concordia Seminary, St. Louis, and now at Christ Seminary—Seminex, St. Louis, dealt with Pauline and Johannine literature.

In surveying the doctrine of the Holy Spirit in Christian thought, William Rusch, associate executive director of the LC/USA Division of Theological Studies, covered the early and medieval periods. Bernard Holm, professor of biblical and historical theology at Wartburg Seminary, continued with the treatment of the Holy Spirit in the Reformation and modern periods.

Warren Quanbeck, professor of systematic theology at Luther Theological Seminary, St. Paul, and Harold Ditmanson, professor of religion at St. Olaf College, Northfield, Minnesota, raised issues on the role of the Holy Spirit in contemporary theology. Olaf Hansen, also a professor of systematic theology at Luther Seminary, analyzed one approach to the doctrine of the Holy Spirit, "Spirit-Christology."

Even though the focus of the study was intended to be biblical, historical, and doctrinal, the conference planners wanted these deliberations to take place in light of present day developments, including neo-Pentecostalism. Therefore, even at the initial meeting, there were presentations on the church and the charismatic movement. The essay by Karlfried Froehlich, professor of church history at Princeton Theological Seminary, was on biblical and confessional aspects of the charismatic movement.

Four Lutheran "charismatic" pastors and teachers had been included in the study process as participants from the outset. Desire was expressed more and more within the entire group to consider together certain theological and pastoral problems relating to charismatic manifestations in the church. The third and fourth conferences were devoted largely to dialogue and to the production of the document which appears in this volume as Appendix A.

To offer the reader an indication of the kind of study on neo-Pentecostalism which has been done within each of the church bodies participating in the Lutheran Council, the appendixes include documentation from The American Lutheran Church, the Lutheran Church in America, and The Lutheran Church-Missouri Synod. A brief bibliography of documents arising from within other churches is also appended.

Gratitude must be expressed to David W. Lotz, Washburn Professor of Church History at Union Theological Seminary, New York City, for valuable assistance in the editorial process.

The essays are the responsibility of their authors and do not claim to represent consensus on the part of all participants, nor do they carry the endorsement of the Lutheran Council Division of Theological Studies. The essayists, participants, and division hope that teachers, pastors, and laity will find these materials of value for their own study and discussion.

> PAUL D. OPSAHL
> Executive Director
> Division of Theological Studies
> Lutheran Council in the USA

Notes

1. The following participants, unless otherwise indicated, attended the four study conferences, (1) November 22-25, 1974; (2) April 25-27, 1975; (3) October 24-26, 1975; (4) April 30-May 2, 1976: Robert Bertram (2, 3), Paul Bretscher, Joseph Burgess, Larry Christenson, Harold Ditmanson, Karlfried Froehlich (2, 3), Eric Gritsch, Olaf Hansen (2, 3, 4), Mark Hillmer (2, 3, 4), Bernard Holm, Horace Hummel, Richard Jensen, Theodore Jungkuntz, Fred Kramer (1), Thomas Kraabel, Edgar Krentz (1, 2, 4), Gerhard Krodel (1, 2, 3), David Lotz (1), Lyman Lundeen (1), Paul Opsahl, Warren Quanbeck (1, 2, 3), William Rusch, Edwin Schick, Robert Schultz, Trygve Skarsten (1, 2), Howard Tepker (1, 4), Robert Tobias (1), Carl Volz (1, 2, 3).

2. Cf. Minutes of the Division of Theological Studies for March 17-18, 1977, pp. 3-4: "In authorizing 'The Holy Spirit in the Life of the Church' for publication, the Standing Committee of the Division of Theological Studies of the Lutheran Council in the U.S.A. is not offering an official statement on the subject, but hopes that these materials may be of help to Lutherans in the United States in rethinking the place and importance of the Holy Spirit in Lutheran theology, and may help Christians give attention to crucial issues in the faith and life to today's church."

Gerhard Krodel

The Functions of the Spirit in the Old Testament, the Synoptic Tradition, and the Book of Acts [1]

I. The Spirit of God in the Old Testament

The Hebrew word *ruah* as well as the Greek word *pneuma* can mean wind, breath of air, breath of the mouth, breath of life, Spirit of God, and spirit of man. It can be used to designate an angel, demon, or the spirit of man after death. When we inquire about the Old Testament understanding of the Spirit, we receive neither a theological definition of the Spirit of God, nor a pneumatology which could logically embrace all statements about the Spirit of God. Old Testament thought is enmeshed in concrete experiences and is expressed in a diversity of historically conditioned traditions. Hence we can indicate only some of the more important aspects of the wind, breath, and Spirit of God which are found in the Old Testament.

A. From Yahweh's storehouses in heaven come rain, hail, snow, and wind (Job 38:22; Psalm 135:7; Jeremiah 10:13; 51:16). Yahweh's *wind* can bring drought and destruction by parching the land (Psalm 103:16), but his wind can also bring clouds and the rain which revitalizes the land (1 Kings 18:45). When God sends forth his life-giving breath, he renews the "face of the ground" (Psalm 104:30). The distinction between a good wind and a destructive wind appears in the distinction between the Spirit as divine power bringing deliverance to Israel from its enemies (Judges 3:10; 6:34; 11:29, etc.), and an evil

10

spirit which also comes from Yahweh causing dissension (Judges 9:23) or moving Saul to attempt to murder David (1 Samuel 19:9). God can put a lying spirit into the mouth of false prophets (1 Kings 22:21-23). He can send a spirit of confusion which makes Egypt stagger like a "drunken man in his vomit" (Isaiah 19:14) and, according to Isaiah, the Lord poured out "a spirit of deep sleep" even over his own people, Israel. In his wrath God can send a spirit which brings disaster. The Old Testament does not know a power of evil which is independent of God, though simultaneously men are held responsible for their actions.

B. God's *ruah* eventually was also understood as *creative force*. "By the word of the Lord the heavens were made and all their host by the *ruah* of his mouth" (Psalm 33:6). The sovereignty of Yahweh would not permit a pantheistic interpretation of the world, where the Spirit of God functions as world soul or as the divine rational principle of the cosmos. The Spirit of God finds his expression in the word of God which commands and it is done. In the creation narrative of the priestly writer, the *ruah* of God was moving over the primeval waters of chaos, indicating that God's creative activity through his word was about to begin (Genesis 1:2). In the earlier Yahwistic narrative, God breathed into Adam's nostrils "the breath *(nesamah)* of life and man became a living being" (Genesis 2:7). In the priestly texts of Genesis 6:17 and 7:15 *ruah* becomes the equivalent to *nesamah*. Hence Job can confess: "The Spirit of God has made me, and the breath of the Almighty gives me life" (Job 33:4). If God withdraws his spirit or breath, all flesh must perish (Job 34:14f.). The animal kingdom is also brought into being through the same principle of life (Genesis 6:17; 7:15, 22). The mystery of life which is expressed by the notion of God's *ruah* breathed into man does not lead to the idea of the immortality of man's spirit or soul in the Old Testament, but it underscores that man is nothing but dust apart from God's *ruah*. Life remains *his* property and not man's inherent possession. "When thou takest away their breath they die and return to their dust. When thou sendest forth thy spirit, they are created" (Psalm 104:29f.).

C. But life is more than being alive. *Mental abilities* and craftsmanship, the arts and poetry, are also understood to be the result of God's creative power. Hence the phrase "filled with the Spirit of God" can

mean to have "ability and intelligence," "knowledge and all craftsmanship" (Exodus 31:3; 35:31). An enlightened attitude, understanding
and wisdom can likewise be perceived as the presence of God's spirit
in man (Daniel 6:3).

The notion of *the presence of God's Spirit* gained importance after
the exile. All of life should be lived out of the power of God's present
Spirit. In the long development of the wisdom traditions, the Spirit of
God now becomes the force which illuminates and guides the individual's mind. "It is the spirit in a man, the breath of the Almighty
that makes him understand" and "constrains" him (Job 32:8, 18). God
"pours out . . . his Spirit onto those who fear the Lord and seek wisdom" (Proverbs 1:23). However, the spirit of man, entrusted to him
by God can be misdirected. "Take heed to your spirit," says Malachi
2:15, "and let none be faithless to the wife of his youth." "Blessed is
the man . . . in whose spirit there is no deceit" (Psalm 32:2).

The presence of God's Spirit means forgiveness of sin, life and salvation. The psalmist therefore prays: "Create in me a clean heart, O
God, and put a new and steadfast spirit within me. Cast me not away
from your presence and take not your Holy Spirit from me . . . but
uphold me with a willing spirit" (Psalm 51:10-12). God's Holy Spirit
is understood in this Psalm as God's presence, the power which trans-
forms a sinful heart and directs man's spirit to God. To the disillu-
sioned people after the exile, Haggai called: "Take courage . . . I am
with you, says the Lord . . . My Spirit abides among you; fear not"
(2:4-5). Thus postexilic writers also regard Yahweh's Spirit as his
agent which had been present with Israel in the past and had led
Israel in its exodus and its journey through the wilderness. Though
Israel "rebelled and grieved his holy Spirit," the "Spirit of the Lord
gave them rest" (Isaiah 63:10-14; Nehemiah 9:20, 30; Zechariah 7:12).
And this promise of the presence of God's Spirit among the covenant
people becomes the pledge for a future fulfillment of worldwide
dimensions, when Yahweh overturns the kingdoms of this world "not by
might nor by power, but by my Spirit, says the Lord" (Zechariah 4:6;
6:1-8). In the meantime, God guarantees that his Spirit and his words
shall endure with his people (Isaiah 59:21; cf. Nehemiah 9:20, 30).

D. Before the belief arose that God's Spirit is his saving and judging
presence among his people, there existed an earlier idea which held

that Yahweh's Spirit manifested itself as *extraordinary ecstatic power* in individuals, be they charismatic leaders in war or prophets. Human actions which are inexplicable indicate the operation of the Spirit of God which empowers men to act beyond their normal capabilities. During the period of the judges and the early monarchy we hear that the Spirit of God moved some specially selected men and women to perform heroic deeds of deliverance in times of national crises and war. "The Spirit of the Lord took possession of Gideon and he sounded the trumpet" of war (Judges 6:34). The Spirit "leaped upon" Samson, who tore a lion asunder and later killed thirty men of Askelon (Judges 14:6, 19). The Spirit turned King Saul "into another man" (1 Samuel 10:6) so that, in a state of ecstasy, he begins to prophesy among a band of prophets (1 Samuel 10:10), stripping off his clothing and falling naked to the ground (1 Samuel 19:24).

This extraordinary divine power can carry a prophet miraculously from one place to another (1 Kings 18:12; 2 Kings 2:16). It produced prophetic, ecstatic utterances (Numbers 11:17, 25; 24:2; 1 Samuel 10:6, 10; 19:20, 23; 2 Samuel 23:2; 1 Kings 22:24; 2 Kings 2:9). The prophetic message "is sent" by the spirit of God (Zechariah 7:12). Likewise visions, auditions, and the performance of miracles are the result of possession by the spirit. Hence a prophet is also called "a man of the spirit" (Hosea 9:7). Anecdotes are told about his divine powers. Meal and oil are miraculously multiplied, dead men become alive, poisoned food becomes innocuous, bad water is turned into good, iron is made to float, to be buried in a prophet's grave is desirable, and Elijah's mantle possesses supernatural power (1 Kings 13:31; 17:9ff.; 2 Kings 1:10; 2:8, 14; 4:4ff., 42ff.; 5:27; 6:5ff., 18; 13:14ff., 21). Obviously many of these anecdotes contain features of primitive magic. However, the chief function of the prophet is proclamation, and miracles merely indicate that the word of God has effective power, bringing about what is announced (cf. Jeremiah 13:1-11).

E. To be grasped by the Spirit of Yahweh was a temporary endowment, not a permanent possession because Yahweh's Spirit is not at man's disposal. The Spirit departed when a task was accomplished. But it should also be noted that in some traditions the Spirit of God appears as a *permanent* possession and can even be transferred from Moses to elders, or from Elijah to Elisha (Numbers 11:17, 25; 2 Kings

2:9, 15). What is equally important is that in certain traditions the Spirit of God became institutionalized in the office of the king (1 Samuel 16:13).

We do not know how widespread the notions were in Israel concerning the transfer of the spirit from the prophetic leader to his disciple, but such notions, together with the idea of the institutionalization of the spirit in the royal office and the ecstatic manifestations of many prophets, could explain the curious phenomenon that the great prophets, beginning with Amos, generally did not base their prophetic authority on the Spirit of God, even though they were concerned about establishing their legitimacy as messengers of Yahweh (Amos 1; Isaiah 6; Jeremiah 1).

In Amos the *ruah* of Yahweh is not mentioned at all. In Hosea, only once (9:7), in an aside made by other people. Micah 3:8 is probably a later addition. Neither Isaiah nor Jeremiah mentions receiving the Spirit of God as an authorization and equipment for their prophetic task. Jeremiah does not speak of the Spirit of God at all. In Nahum and Zephaniah this concept, "the Spirit of Yahweh" does not occur and the same holds true for Leviticus (P), Obadiah, and some other Old Testament books. It may well be true as Walter Eichrodt [2] and Sigmund Mowinckel [3] and others have argued that the great reforming prophets reacted against the appeal to divine inspiration made by popular prophets. Perhaps in the minds of the classical prophets the *ruah* held magical or wild orgiastic, ecstatic connotations. Or it could be that "the concept of the spirit was a characteristic of North Israelite prophecy" as Gerhard von Rad suggests.[4]

Isaiah and Jeremiah speak of "the hand" of Yahweh which came upon them and seized them (Isaiah 8:11 and Jeremiah 1:9), placing them under permanent divine constraint. They emphasize not their own visionary state of mind, which is temporary, but their permanent mission and God's personal address, "the word," coming to the prophet when and where it pleases God. The notion of the word of God coming to the prophet expresses the immediacy of the content of revelation much more forcefully than any appeal to inspiration as foundation of revelation could do. What was decisive to the great prophets of the eighth and seventh centuries was not their own inspiration, but hearing God's word and perceiving his counsel and will. Here lies the distinction between them and the false prophets of their time who "teach lies" and "err in visions" and are "confused with wine" (Isaiah 9:15; 28:7; Jeremiah 28; cf. Ezekiel 13:3).

The exilic prophets, Deutero- and Trito-Isaiah, as well as Ezekiel and others following them, again regarded the spirit as the basis of their prophecy (Isaiah 48:16; 61:1). Ezekiel attributed it both to "the hand" of God and "the Spirit" of God (3:14; 11:5, 24; 37:1). It would seem that for him Yahweh's hand and his spirit are synonymous. For him the spirit is also the power which miraculously lifts him up and transports him to different places (3:12; 8:3) and he, more than Isaiah and Jeremiah, dwells upon the fantastic visions which he experienced.

F. The prophetic hope for God's ultimate triumph assigned to the Spirit an *eschatological function*. In the messianic age, the Spirit will come in a new fullness, creating life and righteousness. For Isaiah "the Spirit of God will rest upon" the messianic king, endowing him with extraordinary power, insight, and wisdom, so that he can rule in righteousness and faithfulness over a paradise restored (Isaiah 11:2-9). In Deutero-Isaiah, God says of his chosen servant: "I have put my Spirit upon him, he shall bring forth justice to the nations . . . a bruised reed he will not break and a dimly burning wick he will not quench . . . he will faithfully bring forth justice" upon all the earth "and the coastlands wait for his law" (Isaiah 42:1-4). Not only shall the ideal eschatological ruler be endowed with the Spirit, but God shall also pour his Spirit upon his people (Isaiah 32:15; 44:3; Ezekiel 36:26f.; 39:29; Joel 2:28). The effects of this "democratic" outpouring of the Spirit will be righteousness, justice, and peace on earth (Isaiah 32:16f.). It will be a re-creation of God's people (Isaiah 44:3), with obedience to God's statutes and ordinances (Ezekiel 36:27) on the basis of "a new heart" and "a new spirit" (Ezekiel 36:26).

In Ezekiel's vision of the valley of dry bones, the eschatological salvation is like a resurrection from the dead. God's *ruah* will raise up his people again. He will put his Spirit within them (Ezekiel 37:14) and "they shall be my people," gathered as one nation in their own land under one king, and "I will be their God" (Ezekiel 37:21-23). Because Spirit and prophecy became closely related to each other, therefore the eschatological outpouring of the Spirit in Joel means that "your sons and your daughters shall prophesy, your old men shall dream dreams and your young men shall see visions" (Joel 2:28). Then it shall be fulfilled what at present can only be wished: "would that all the Lord's people were prophets, that the Lord would put his Spirit upon them" (Numbers 11:29).

In conclusion, it should be pointed out that a prayer addressed to the Holy Spirit would be out of place in the Old Testament. The same would be true for prayer to the "hand" of Yahweh. Furthermore, nowhere does the Old Testament speak of the Messiah giving or mediating the spirit. It should be noted that the eschatological salvation can be proclaimed in the Old Testament without mentioning either a Messiah or an outpouring of God's spirit, and when they are mentioned, then their fulfillment in Christ Jesus is different from their announcement.

Moreover, the spirit of God is understood in the Old Testament not only as the awe-inspiring power of God which intermittently takes possession of persons especially chosen and which is manifest in physical strength, courage, revelations, insights into God's counsel, wisdom, and will. It is also perceived as God's saving presence which renews individuals, or as an ethical force which establishes righteousness, justice, a clean heart in Israel.

Finally, the Spirit of God functions also as the principle of life and of God's cosmological activity. It is then understood as the creating or sustaining power of all life, or as vitality which can be increased or diminished and which is ultimately taken away in death.

II. The Spirit in First Century Judaism

The historical context within which Christianity arose is made up of a bewildering variety of religious movements. We can indicate only some of the more pertinent Jewish traditions which seem important for an understanding of the Holy Spirit in early Christianity.

A. Some traditions of rabbinic Judaism identified the Spirit of God with the Spirit of prophecy which had spoken in the sacred past and had become incarnate, so to speak, in the divinely inspired Scriptures.[5] Simultaneously it was hoped that in the future age of salvation the Spirit of God would return again, bringing about the resurrection of the dead according to Ezekiel 36:26f. and 37:14, taking away the "evil impulse" by transforming man's heart, and granting the power of prophetic inspiration to all members of the people of God according to Joel 2:28.[6] But the present was regarded as a time when the prophetic Spirit was absent. Its place was taken by the divinely inspired Scripture and the tradition. Hence the Syriac Apocalypse of Baruch (85:3-4) laments: "The prophets have fallen asleep . . . we have nothing now except the Mighty One and His Law." Rabbis declare: "When Haggai, Zechariah, and Malachi, the last prophets, died, then the Holy Spirit disappeared from Israel." [7] Some rabbinic traditions flatly state that the prophetic Spirit ceased with the destruction of the first temple and hence was not even present in the second.[8] Others dated the absence of the Spirit with the rise of Alexander's empire.[9]

In general New Testament scholarship tends to absolutize these rabbinic traditions [10] and consequently it paints a picture of Judaism as a spiritless, arid desert. Frequently scholars have misinterpreted texts [11] which speak of a temporary absence of prophets as though these texts were speaking of an absence of the Holy Spirit until the eschaton. Furthermore, the notion of the absence of the Spirit until the eschaton received a powerful impetus not only through the catastrophes which Spirit-filled Zealots and prophets brought upon Judaism, but also through the victory of rabbinic orthodoxy in the period of reconstruction after A.D. 70 when the idea of the book and the tradition as substitute for the presence of the Spirit gained prominence.

Finally, we must recognize that there are rabbinic traditions which speak of the *presence of the Holy Spirit* in especially pious individuals. Fulfillment of the commandments of God, good works, and an exemplary, pious life are rewarded with the gift of the Holy Spirit.[12] Of Rabbi Gamaliel I, Rabbi Akiba, Rabbi Meir, and Rabbi Schimon ben Jochai, it is said that on particular occasions they had visions "in the Holy Spirit." [13] Other texts invite people to obey the Torah and perform good works in order to become worthy of receiving the Holy Spirit, not merely in the life to come, but already in the present age. These rabbinic traditions do not speak of the presence of the prophetic Spirit. True enough, but neither does Psalm 51 speak about it when the petition is offered: "Take not thy Holy Spirit from me." In Psalm 51:11, however, the presence of the Holy Spirit is not the reward for piety, but the presupposition for renewal and the basis for a life in God's presence.

B. But also the *prophetic* Spirit was thought to be active in certain individuals from the time of Daniel to Rabbi Akiba. At least some circles within Judaism believed that the prophetic Spirit had not departed from Israel. While the evidence for Jewish prophets and seers in the first centuries B.C. and A.D. is extremely scanty, it has been presented in convenient form by Rudolf Meyer.[14] Through Josephus we know at least the names of some of them.[15] Zealotic prophetic leaders fanned the flames of revolt against Rome,[16] but we also know of "peaceful" prophets. The Teacher of Righteousness in Qumran claimed divine inspiration for his interpretation of Scripture. "God has revealed to him all the mysteries of the words of his servants, the prophets," [17] so that he would actually know more than the prophets themselves who merely wrote the words of Scripture. He knows their true meaning, a meaning which is hidden from all who are outside the community of Qumran, through revelations given by God.[18]

Evidence for first century Jewish prophets is also found in the New Testament itself. Luke 1 and 2 speak of prophetic inspiration granted to chosen individuals. Apparently Luke never heard of the idea that the prophetic Spirit was absent in Israel at the time of Jesus' birth. Furthermore, the Marcan apocalypse (Mark 13:6-22) refers to "false Christs" and "false prophets" who "arise and show signs and wonders" reflecting the situation during the first revolt in A.D. 66-70. In conclusion, the notion of the absence of the prophetic Spirit in the present was a belief held by some Jewish groups, but by no means was it characteristic of first century Judaism as a whole.

C. The Qumran community [19] expressed an eschatological self-understanding which believed that salvation is already present in the community. As Bertil Gaertner has shown [20] the community thought of itself as the "new temple," the "foundation of truth," the "sanctuary in Aaron" in an exclusive sense.[21] The community's existence was determined by the "Spirit of Truth" who is the "prince of light," while the "sons of perversity" are under the dominion of the Spirit or angel of darkness.[22] Though both Spirits were made by God,[23] the Spirit of darkness will be destroyed in the end.[24]

Upon entering the community, man's sinful self, the "perverted spirit," the "spirit of the flesh" [25] is purified through "the Holy Spirit of the community in His Truth." [26] The community is called the "community in His Truth" (1 QS 2:26) because it possesses the knowledge of God's mysteries.[27] The Spirit is called "Holy Spirit of the community" because it mediates the truth, the revelation, to the community, and the community expresses the presence of the Holy Spirit by exhibiting a spirit of rightness and humility (1 QS 3:8).

The notion of two opposing Spirits converges with the idea of the purifying Spirit of God in 1 QS 4:18-23. In the eschaton, God will cleanse by "the Holy Spirit" those whom he has chosen for an everlasting "covenant," free from every defilement. It is important to note that this seems to be the only text in the Community Rules and in the Hymns which assigns an eschatological function to the Spirit. Furthermore, nowhere is it stated that the presence of the Spirit in the community is the eschatological fulfillment of prophetic promises. This is all the more surprising because Qumran does understand itself to be the eschatological community of the sons of light. The reason for the lack of emphasis on the Spirit's eschatological function lies in the fact that the Spirit is understood primarily as the mediator and enabler of esoteric truths in the present. Since in other apocalyptic texts the Spirit played no role, we can conclude that the Qumran community did not understand the Spirit's presence as anticipation and sign of the eschaton. In Qumran the Spirit is perceived as the agent of revelation and purification; second, as endowment, and; third, as cosmic principle. The cosmic dimension of Qumran's dualism as well as the hypostatization of the Spirits goes far beyond the Old Testament and rabbinic thought.[28]

D. Jewish *apocalypticism* [29] understood itself to be in succession to the prophets. We would therefore expect that the prophetic promise of an eschatological outpouring of the Spirit upon the community would play a central role in its message. But this is not the case. Only on the fringes of apocalypticism can we discover the idea of an eschatological renewal of the people through the Spirit of God or its endowment with the Spirit of God.[30] If a Messiah is mentioned in this literature, we usually find him described in the language of Isaiah 11:2 as recipient of the Spirit of God.[31] But, as in the Old Testament, we never find that he, or God through him, bestows the Spirit upon the community.

Naturally we hear that apocalyptic writers believed themselves to be inspired by the Spirit of God,[32] but even more frequently they take recourse to angels, dreams, trances, visions, auditions, and even to special potions,[33] and, above all, to translations [34] into heaven in order to present the basis for the authority of their message. Who needs the Spirit as agency of inspiration when one can be miraculously translated into heaven?

The dearth of a pneumatology in apocalypticism is offset, however, by an explosion of good spirits and evil spirits, especially the latter, who are organized in a bewildering variety of angelic or demonic hierarchies and are given different names, stations, and functions [35] with God reigning as the "Lord of the Spirits." [36] These spirits are cosmic forces which influence the course of history and the individual's life for good or ill.[37] The evil spirits are no longer envoys of God's wrath, but fallen angels, rebels against the Almighty. Human ills, be they suffering, idolatry, fornication, or wars, were interpreted as part of a cosmic disorder. Man's actions are not merely the result of his choice, but also the result of forces acting on him. On the other hand, good spirits could also affect man's destiny.

The lack of need to speak about the Holy Spirit becomes even more apparent when we turn to a new development in the anthropological use of the word "spirit" during our period. In some traditions the Greek idea of the immortality of man's spirit slowly gained in importance.[38] It can be said of these discarnate spirits or souls that they cry, feel pain, and grieve, wander about in torture.[39] While the bones of the righteous rest in the earth, "their spirits shall have much joy" (Jubilees 23:31) in the "garden where the elect and righteous dwell" (1 Enoch 60:8). This belief could quite easily be related to the notion of the resurrection of the body.[40] In these traditions spirit is understood as man's true self which is a divine, heavenly substance and which survives death. Hence, if man's spirit or soul is already divine and immortal, then man is not primarily in need of God's renewing Spirit, but of secret revelations, knowledge, and good works in order that his immortal spirit may enter paradise as the reward for keeping itself undefiled.

E. Two distinct traditions concerning the Spirit are interwoven in the *Wisdom of Solomon*. On one hand we hear that it is God alone who grants wisdom by sending his Holy Spirit from on high (9:17).

On the other hand the Stoic idea of the Logos which as pneuma substance permeates the cosmos is taken up so that Wisdom/Spirit can also function as the cosmic principle.[41] The Spirit which "penetrates all things" (7:24) is combined in this writing with the Spirit which can "pass into holy souls making them friends of God and prophets" (7:27), who had been predestined for immortality.[42] Two further insights are important. As principle of divine energy in creation Wisdom/Spirit became personified and functioned as mediator in creation (7:22; Sirach 24:3-6). Second, the Wisdom/Spirit was not brought into any relationship to the Messiah, for the Messiah has no place in the Wisdom traditions.

In conclusion:

1) The Spirit of God as creative power and as principle in the life of every man should be distinguished from

2) The Spirit of God as agent and as endowment in salvation history in its past, present, and future dimension. As agent of salvation the Spirit effects prophetic inspiration, revelation, miracles, the Scriptures, righteousness, moral renewal, a new creation. As endowment, the Spirit is the gift of supernatural qualities or abilities such as a new heart, a new will, a new insight, righteousness, etc.

3) The influence of a cosmological dualism upon the understanding of the Spirit of God issued on one hand in an understanding of the Spirit as the power and knowledge of that which is true and good; on the other hand it led to a distintegration of the Spirit of God into a multitude of spirits.

4) While rabbinic Judaism expected an eschatological endowment of the people of God with the Spirit of prophecy, other traditions which acknowledged the presence of the Spirit of Wisdom or of the Spirit of Truth in their midst held a non-eschatological understanding of the Spirit.

5) The development of the spirit as an impersonal power to the Spirit as divine hypostasis did not lead to an identification of the Spirit with the Messiah, nor to the notion of the mediation of the Spirit through the Messiah.

6) Finally, Judaism, as well as the Old Testament, could speak of salvation without mentioning the Spirit of God.

III. The Holy Spirit in the Synoptic Tradition

A. *Jesus and the Spirit*

All four Gospels agree that during Jesus' earthly life, his disciples did not receive the Holy Spirit (cf. also John 7:39). Furthermore, they agree that the Holy Spirit was present in Jesus in a unique way. It is therefore surprising that the Synoptic Gospels contain only a few sayings in which Jesus himself mentioned the Spirit as the source of his authority and power, or in which he promised the Spirit to his disciples. They are Matthew 12:28; 28:19; Mark 13:11; and parallels; Luke 4:18; 11:13; 12:10 and parallels.

A traditional, historical analysis would show that probably none of these sayings can be traced back to the historical Jesus, which means that Jesus did not speak of the Holy Spirit at all.[43] Even though it cannot be doubted that Jesus was aware not only of his unique relationship to God when he called God his *abba*,[44] but also of his unique mission, still the absence of evidence that the historical Jesus spoke of the Holy Spirit needs to be explained.[45]

We can only offer a hypothesis to this question. The mission of Jesus consisted not in making claims for himself, for his own powers and inspiration, but in fulfilling a task, namely to proclaim and enact and represent the kingdom of God. The concentration of Jesus, like the great prophets of the eighth century, lay on the content of his message and action, not on the agency by which that content was enacted. Moreover, quite a few of his contemporaries also claimed to possess the Spirit, either by virtue of their moral life or through membership in a religious community like the people of Qumran or by prophetic inspiration like the zealotic prophets. It is not so that Jesus rejected the idea of the Holy Spirit. He was aware of God's saving reign in his own life and mission; however, he concentrated not on himself but on the task of proclaiming and enacting the will of God, the saving and judging rule of God as king. Therefore, he did not speak about the Holy Spirit, but he spoke about the kingdom of God.

B. *Jesus and the Spirit in the Synoptic Tradition*

Because the early church experienced the miracle of the coming of the Holy Spirit in consequence of the resurrection-exaltation of Jesus, therefore, it connected the Spirit with the person and mission of Jesus.

1) In *Mark* the baptism of Jesus is the central event of Mark's introduction and forms the basis of the Baptist's promise that the eschatological Lord shall baptize "with the Holy Spirit" (1:8). The descent of the Spirit like a dove [46] "into him" expresses the unique manifestation and union of the Spirit with Jesus and indicates that in this event, which Christian faith narrates, we are dealing not with the account of another prophetic call, but with the anointing of the messianic Son of God whose ministry ushers in the eschatological kingdom of God. The voice from heaven in Mark is addressed to Jesus only, in contrast to Matthew, and signifies the beginning of his messiahship.[47] Because Jesus received the Holy Spirit in a unique and permanent way, therefore everything which is said and done by the Marcan Jesus is accomplished by the power of the eschatological Spirit present in Jesus. Hence, to call Jesus possessed by Beelzebub is to commit the blasphemy against the Holy Spirit which is present in him and through which he expels demons (Mark 3:28-30).

2) In *Matthew* and also in *Luke* the union between Jesus and the Holy Spirit does not begin with his baptism, but at the very beginning with his conception. These two evangelists begin their stories of Jesus by pointing to the Holy Spirit as the power which created this child in a virgin. Because of Jesus' miraculous conception, "*therefore* the child to be born will be called holy, the Son of God" (Luke 1:35). Matthew saw in this gynecological miracle [48] the fulfillment of the Septuagint text of Isaiah 7:14, and, like Luke, connected it with his Son-of-God Christology. The meaning of the descent of the Spirit upon Jesus after his baptism [49] has now been altered slightly. In Matthew and Luke the Spirit's descent no longer marks the beginning and origin of Jesus' messianic career, but now it indicates that Jesus enters on a new phase of his messianic career. Because of the Spirit's descent, Jesus, in comparison to John the Baptist, is the mightier one. Matthew specifically emphasized that the Spirit is the power through which Jesus performed his miracles (Matthew 12:18, 28). Because his exorcisms are performed by the Spirit of God, the kingdom of God is present already now.

3) *Luke* continued the trend of speaking more frequently about the indwelling of the Spirit in Jesus. Not only does the virginal conception receive more space in Luke than in Matthew, but the beginnings of the ministry of Jesus contain three additional Lucan statements. Jesus

returned from his baptism "full of the Holy Spirit" and he returned from his temptation "in the power of the Spirit." In his opening sermon in Nazareth, he declared himself to be the prophet of Isaiah 61:1f., who will proclaim good news and perform miracles because the "Spirit of the Lord is upon" him (Luke 4:1, 14, 18). Since the Nazareth pericope in the third Gospel functions as a summary of the whole Gospel, even as the Pentecost narrative in Acts 2 summarizes the Book of Acts, therefore we can conclude that the whole ministry of Jesus—his words, miracles, and actions—is determined by the power of the Spirit[50] working in him.

A threefold relationship between the Spirit and Jesus is found in Luke. First, Jesus is conceived by the Holy Spirit. The *Spiritus Creator* created a new man, the Son of God, the son of Adam, who belonged to God (1:35; 3:38). Second, the Spirit took possession of Jesus after he was baptized with water (3:21f.). According to Luke, Jesus, in a unique way during his ministry, is the sole possessor of the Spirit, which he committed at death into his Father's hands. Also after Easter Jesus speaks[51] "through the Holy Spirit" (Acts 1:2). Third, on Pentecost the exalted Jesus pours out the Holy Spirit which he had received from the Father (Acts 2:33). The same Spirit which had spoken through the prophets and was uniquely present in Jesus is given through Jesus to the church. This outpouring of the Spirit which had been promised by the prophets and by John the Baptist and by Jesus (Acts 1:5) is the goal of the ministry of Jesus. Its presupposition is his ascension into heaven. The age of the Spirit was already present in the Son and was made possible through the Son and is inaugurated on Pentecost by the exalted Son and finds its climax and conclusion in his parousia.

C. The Spirit and the Community in the Synoptic Tradition

Mark, as well as "Q" and John, preserved a word of John the Baptist (Mark 1:8; Luke 3:16; John 1:26, 33). Its original form probably was:

> I baptize you with water
> but he shall baptize you with the Holy Spirit and fire.

The Marcan version which omitted "fire" is secondary, but its form is primary. This saying contrasts the Baptist with Jesus, the present time with the future, water with Spirit and fire. It is important to notice that the parallelism demands that water, Spirit, and fire are understood to be instruments. They are not to be interpreted as gifts. In this saying the Holy Spirit is the means by which "he" shall baptize. In tracing this saying through its history, we can discover several levels of meaning.

1) *The historical Baptist* probably regarded himself as the herald "of the great and terrible day of the Lord" (Malachi 4:5f.), rather than as forerunner of a Messiah.[52] He announced an imminent baptism with "Holy Spirit[53] and fire." In 2 Esdras 13:10, we hear of "a *fiery* stream, a flaming breath, a violent *storm*" which will destroy God's enemies; and Isaiah 4:4 speaks of "a *spirit* of judgment and a spirit of *burning*" which will purge Israel, with which the Lord "shall wash away the filth of the daughters of Zion . . . the bloodstains of Jerusalem." However, the symbol of fire was used not only as means for divine destruction, but also for purification (Malachi 3:2). John announced to the people who were baptized that they too would undergo the judgment of God in which God will separate the wheat from the chaff by means of his eschatological Spirit-windstorm and fire. Simultaneously, with his Spirit God shall purify repentant sinners and with his eschatological fire he shall cleanse them. However, the "brood of vipers" shall be utterly destroyed by his Spirit and fire. In short, John the Baptist did not promise the Spirit as the eschatological gift, but rather Spirit and fire are the eschatological instruments of cleansing and of judgment. Baptism with Spirit and fire is therefore a metaphor.

How was John's baptism with water related to the coming baptism with the Spirit? His water baptism symbolized turning to God in preparation for the judgment to come. Repentance, expressed by undergoing baptism, was meant to result in forgiveness of sins and also in commitment to bring forth "fruits of repentance" (Luke 3:8). Thus water baptism prepared the penitent for the Spirit baptism to come.

2) For the communities who used the *Q traditions,* the one who shall baptize with the Holy Spirit and fire was none other than the Son of man at his parousia, whose words these communities proclaimed in the conviction that those who reject their message are committing the blasphemy against the Holy Spirit which will never be forgiven (Luke 12:10). Hence, the "Q" communities were aware of the presence of the Spirit in their proclamation. Simultaneously, they

looked forward to an eschatological sanctification by the Spirit. Perhaps in their reinterpretation of the Baptist's prophecy, the Q communities distinguished baptism with Spirit from baptism with fire, understanding the Spirit as the instrument of God's eschatological cleansing activity upon those who now listen to and obey the words of the Son of man, and reserving baptism with fire for those who now commit blasphemy against the Holy Spirit by rejecting God's last call.[54]

3) In *Mark* the words "and fire" are omitted (1:8), and hence it would seem reasonable to suppose that Mark saw the fulfillment of the Baptist's promise in the endowment of the community with the Holy Spirit in the present rather than at Christ's parousia. How does Jesus' baptism with the Holy Spirit manifest itself according to Mark? Only one text deals with that question. Jesus on his way to the cross will experience a "baptism" in which his disciples will likewise share (10:39). As Jesus will be "delivered up" (9:31; 10:33; 14:41; 15:1), so will his disciples (13:9, 11) if they follow in his path. In that hour when they are "delivered up" for Christ's sake and share in "his baptism," then the Holy Spirit will be the power of their speech and of their witness to their accusers and judges (13:11).

Mark apparently wished to restrict baptism with the Spirit to the special occasion of the persecution of Christ's followers. Perhaps we might say that for him, Christian claims concerning baptism with the Spirit find their test when the birthpangs of the new age produce persecutions of the disciples. When they are "delivered up," when the limits of endurance are reached, then the Spirit will manifest itself as the extraordinary power of God in the witness of Christ's disciples.

4) Also *Luke* related the prophecy of a baptism with the Holy Spirit and fire no longer to the final consummation, but in contrast to Mark he saw its fulfillment taking place[55] at Pentecost. In accordance with Jesus' promise (Acts 1:5) all the disciples were "filled with the Holy Spirit" (Acts 2:4) by receiving the "power from on high" (Luke 24:49). For Luke to be "baptized with the Holy Spirit" (Acts 1:5; 11:16) meant that the Spirit is both instrument and gift (Acts 1:8). The Spirit, however, is not received mechanically. Hence, the foremost request which Christians should make in prayer is for the gift of "the Holy Spirit" (Luke 11:13).[56] Prayer is the means by which the energy of the Spirit is apprehended[57] ever anew. God's supreme gift dare not be misused. Because of the Spirit's presence in the commu-

nity, therefore Christians who blasphemed against the Spirit by denying Jesus or by lying to the church have committed a sin which will
not be forgiven (Luke 12:8-13; Acts 5:3, 5, 9).[58]

5) In the Gospel according to *Matthew* we discover that in contrast
to the emphasis upon the Spirit's activity in Lukan and Johannine
theology, the first evangelist did not emphasize the Spirit's operation
in the community at all. On the contrary, Matthew deliberately down-
played the function of the Holy Spirit in the church by focusing his
attention upon the role of the teachings of Jesus for discipleship.
Though the first evangelist delineated the Spirit's relationship to
Jesus, he remained almost completely mute on the subject of the
Spirit's role in the church. Aside from traditional sayings (3:11; 10:20;
12:31f.), he himself referred to the Spirit's ecclesiological significance
only in conjunction with the great commission (28:19). Nothing shows
Matthew's anti-enthusiastic bias more clearly than his version of the
testament of Jesus (28:18-20) which finds its climax in the injunction
"teach them to obey all that I have commanded you," and contains the
promise not of the Spirit's presence but of the presence of Jesus.

Matthew was well aware of Christian prophets who, like all prophets, claimed divine inspiration, but whose teachings and whose life-
style were contrary to Jesus and his word—hence, "beware of false
prophets" (7:15), for "many false prophets will arise and lead many
astray" (24:11). The criterion which enabled the Matthean church to
distinguish between false prophets and the true "prophets, wise men
and scribes" (23:34) sent by God has been given once and for all in
the teachings of Jesus and in the obedience demanded by his teaching
(7:21-27).

While the promise of the presence of the Holy Spirit is central to
the Lukan version of Jesus' testament (Luke 24:44-49; Acts 1:7-8) we
find that in Matthew the promised divine presence refers not to the
Spirit but to Jesus himself (28:20; 18:20; cf. 1:23). For Matthew the
criterion of the Spirit is the Son of God, his word and authority. He
is the basis of the church's mission (28:18) and he is present with his
church in her mission (28:20). The mission charge given to her is
threefold: 1) Go and make disciples of all nations, 2) baptizing them
in the name of the Father and of the Son and of the Holy Spirit,[59]
3) teaching them to obey all that I have commanded you. While the
pre-Easter disciples were engaged in mission to Israel only (10:5),

the post-Easter disciples' mission has a universal dimension. Its basis is the all-encompassing authority of Jesus, the Son [60] (28:18). The means of making disciples of all nations are baptism and teaching.

 For Matthew baptism in the name of the triune God corresponds to the call of Jesus issued to his first disciples: "Follow me." This call is a gracious invitation (Matthew 11:28) and simultaneously, it involves lifelong discipleship and obedience. The command to baptize in the name [61] of the Father, Son, and Holy Spirit recalls the baptism of Jesus when the Father proclaimed Jesus to be his Son and granted him the power of the Spirit for his ministry. Hence through baptism in the name of the "triune" God, a person becomes a disciple of Jesus and a son of the Father. As such we would expect him to be empowered by the Spirit to do ministry in obedience to Jesus, but that is not emphasized in Matthew. He merely quoted a formula. For the first evangelist baptism is the gracious act which calls and transfers the baptized person into the possession of and under the authority of Father, Son, and Holy Spirit.

It is indeed at first surprising that the mandate "teach them to obey all" does not precede the injunction to baptism as in Didache 7:1.[62] To Matthew the instruction subsequent to baptism is of central interest because Jesus himself is present in his word and because the righteousness of the disciples (5:20) consists of obedience to his teachings, foremost to his interpretation of the two commandments on which all the law and the prophets depend—love toward God and love toward the neighbor (22:37-40; 5:21-48).

IV. The Holy Spirit in the Book of Acts

Just as the second article of the Apostles' Creed is followed by the third, so the Gospel of Luke is continued in the Book of Acts, which deals less with acts performed by apostles than with acts of the Spirit. The Spirit which had spoken through the Old Testament prophets (Acts 1:16; 4:25; 28:25; Luke 1:41, 67; 2:25-32, 36) and which had descended upon Jesus in a unique way at his baptism and which had been surrendered to the Father by the Son on the cross (Luke 23:46) is given to the church. In consequence of Christ's ministry, death, resurrection, and exaltation, God bestows the Holy Spirit through Christ upon all believers and inaugurates the third and last period of salvation history which is distinct from and simultaneously in continuity with the period of the Old Testament and the period of Jesus' ministry. The Holy Spirit demonstrates the continuity of salvation history and indicates the distinctiveness of its three periods.[63] In the period of the Old Testament which, according to Luke, also includes the time covered by the first two chapters of his Gospel, the Holy Spirit was bestowed upon certain individuals who spoke as prophets. In the center of time which began with Jesus' baptism and ended with his ascension, Jesus himself was the sole bearer of the Spirit. At Pentecost the Holy Spirit created the church and was promised to the church until the parousia.[64] No longer did only specially elected persons receive the Holy Spirit. Since Pentecost the Holy Spirit is poured out democratically upon every believer. Pentecost marked the fulfillment of the promise made in the Old Testament and by Jesus himself (Acts 1:5; 2:16-21).

A. The Pentecost Narrative

1. Some Problems

Luke's Pentecost narrative poses problems. To begin with, we should note that it contradicts the Johannine account according to which the gift of the Spirit was imparted by the resurrected Christ breathing the Spirit on his disciples on Easter evening (John 20:22), not fifty days later by the ascended Lord (Acts 2). It should be recognized that efforts to harmonize Acts 2 with John 20:22 lead nowhere because Luke deliberately separated what originally was viewed as being one event, namely, resurrection, exaltation, and bestowal of the Spirit. Since Luke separated the resurrection from the exaltation by 40 days, he also had to separate the bestowal of the Spirit from the resurrection. Hence, he chose the next Jewish festival for the imparting of the Spirit.

It has frequently been asserted that Luke's narrative should be interpreted against the background of Pentecost as the festival of the renewal of the Sinai covenant.[65] Pentecost would then mean the renewal of Israel's covenant or the inauguration of a new covenant. The gift of the Spirit could then be interpreted as the counterpart of the gift of the Torah, or else the law could be understood as having been fulfilled or abrogated by the writing of a new law into the hearts of believers. The glossolalia of Pentecost could function as a counterpart to the voice of God from Mt. Sinai which, according to some traditions, changed into fire and spirit and even into understandable speech so that it could be heard by those near and far.

However, Pentecost was not celebrated prior to A.D. 70 as a festival of the renewal of the Sinai covenant.[66] Moreover, Peter's speech in Acts 2:14-40 which interpreted the narrative did not refer to the Sinai covenant at all. Hence, a Sinai covenant typology is to be excluded from Luke's narrative in Acts 2:1-13. Luke did not deal with ideas of covenant renewal, and the notion of a new covenant with a new law is foreign to his thought. His Pentecost narrative is filled with motifs from the description of theophanies as found, for instance, in Isaiah 66:16ff. and in Philo.[67] The point of these theophany motifs is to indicate that Pentecost is a miracle which begins the new age of the Spirit.

Occasionally the miracle of glossolalia has been thought to signify the end of the confusion of languages.[68] Pentecost would then mean Babel in reverse. But this was not Luke's opinion. The notion that *one* language, namely, Hebrew, will be established in the end as it was in the beginning [69] is not present in Acts 2. On the contrary, Luke assumed that the apostles and disciples spoke miraculously in a multitude of languages. Nor are merely two or three languages involved as some interpreters proposed.

The language miracle of Pentecost should not be interpreted as constituting a miracle of audition through which each foreign visitor merely heard in his own language what the apostle said in Aramaic. On the contrary, Luke presented us with a miracle of proclamation because he was well aware that preaching creates faith and causes division. Therefore, the gospel is to be proclaimed in understandable language. The author of Acts sees the chief effect of the Spirit's coming upon the disciples in their bold proclamation of the mighty acts of God.

The inspired speech of Acts 2:4-11 calls to mind the phenomenon of glossolalia which Paul addressed in 1 Corinthians 14. Both are brought about by the Spirit. Yet the differences between the two phenomena should be noted. In 1 Corinthians 14 glossolalia is unintelligible prayer which needs a "translator" in order to be understood. In Acts 2:4 "speaking in other tongues" is intelligible speech, proclamation, in foreign languages (2:6, 8).[70] Luke played with the double meaning of *glossa*, tongues of fire, and "other tongues." The latter he

identified with *dialektos,* native language. In short, the tongues of
Acts 2 are not identical with those of 1 Corinthians 14.[71]

We should also recognize that the Pentecost narrative is not a realistic account. To begin with, one might ask: When did "the sound" and
"the rush of a mighty wind" disappear? When the disciples began to
speak (v. 4), or when Peter began to speak (v. 14), or when? Where
in Jerusalem could such a mass of people of which 3000 were con-
verted be assembled? How was it possible that neither the Roman
nor the Jewish authorities would interfere in the face of such a challenge? How could Peter address such a multitude without a loud-
speaker system? How could those diaspora Jews know that the disciples
speaking in their dialects were Galileans? Incidentally, the Medes
and the Elamites [72] had long disappeared from the scene of world
history; nor is it realistic to suppose that the diaspora Jews would tick
off a long list of peoples representing "every nation under heaven"
(2:9-11). In short, Luke's Pentecost account is not a realistic narrative
which conveys to us what actually happened.

We should therefore interpret Acts 2 by inquiring into the theological message which Luke sought to convey to the reader by means of
his Pentecost narrative and Peter's interpretive speech.

2. The Message of Acts 2

A careful study of Acts 2 shows that it summarizes the Book of Acts
even as the Nazareth pericope of Luke summarizes the third Gospel.
We have already indicated several Lukan themes which are brought
out in Acts 2, such as the outpouring of the Spirit as fulfillment of
prior promises by Jesus (Acts 1:5, 8; Luke 24:49), by John the Baptist
(Luke 3:16), and by Joel (Acts 2:16-21). Moreover, Luke retained
the christological basis of the Spirit in Acts 2:33. The Holy Spirit is
received by Jesus from the Father and poured out by Jesus upon the
disciples. Hence, the Holy Spirit (16:6) can be called "the Spirit of
Jesus" (16:7). As eschatological gift it is granted to every believer
(2:17-18). The primary effect of the Spirit is the proclamation of the
mighty acts of God in understandable language. Since all Christians
are recipients of the Spirit, therefore all are prophets as Peter declared
by adding to the Joel quotation the words "and they shall prophesy"
(2:18). The mandate of witnessing to Christ is laid on all disciples
(1:5) and hence we hear later on in Acts of nameless Christians who

were scattered like seeds across the region "preaching the word" (8:4; 11:19-21). Therefore Peter found Christians already when he came to Lydda and Joppa (9:32, 36) even as Paul was met by believers living in Ephesus and Rome. The task of witnessing to Christ in the power of the Spirit is not restricted to Peter and Paul, the chief figures in the two parts of Acts.

Furthermore, from one perspective Pentecost was for Luke a unique miracle, similar to the virginal conception of Jesus. It was the miracle of the church's birth and of the beginning of the age of the Spirit. This first outpouring of the Spirit upon the disciples is therefore unrepeatable, for it erupted not in consequence of preaching, but directly and unmediatedly. Its visible and audible manifestations were likewise unique. Later on, Luke will narrate several "mini-Pentecosts" (10:44; 19:6), but these took place after preaching and the theophany motifs of Acts 2:2f. are absent. The speaking in tongues in these cases is not designated as speaking in foreign languages either. It can therefore be understood as glossolalia in the Pauline sense of 1 Corinthians 14.

The Pentecost account also serves as pre-enactment of the universality of the church's mission. The list of nations of 2:9-11, the proselytes of 2:10, the reference to "those who are afar" in 2:39 indicate the worldwide dimension of the church.[73] Later on Luke would narrate how the church, under the direction of the Spirit, broke through barriers of Judaism and was led across racial frontiers (8:5-39; 10:1-11:18).

The Spirit which directs the church in its mission (Acts 10; 13:1-3; 16:6-7; 19:21) also guides its decision. The most important decision made by the apostles in the Book of Acts is introduced with: "It seemed good to the Holy Spirit and to us" (Acts 15:28ff.). Also the appointment of elders is made "by the Holy Spirit" (20:28). The Spirit legitimates the ecclesiastical office insofar as the officeholder faithfully declares the whole counsel of God (20:26f., 29f.) [74] as Peter had done paradigmatically at Pentecost.

B. *Water Baptism and Spirit Baptism* [75]

When we inquire into Luke's understanding of the relationship between water baptism and Spirit baptism, we receive at first a bewildering number of contradictory answers.

1) In Acts 2:38f. Peter announced: "Repent and be baptized every one of you in the name of Jesus Christ for the forgiveness of your sins; and you shall receive the gift of the Holy Spirit." Here the gift of the Spirit appears to be given *simultaneously* with baptism. Repentance (in other Lukan texts, faith) is the presupposition for baptism and the reception of the Spirit. Together these elements form a unity of thought. Forgiveness and the gift of the Spirit do not belong to two separate stages in the development of believers, but are two aspects of the same divine action. Luke did not contrast water baptism "in the name of Jesus" with Spirit baptism, but he connected them and he understood the Spirit to be both agent and gift. As agent he is the *Spiritus creator* who through preaching creates faith and directs the church. As gift, the Spirit is endowment with divine power which presupposes faith. In distinction to rabbinic Judaism, the gift of the Spirit is not to be understood as a reward for piety. The interrelatedness of repentance, faith, and the Spirit as gift in a unity of thought comes to expression also in texts such as 11:17f. "God gives the same gift [the Holy Spirit] to them as he gave to us when we *believed* in the Lord Jesus Christ." This means that "God has granted *repentance* unto life also to the Gentiles" (11:18). Faith, repentance, the reception of the Spirit belong together. In this Luke agrees with his tradition as well as with Paul and John.

2) While in Acts 2:38 the Spirit is given simultaneously with repentance, baptism, and forgiveness, in Acts 8:12-17 we find an interval between them. Here the Spirit comes upon the Samaritans *after* their baptism and is separated from their baptism and faith by a new action, the apostles' prayers and laying on of hands. This incident which serves as scriptural foundation for the Pentecostal separation of water baptism from Spirit baptism has resulted in a variety of interpretations.[76] Dunn's solution to the riddle in Samaria is that the faith of the Samaritans was defective.[77] They "gave heed" to Philip (8:6) because of his miracles, just as they formerly "gave heed" to Simon the magician (8:10-11). They, like Simon, believed Philip (8:12-13) and were baptized, but they did not believe in the Lord. Hence they were only nominal Christians without true faith, and therefore the Spirit was not received by them when they were baptized but only later when they came to true faith in Jesus Christ. However, Luke's narrative does not speak of a defectiveness of the Samaritans'

faith, nor does it indicate that through the apostles' prayer and laying on of hands the Samaritans came at last to true faith in Jesus, nor does it mention additional instruction given to them by the apostles in contrast to 19:4. Hence the solution to the riddle in Samaria must be sought elsewhere.

Following Bultmann [78] and Conzelmann,[79] Dale Bruner correctly saw that 8:16 presupposes the unity of water baptism and Spirit baptism.[80] Since the Spirit "had *not yet* fallen," but the Samaritans "had *only* been baptized" [81] an impossible situation had arisen. Baptism in the name of Christ remains also for Luke baptism in the Holy Spirit. Otherwise Christ would be a Christ without the Holy Spirit. But how should we understand the anomaly of the temporary separation of baptism from the reception of the Holy Spirit? The answer lies in Luke's view of the expansion of the church,[82] rather than in his doctrine of baptism. Christian preaching had crossed the frontier of Judaism and entered Samaria. The holy irregularity of Acts 8:16 had an ecclesiological function, namely, to testify to the representatives of the Jerusalem church and in their presence that the Spirit is received also by Samaritans. "To teach this basic and important fact . . . God withheld his gift until the apostles should see with their own eyes and . . . be instrumental with their own hands in the impartation of the gift of God, merited by nothing, least of all by race or prior religion." [83] But precisely the anomaly of Acts 8:16 points to the unity of water baptism and Spirit baptism as norm.

3) Whereas in Acts 8:17 the Spirit is received after baptism we read in Acts 10:44-48 that it came *prior* to the baptism of Cornelius. For Luke the conversion of the gentile Cornelius by Peter the apostle is the basis and legitimation of the gentile mission (see 11:17; 15:7, 14). The conversion of the Ethiopian Eunuch by Philip is, in Luke's scheme, merely the prelude to this decisive incident which is told twice in great detail (10:1-11:18). Luke shows his readers that Peter had not been an innovator seeking new actions and planning by himself to move across the frontier into the gentile world. Rather Peter had to be pushed across the barrier which separated Judaism from the gentile world by a series of divine interventions. The last intervention was the holy irregularity of the Spirit falling upon Cornelius and his household (10:44-46) and thus forcing Peter to baptize those gentiles. "Who was I that I could withstand God?" (11:17), Peter

asked those who criticized his actions in Jerusalem (11:2). Acts 10:44-48, which is the counterpart to Acts 8:16-17, is ecclesiologically motivated (10:45) and presupposes the unity of water baptism and Spirit baptism as norm.

We should also note that proclamation serves as the instrument through which the Spirit is mediated to Cornelius; and furthermore, that he is baptized even though the Spirit had already fallen on him. The irregularity of Cornelius' conversion, in which the Spirit came prior to his baptism, dramatizes the breakthrough of the gospel into the gentile world and illustrates that, in the decisive moments of the church's history, the Spirit directs the church in accordance with the logic of the gospel.

In passing, one might also point out that Peter was criticized not primarily for preaching the gospel to gentiles, nor even for baptizing them, but rather for eating with them (11:3). Luke had placed a vision about eating and drinking into the middle of this conversion narrative (10:9-16) because he understood that the gospel is preached rightly only if the missionary preacher is willing to eat with the people to whom he preaches. The solidarity created by the gospel embraces social relationships, including eating.

4) In Acts 19:1-5 we hear that Paul *rebaptized* the Ephesian disciples [84] and in conjunction with the laying on of hands the Spirit is received. In this narrative we find a defective faith and also a defective baptism. Since the Ephesian disciples had never heard "that there is a Holy Spirit" (19:2), Paul inquires about their baptism because baptism and the Spirit belong together. Paul's question "into what then were you baptized" (19:3) makes sense only if the unity of faith (19:2), baptism in Jesus' name and the Holy Spirit is taken for granted by him. Since the baptism as well as the faith of the Ephesian disciples is defective, they are instructed by Paul (19:4). The instruction summarized in one verse deals with the testimony of John to Jesus and faith in Jesus. The latter is the prerequisite of baptism in the name of Jesus which is baptism with the Spirit (19:5-6). The laying on of hands (19:6) was a customary part of baptism attended by prayer. [85] It was not yet a separate or additional rite which bestowed the Holy Spirit. Paul therefore did not ask those disciples, "Who laid hands on you?" [86] but rather, "Into what then were you baptized?" In short, the absence of the Holy Spirit in these disciples was not the result of

faulty laying on of hands by unauthorized persons. It was the result of a defective faith and of the absence of baptism in Jesus' name.

5) Correspondingly, a rebaptism of the 120 disciples of Acts 1:15 is not mentioned (even though they had been baptized presumably only with John's baptism) because these disciples believed in Jesus and received the Spirit at Pentecost.

C. The Relationship Between God, Christ, and the Spirit in Acts

Building blocks for the later trinitarian dogma are scattered across the pages of Acts. For Luke to speak of God adequately demanded that he speak of the Creator (17:24) in whom we live and move and have our being. He is the God of his people Israel, the God of Abraham, Isaac, and Jacob (3:13) who as Lord of history brought to Israel a Savior (13:23). To speak of God, therefore, means to speak of Christ and his work. The Christ who is "exalted at the right hand of God, having received from the Father the promise of the Holy Spirit" has poured out the Spirit upon all believers (2:33). To speak of God, therefore, includes speaking about the Holy Spirit.

1) The unity of purpose without losing sight of the distinctions between Father, Son, and Spirit can be perceived in the ease in which Luke relates the same event or similar events to the Father or to Christ or to the Spirit. For instance, Paul's conversion and mission are related by Luke to *Jesus* (9:17), or to the *God of our fathers* (22:14), while in 13:2-4 it is the *Spirit* which commissions him and Barnabas. A directive given by the *Spirit* means that "*God* has called us to preach the gospel to them" (16:10); yet Luke can in the same context speak of "*the Spirit of Jesus*" (16:7). Or, to give another example, in his final journey to Jerusalem and Rome, Paul is "bound in the *Spirit*" (20:22; 19:21), directed by the Lord *Jesus* (23:11), or an angel of *God* (27:23).

2) The unity of purpose does not negate the peculiar functions of Jesus and the Spirit. The Spirit functions as Jesus' extension and representative in and through the church. Theologically this means that Luke would have us distinguish between God's general governance over his creation (17:24-29) and his eschatological saving activity through Christ and the Holy Spirit. The eschatological outpouring of the Spirit at Pentecost is not related to creation as such, but to the church.

3) Because the Holy Spirit in Acts fulfills functions which can also

be ascribed to God and Christ, therefore we find a number of personifying expressions in conjunction with the Spirit's work:

- 1:16—the Holy Spirit *"spoke* beforehand"
- 2:4 —"the Spirit *gave* them *utterance,"* (cf. 8:29; 10:19; 11:12, the "Holy Spirit *said.")*
- 4:25; 28:25—prophecy through the mouth of David
- 5:3 —Annanias *"lied to* the Holy Spirit"
- 5:32—"we are *witnesses* and so is the Holy Spirit"
- 7:51—"you always *fight against* the Holy Spirit"
- 13:2, 4—The Holy Spirit *"said" . . .* and *"sent out"*
- 15:28—*"It seemed good to* the Holy Spirit and to us"
- 16:7 —"The Spirit of Jesus *did not permit* them" to enter Bithynia
- 20:23—"the Holy Spirit *testifies* to me"
- 20:28—"the Holy Spirit *has made* you guardians" over the church at Ephesus.

Alongside these personifying expressions we find a dynamistic view in which the Spirit appears as impersonal gift and power which believers "receive" (2:38; 8:15, 17, 19; 10:47; 19:2), which "comes upon" disciples (1:8; 19:6), which God or the exalted Christ "pours out" (2:17, 33; 10:45), which he "gives" (5:32; 8:18; 11:17; 15:8), which "falls on" believers (8:16; 10:44; 11:15), with which they are "baptized" (1:5; 11:16). They are "full with" (6:3; 7:55; 11:24) or "filled with" the Holy Spirit (2:4; 4:8, 31; 9:17; 13:9, 52).

The personifying expressions indicate the Spirit relates the church or individual believers to God and Christ himself and vice versa—the Spirit is the creator and sustainer of the church's existence. The impersonal expressions emphasize that God's eschatological gift is received as power by grace through faith which enables the church and individual believers to witness truthfully and boldly on the way from Jerusalem to Rome.

In conclusion we might also note that Luke was aware of the problem of the relationship between tradition and Spirit. Because he desired to write "accurately" (Luke 1:3) what was transmitted by the eyewitnesses and to show what the apostles and Paul preached and did under the prompting of the Holy Spirit, therefore, he presented to Theophilus and to his church a mini-canon in two volumes. For

Luke the Spirit was present where the true tradition was present. Hence it was important for him that Peter and Paul proclaimed the same (Lukan) message. Therefore Paul warned the Ephesian elders to watch out for heretics who "speak perverse things" (20:28-30). False tradition blocks the operation of the Spirit because the Spirit operates through that word which is in continuity with Paul, Peter, and the teachings of Jesus.

Notes

1. Bibliography:

   a) *General articles:*

   Kleinknecht, Baumgärtel, Bieder, Sjöberg, Schweizer, *Pneuma, Pneumatikos, Theological Dictionary of the New Testament,* Eng. trans. by G. W. Bromiley (Grand Rapids: Eerdmans, 1968), vol. 6, pp. 332-454. This outstanding article is preceded by a detailed bibliography. An abbreviated translation of this article was published under the title *Bible Key Words* tr. by A. E. Harvey, London: Black, 1960).

   G. W. H. Lampe, "Holy Spirit," *The Interpreter's Dictionary of the Bible* (New York: Abingdon, 1962), vol. 2, pp. 626-639.

   S. V. McCasland, "Spirit," *The Interpreter's Dictionary of the Bible,* vol. 3, pp. 432-434.

   E. Schweizer, "Gegenwart des Geistes und eschatologische Hoffnung bei Zarathustra, spätjüdischen Gruppen, Gnostikern und den Zeugen des Neuen Testaments," in W. D. Davies and D. Daube (ed.), *The Background of the New Testament and Its Eschatology. Studies in Honor of C. H. Dodd* (Cambridge, 1956), pp. 482-508. Reprinted in: E. Schweizer: *Neotestamentica* (Zürich, 1963), pp. 153-179.

   b) *Old Testament:*

   W. Eichrodt, *Theology of the Old Testament,* tr. by J. A. Baker (Philadelphia: Westminster, 1967), vol. 2, pp. 46-68.

   L. Köhler, *Theologie des Alten Testaments,* second ed. (Tübingen, 1947), pp. 95-104.

   G. von Rad, *Old Testament Theology,* tr. by D. W. G. Stalker (New York: Harper, 1962-65), vol. 1, pp. 93-102; vol. 2, pp. 50-79.

   M. Burrows, *An Outline of Biblical Theology* (Philadelphia: Westminster, 1946), pp. 119-130, 139-141.

   J. Hehn, "Zum Problem des Geistes im Alten Orient und im Alten Testament," *Zeitschrift fur Alttestamentliche Wissenschaft,* new series, vol. 2 (1925), pp. 210-225.

   c) *Intertestamental Period:*

   G. F. Moore, *Judaism in the First Centuries of the Christian Era* (Cambridge: Harvard University Press, 1927), vol. 1, pp. 402-422; vol. 2, pp. 323-376.

H. Strack and P. Billerbeck, *Kommentar zum Neuen Testament aus Talmud und Midrash* (Munich, 1922-1926, 4 vols.), vol. 2, pp. 126-138, 614-617 (on Acts 2); vol. 4, pp. 435-451 (on the inspiration of Scripture); vol. 1, pp. 123-134 (on the dove, bath gol, and absence of the Spirit). (Hereafter abbreviated Billerbeck.)

Peter Schäfer, *Die Vorstellung vom Heiligen Geist in der Rabbinischen Literatur. Studien zum Alten und Neuen Testament,* vol. 27 (Munich, 1972).

A. Marmorstein, *Studies in Jewish Theology,* edited by J. Rabbinowitz and M. S. Lew (London, New York, Toronto, 1950), pp. 122-144.

G. Vermes, *The Dead Sea Scrolls in English* (Pelican paperback A551, Baltimore: Penguin Books, 1962).

A. Dupont Sommer, *The Essene Writings from Qumran,* tr. by G. Vermes (New York: Meridian Books, 1962).

W. D. Davies, "Paul and the Dead Sea Scrolls: Flesh and Spirit," in K. Stendahl, ed., *The Scrolls and the New Testament* (New York: Harper, 1957).

W. Foerster, "Der Heilige Geist im Spätjudentum," *New Testament Studies* (Cambridge, England, and Washington, 1962), vol. 8, pp. 117-134.

A. A. Anderson, "The Use of Ruah in 1Qs, 1QH, 1QM, *Journal for Semitic Studies,* vol. 7 (1962), pp. 293-303.

R. H. Charles, *The Apocrypha and Pseudepigrapha of the Old Testament in English,* vol. 2 (Oxford: Clarendon Press, 1913).

D. S. Russell, *The Method and Message of Jewish Apocalyptic, 200 BC-AD 100* (Philadelphia: Westminster, 1964).

d) *New Testament, including Acts:*

H. B. Swete, *The Holy Spirit in the New Testament* (London, 1907).

E. F. Scott, *The Spirit in the New Testament* (New York: Doran, 1923).

C. K. Barrett, *The Holy Spirit and the Gospel Tradition* (London, 1958).

G. W. H. Lampe, "The Holy Spirit in the Writings of St. Luke," in *Studies in the Gospels. Essays in Memory of R. H. Lightfoot.* D. E. Nineham, ed. (Oxford, 1955), pp. 159-200.

S. Smalley, "Spirit, Kingdom, Prayer in Luke-Acts," *Novum Testamentum* (Leiden, 1973), vol. 15, pp. 59-71.

R. Bultmann, *The History of the Synoptic Tradition* (tr. by J. Marsh, New York: Harper, 1963).

E. Haenchen, *The Acts of the Apostles,* tr. by B. Noble et al. (Philadelphia: Westminster, 1971).

H. Conzelmann, *Die Apostelgeschichte, Handbuch zum Neuen Testament,* vol. 7 (Tübingen, 1963).

F. F. Bruce, "The Holy Spirit in the Acts of the Apostles," *Interpretation*, vol. 27 (1973), pp. 166-183.

E. Schweizer, "The Spirit of Power," *Interpretation*, vol. 6 (1952), pp. 259-278.

J. D. G. Dunn, "Baptism in the Holy Spirit," *Studies in Biblical Theology*, 2nd series, no. 15 (Naperville, Illinois: Allenson, 1970).

F. D. Bruner, *A Theology of the Holy Spirit; The Pentecostal Experience and the New Testament Witness* (Grand Rapids: Eerdmans, 1970).

2. W. Eichrodt, *op. cit.*, vol. 2, p. 24f.
3. *Journal of Biblical Literature*, vol. 53 (1934), pp. 199ff.
4. G. von Rad, *op. cit.*, vol. 2, p. 57, note 11.
5. P. Schäfer, *Die Vorstellung vom Heiligen Geist in der Rabbinischen Literatur, Studien zum alten und neuen Testament* (Munich, 1972), and the literature there.
6. Billerbeck, *op. cit.*, vol. 2, p. 134, 616; vol. 4, p. 915; Barrett, *op. cit.*, p. 21; *Theological Dictionary of the New Testament*, vol. 5, p. 885.
7. Billerbeck, *op. cit.*, vol. 1, p. 127.
8. P. Schäfer, *op. cit.*, pp. 89ff.; 99ff.
9. P. Schäfer, *op. cit.*, pp. 96-99.
10. This is also true of Schweizer's article in *Theological Dictionary of the New Testament*, vol. 5, p. 400, and *Interpretation* 6 (1952), p. 261.
11. See *Theological Dictionary of the New Testament*, vol. 5, pp. 813-816 where it is shown that Psalm 74:9, Zechariah 13:2-6; 1 Maccabees 4:46; 9:27; 14:14 cannot be used as evidence for the belief that the Spirit is absent in Judaism until the eschaton.
12. P. Schäfer, *op. cit.*, pp. 125-133.
13. *Ibid.*, pp. 121-123, *pace* W. Foerster, pp. 117f.
14. *Theological Dictionary of the New Testament*, vol. 5, pp. 819-827.
15. *The Jewish Antiquities* 13:311ff.; 15:373ff.; 17:345; *The Jewish War* 6:283-286; 6:299; *The Jewish Antiquities* 20:97; cf. Acts 5:36.
16. *The Jewish Antiquities* 20:169; cf. Acts 21:38; *The Jewish War* 7:437; *Theological Dictionary of the New Testament*, vol. 5, p. 824.
17. 1 Q Hab 7:4-5. In subsequent references to the Qumran scrolls, the standard system of abbreviation is used. For further information, the reader should consult *New Catholic Encyclopedia*, vol. 4, pp. 678-680.
18. 1 QH 5:25; 9:24.
19. A. A. Anderson, *op. cit.*; D. W. Davies, "Paul and the Dead Sea Scrolls: Flesh and Spirit" in K. Stendahl, *The Scrolls and the New Testament* (New York: Harper, 1957), pp. 157-182; W. Foerster, *op. cit.*; above all, H. Braun, *Qumran und das Neue Testament*, 2 vols. (Tübingen, 1966).
20. B. Gaertner, *The Temple and the Community in Qumran and the New Testament, Supplement—New Testament Studies*, Monograph 1 (Cambridge, England, 1965), pp. 4-46.
21. 1QS 5:5ff.; 9:3; 4 Q Floril.

22. 1QS 3:18f.
23. 1QS 3:25.
24. 1QS 4:18.
25. 1QH 3:21; 13:15.
26. 1QS 3:7. We read that God has "poured out" his Holy Spirit upon the Qumran member (1QH 7:6) or has "given" him the Spirit (1QH 12:11f.). has "cleansed" him through his Holy Spirit (1QH 16:12) and through this Spirit he can "appease" God's face (1QH 16:11), "go forward" in doing God's will (1QH 16:12), and walk upon "the ways" of the Spirit of Truth (1QH 4:5-7), exhibiting a "spirit of humility and forebearance" and "a spirit of knowledge in every design" as well as "abundant love for all the sons of truth" and, one might add, abundant hatred for all the sons of darkness outside of Qumran (cf. 1QS 2:5-18).
27. 1QH 1:21; 4:27; 1QS 11:3-6; CD 3:7, etc.
28. But Qumran's Spirit of Truth also has little in common with the Spirit of Truth in John's Gospel, except the name and the dualistic context. In Qumran the Spirit of Truth is not given to the community through either of the two Messiahs even though the Messiah of Israel possesses the Spirit in accordance with Isaiah 11:2; 1QSb 5:25f. Furthermore, in Qumran the Spirit precedes, in John it succeeds, the Messiah. Finally, in John the Spirit is not a creature (as in 1QS 13:24) but God's spotlight on Jesus and his presence when he is absent.
29. K. Koch, *The Rediscovery of Apocalyptic, Studies in Biblical Theology,* 2nd series, no. 22 (1972), pp. 49-56; D. S. Russell, *The Method and Message of Jewish Apocalyptic* (Philadelphia: Westminster, 1964), pp. 73-103.
30. M. de Jonge, "Christian Influence in the Testaments of the Twelve Patriarchs," *Novum Testamentum,* 4 (1960), pp. 199-208, 225-227; J. Becker, *Untersuchungen zur Entstehungsgeschichte der zwölf Patriarchen. Arbeiten zur Geschichte des antiken Judentums und des Urchristentums,* vol. 8 (1970). Jub. 1:23 and 2 Esd. 6:26 allude to Ezek. 36:26f. Sibylline Oracles 3:582 says once that all inhabitants of Jerusalem shall be prophets; cf. Joel 2:28; 3:1. Otherwise only the Test. of the Patriarchs refers to an eschatological endowment of the community with the Spirit—Test. Levi 18:6f.; 10ff.; Test. Jud. 24:1ff.; Test. Benj. 9:4. But these texts are probably Christian interpolations.
31. Psalms of Solomon 17:37; 18:7; 1QSb 5:24ff.; Enoch 49:3; 62:2.
32. Thus the Holy Spirit is sent into Ezra's heart to write 24 public books and 70 secret books during 40 days, 2 Esdras 14:22-48. The other texts are conveniently listed by Russell, *op. cit.,* p. 402, and discussed on p. 160.
33. 2 Esdras 14:38f. Ezra received a cup "full of something like water, but its color was like fire." He drank it and his heart "poured forth understanding and wisdom increased in his breast." Firewater can do strange things to people and so can drugs; cf. Martyrdom of Isaiah 2:11; 2 Esdras 9:24.

34. 1 Enoch 14:8; 71:1, 5, etc.; Testament of Abraham 8; 2 Baruch 6:3f., etc., see Russell, *op. cit.*, pp. 162-173.
35. Jubilees 2:2, etc.; see Russell, *op. cit.*, pp. 235-262.
36. This title occurs over one hundred times in 1 Enoch.
37. E.g., Testament of Reuben 2:1-3:10.
38. 1 Enoch 103:4f.; 2 Esdras 7:78; Adam and Eve 32:4, "Rise up Eve; behold Adam, your husband, has gone out of his body. Rise up and behold his spirit, borne aloft to his maker."
39. 2 Esdras 7:80ff.; 1 Enoch 9:10.
40. The popular modern alternative of either immortality of the soul or resurrection of the body does not apply to 1 Enoch, 2 Esdras, 2 Baruch or Apocalypse of Moses which all have both.
41. Wisdom of Solomon 1:7; 12:1; 7:22-25.
42. Wisdom of Solomon 2:23; 5:15; 8:13, 17, 19f.
43. In the Q saying of Matthew 12:28 (equals Luke 11:20) the first evangelist changed "finger" of God into "Spirit" of God in order to bring it into line with the preceding quotation from Isaiah which refers to God's Spirit and the following section on the blasphemy against the Spirit. To suppose that it was Luke who changed Spirit to finger is an unlikely hypothesis, because Luke never refers any other miracles in his two-volume work to God's "finger." To suppose, as Schweizer does, that Luke made the change because he did not wish to connect the Spirit with miracles is even less likely in view of Luke's idea of the Spirit as divine power which produces a virginal conception. For the explicit connection between Spirit and power see Luke 1:17, 35; 24:49; Acts 1:8. Likewise Spirit and miracles are clearly connected in Luke 4:18, Acts 6:3-8; 8:39; 10:38. That the Spirit in Luke-Acts is also miracle working power should not be denied. Since Mark 13:11 presupposes the existence of the church, it would hardly seem to be an authentic word of Jesus prior to Easter. For a contrary view see Schweizer, *Theological Dictionary of the New Testament*, vol. 6, p. 398. Luke 4:18 and 11:13 are clearly redactional. The Q tradition of Luke 12:10 (equals Matthew 12:31f.) presupposes two periods, prior to Easter and after Easter, and is therefore not an authentic saying of Jesus. Its parallel in Mark 3:28ff. is a secondary development as Tödt has shown: *The Son of Man in the Synoptic Tradition* (Philadelphia: Westminster, 1965), pp. 118f.
44. See Jeremias, "The Prayers of Jesus," *Studies in Biblical Theology*, 2nd series, no. 6 (1969), pp. 11-65; esp. 57ff.
45. For the answers given by Windisch, Taylor, Flew, E. F. Scott, and others see: Barrett, *op. cit.*, pp. 3f., 95f., 135ff., 140f., etc. Barrett's own answer is dependent upon the historicity of the messianic secret, namely, that Jesus kept both his messianic office and his endowment with the Holy Spirit secret, but occasionally he let the secret slip, as at Matthew 12:28. Yet, Barrett's book contains many valuable insights.
46. The symbolism of the dove is not clear to us any longer. The Hebrew letters for the *shekinah*, the presence of God, were equated in a very

late text with "what is like a dove," *Theological Dictionary of the New Testament*, vol. 6, p. 382, esp. note p. 260.

47. On Mark 1:11, see Mona D. Hooker, *Jesus and the Servant* (Naperville, Illinois: Allenson, 1959), pp. 68-73.

48. For the historical background of conceptions by the Spirit of God see *Theological Dictionary of the New Testament*, vol. 5, p. 830f.; vol. 6, pp. 342, 402, and the literature there.

49. This is certainly true in Luke. In Mark baptism and descent are more closely related than in Luke. Yet also in Mark the descent does not occur while Jesus is being baptized, but as he is leaving the Jordan. John 1:31 does not even mention the baptism of Jesus.

50. For Luke it would be inappropriate to speak of Jesus "growing" in the Holy Spirit. Cf. Luke 1:30 with 2:40; so Schweizer in *Theological Dictionary of the New Testament*, vol. 6, p. 404f. But on the other hand if Luke intended to speak of John's growth in the Holy Spirit, we would expect him to write *en tō pneumati*, not *en pneumati*. Hence an anthropological use of *pneuma* in 1:30 seems probable, and with respect to 2:40 we note that some codices contain also the word *pneuma*. Schweizer also calls attention to Luke's stylistic change of Mark 1:12 in Luke 4:1, and concludes that "Jesus becomes the subject of an action *in* the Holy Spirit . . . he is the Lord of the *pneuma*." He based this conclusion upon the translation, "Jesus is led *in*, not by, the Spirit," but this introduces a false alternative into the text. Luke can say the same of Simeon, that he "came *in* the Spirit into the temple," Luke 2:27. But that does not make Simeon "Lord of the *pneuma*" either. In the third Gospel Jesus is not "Lord of the *pneuma*," but filled with *pneuma* in a unique way. The passive voice in 4:1 makes that rather clear. He becomes the "Lord of the *pneuma*" in Acts.

51. E. Haenchen wrongly connects the Spirit with the election of the apostles in this verse. *The Acts of the Apostles*, tr. by B. Noble et al. (Philadelphia: Westminster, 1971), pp. 135, 138f.

52. See John Reumann: "The Quest for the Historical Baptist," in *Understanding the Sacred Text*, Enslin Festschrift (Valley Forge: Judson Press, 1972), pp. 183-199.

53. Some interpreters held that the phrase "Holy Spirit" was a Christian addition; others hold that only "holy" was a Christian addition. In that case *pneuma* might not refer to Spirit, but to the eschatological windstorm and its winnowing function which separates the wheat from the chaff. But these hypotheses are not necessary.

54. The above interpretation is dependent on the recognition that the Q form of this saying (Luke 12:10 parallel) distinguished between two periods. To speak against the Son of man will be forgiven, if after Easter one accepts his word, but to reject the Holy Spirit present in the message of the Q community cannot be forgiven. The future Son of man will bring a baptism of fire upon the unbelievers who reject the message of Q (cf. Luke 17:26-30). In Mark's version (3:28-30), a different

point is made. There, blasphemy against the Holy Spirit consists in denouncing the earthly Jesus' exorcisms as demonic manifestations. In Mark, as in Q, this sin is committed by non-Christians.

Luke, however, went one step further by placing this saying in a new context (Luke 12:4-12), immediately after the word about confessing Jesus (v. 8). His meaning is that Christians who once acknowledged Jesus, but who subsequently denied him, have blasphemed against the Holy Spirit. Hence, even when Christians are placed on trial, they may not deny him but they can speak boldly because the Holy Spirit will empower them (vv. 11-12). In Luke, Hebrews 6:4-6, 1 John 5:16, this sin is committed only by Christians who had been under the Spirit's influence.

Barrett argues that the same applies to Q (Barrett, *op. cit.*, pp. 103-107). His interpretation would demand that the sequence of Luke 12:8-10 was identical with the sequence of the sayings in Q. However, Luke shifted Mark 13:11 to its present position in Luke 12. Furthermore, also v. 10 did not originally follow v. 8 because of the different meanings which the title "Son of man" has in these verses. In v. 8 it is the future Son of man who in judgment will acknowledge those who confessed him. But in v. 10, the Son of man is Jesus prior to Easter, and to speak against this Son of man is a pardonable offense in v. 10. Therefore, we conclude: In Q, as in Mark, this saying was probably directed against unbelievers. In Luke this saying is applied to Christian renegades.

55. *Pace* Schweizer, *Theological Dictionary of the New Testament*, vol. 6, p. 398. See Acts 1:5; 11:16.

56. A Lukan addition to Q. A variant reading in place of the second petition of the Lord's Prayer in Luke 11:2 reads: "Thy Holy Spirit come upon us and cleanse us." It is found in Marcion, Tertullian, some church fathers of the 4th and 5th centuries, and two minuscules. In the light of 1 QS 4:21, it can no longer be affirmed that the idea expressed in the variant could not have been held by a first century Jew prior to Easter. But simultaneously, it is even more difficult to understand why this reading should have been supplanted if it had been original.

57. G. W. Lampe, "The Holy Spirit in the Writings of St. Luke," in D. E. Nineham (ed.), *Studies in the Gospels: Essays in Memory of R. H. Lightfoot* (Naperville, Illinois: Allenson, 1955), p. 169 f. See also J. H. E. Hull, *The Holy Spirit in the Acts of the Apostles* (New York: The World Publishing Co., 1968), pp. 15-40.

58. Schweizer, *Theological Dictionary of the New Testament*, vol. 6, p. 408, holds this interpretation of Acts 5:30 to be "highly unlikely."

59. Eusebius frequently quoted Matthew 28:19 without the trinitarian formula, writing "make disciples in my name teaching them to obey," (e.g., *Ecclesiastical History* III,5,3), etc. Hence F. C. Conybears in *Zeitschrift für neutestamentliche Wissenschaft* 2 (1901), pp. 275-288, and J. Jeremias, *The Origins of Infant Baptism*, Studies in Historical The-

ology 1, 1963, 57, and others argued for the originality of the text as found in Eusebius. Still others like Stendahl (Peake's Commentary on the Bible, New York: Nelson, 1962, p. 798) wish to omit only the trinitarian formula and would then read "make disciples baptizing them in my name, teaching them," etc. For the difficulties inherent in such hypotheses, see Barrett, op. cit., p. 103.

60. For Matthew's Son of God Christology see J. D. Kingsbury: *Matthew; Structure, Christology, Kingdom* (Philadelphia: Fortress, 1975), pp. 40-83.

61. For various interpretations of the formula "baptizing in the name of," see W. Heitmuller, *Im Namen Jesu, Forschungen zur Religion und Literatur des Alten und Neuen Testamentums* 12 (1903); G. Delling, *Die Zueignung des Heils in der Taufe* (Berlin, 1961); Bietenhard in *Theological Dictionary of the New Testament*, vol. 5, pp. 242-280; L. Hartmann, "Into the name of Jesus," *New Testament Studies*, vol. 20 (1974), pp. 432-440; R. Bultmann, *Theology of the New Testament* (New York: Scribners, 1951), vol. 1, pp. 39ff.

62. Cf. G. Bornkamm, "Der Auferstandene und der Irdische, Matt. 28:16-20," in *Zeit und Geschichte*, edited by E. Dinkler (Tübingen, 1964); pp. 171-192; J. D. Kingsbury: "The Composition and Christology of Matt. 28:16-20," *Journal of Biblical Literature* 93 (1974), pp. 573-584.

63. H. Conzelmann, *The Theology of St. Luke* (New York: Harper, 1960); J. Rohde, *Rediscovering the Teachings of the Evangelists* (Philadelphia: Westminster, 1968), pp. 153-239.

64. With Conzelmann, *Apostelgeschichte*, pp. 28f. we read in Acts 2:17, "in the last days," instead "after these things," so Haenchen, but contrary to Conzelmann we think that Luke understood the time of the church to be eschatological time, which ushers in not just a new age (so Schweizer, *Theological Dictionary of the New Testament*, vol. 6, p. 411) but the new age, which finds its climax at the parousia.

65. Thus Schweizer, *Theological Dictionary of the New Testament*, vol. 6, p. 411; J. Munk, *The Acts of the Apostles* in *The Anchor Bible*, 31 (Garden City: Doubleday, 1967), p. 272.

66. See E. Lohse, "pentēkostē," *Theological Dictionary of the New Testament*, vol. 6, pp. 44-53; S. M. Gilmour, "Easter and Pentecost," *Journal of Biblical Literature*, vol. 81 (1965), pp. 62-66.

67. Philo, *De Somniis* 1, 238; *De fuga et inventione* 5.

68. C. S. C. Williams, *A Commentary on the Acts of the Apostles*, Harper's New Testament Commentaries (New York, 1957), p. 62; also Schweizer, *Theological Dictionary of the New Testament*, vol. 6, p. 410.

69. Cf. Isaiah 66:18; Testament of Judith 25:3.

70. K. Lake, "The Gift of the Spirit on the Day of Pentecost," note X in vol. 5 of *The Beginnings of Christianity* (London: Macmillan, 1933).

71. Lake, *op. cit.*, p. 117f., and others assume that Luke changed an earlier account which referred to glossolalia into the present narrative. Behind

this hypothesis lies the consideration that a mass outburst of glossolalia is at least imaginable.

It is more probable that 2:1-13 is a Lukan construction which incorporated some traditional elements, like theophany, motifs, the phrase "speaking in other tongues" and a list of nations. See Conzelmann, *Apostelgeschichte,* p. 27; R. F. Zehnle, *Peter's Pentecost Discourse. Tradition and Lukan Reinterpretation in Peter's Speeches of Acts 2 and 3.* Society of Biblical Literature Monograph Series 15 (New York: Abingdon Press, 1971), pp. 111-123.

72. Elamites are mentioned by Tacitus, *Annales* VI, p. 44. Haenchen, *Acts, op. cit.,* p. 170.
73. Contrary to Haenchen, *Acts,* p. 184.
74. H. J. Michel, *Die Abschiedsrede des Paulus an die Kirche, Apostelgeschichte 20:17-38,* in *Studien zum AT und NT,* 35 (Munich, 1973).
75. F. D. Bruner, *A Theology of the Holy Spirit, The Pentecostal Experience and the New Testament Witness* (Grand Rapids: Eerdmans, 1970).
    James D. G. Dunn, *Baptism in the Holy Spirit, Studies in Biblical Theology,* 2nd series, no. 15 (London, 1970).
76. Listed and discussed by Dunn, *op. cit.,* pp. 55-68.
77. Dunn, *op. cit.,* pp. 63-65
78. R. Bultmann, *op. cit.,* p. 139.
79. Conzelmann, *Apostelgeschichte,* p. 55.
80. Bruner, *op. cit.,* pp. 173-181.
81. Bruner, *op. cit.,* pp 177-178. He speaks of a "temporary suspension of the normal."
82. Conzelmann, *op. cit.,* p. 55.
83. Bruner, *op. cit.,* pp. 175-176.
84. In addition to Bruner and Dunn see E. Käsemann, "The Disciples of John the Baptist in Ephesus" in *Essays on New Testament Themes, Studies in Biblical Theology* (1st series), no. 41 (Naperville, Illinois: Allenson, 1964), pp. 136-148.
85. E. Lohse, *Die Ordination im Spätjudentum und im Neuen Testament* (Göttingen, 1951), p. 67.
86. Bruner, *op. cit.,* p. 211.

Edgar Krentz

The Spirit in Pauline and Johannine Theology

I. The Spirit in Paul

In the New Testament Paul the Apostle above all others develops and extends the understanding of the role of the Holy Spirit. For Paul the Spirit is the dynamic presence of Christ in the post-resurrection church. He empowers, shapes, and norms the confession, life, and hope of both the individual Christian and the community.[1]

A. *The Eschatological Dimension*

The presence of the Spirit is evidence for Paul that the old age is over and gone.[2] The book of Galatians is a key index to this side of Paul's thought. Christ has rescued us from "this present evil age" (1:4). There was a time when Christians were "under law" (4:5) and under "the elemental spirits of the universe" (4:3). "But when the fullness of the time had come, God sent out his Son, who came into being from a woman, under law, in order that he might buy back those who were under law, that we might receive sonship by adoption" (4:4-5). The decisive turn has taken place; the curse of the law has done its worst (3:13). The Christian lives in the post "evil æon" age.

The Spirit is the dynamic by which this sonship and all that it entails is given to the individual Christian. "But because you are sons, God sent out the Spirit of his Son into our hearts, shouting Abba, Father. So then, you are no longer a slave, but a son; and if you are a son, you are also an heir through God" (4:6-7). The parallelism of verses 6-7 with verses 4-5 is striking. What the Son does for the whole

47

of mankind, the Spirit does for the individual; he brings the promise of sonship to the individual. As the Son was sent, so is the Spirit; as the Son brought adoption, so the Spirit teaches the acclamation "Abba, Father." We are made sons by the Spirit within our hearts.[3] (The parallel in Romans 8:15-16 is striking; there the Spirit witnesses with our spirit that we are sons of God by enabling the acclamation.) Galatians stresses that the force for sonship comes from outside of us (cf. "the Spirit who is given us" in Romans 5:5), from God. The Holy Spirit is thus "the actual . . . conveyance of salvation." [4] *Conzelmann*

This coming of the Spirit cannot be separated in Paul from the coming of Jesus Christ (4:4). The Spirit comes only when "Christ is vividly painted before one's eyes as crucified" (3:1-2). His being a curse under the law for us is the condition for the blessing of Abraham coming to the Gentiles. Thus we "receive the promise of the Spirit by faith" (3:13-14). Therefore an appeal for action on the basis of the Spirit is often coupled with the appeal to the Lord Jesus (cf. Romans 15:30; Philippians 2:1).

The Spirit leads to confession of Jesus. "No man can say that Jesus is Lord except by the Holy Spirit" (1 Corinthians 12:3).[5] Just as the Spirit teaches the acclamation "Abba, Father," so he teaches the Christian to own Christ as his Lord.[6] That confession separates the Christian from his past life and the false spirit that lead him to say "anathema on Jesus." It delivered him from idolatry and slavery to false lords (12:2). The Thessalonians had turned to the living and genuine God from idols and were awaiting his Son (1 Thessalonians 1:9-10). That happened because Paul's gospel came to them accompanied "by power and Holy Spirit and great assurance" (1:5). The Spirit that leads to confession is a Spirit of power who convicts the hearer of the truth of the confession. He leads to acceptance.

The Spirit is so intimately related to Christ because Christ is himself a dynamic Spirit after the resurrection. He is a *pneuma zōopoioun* (1 Corinthians 15:45). Thus Christ as well as the Spirit can be used to describe the motive power and the sphere in which the Christian finds himself. The confessing Christian can speak of being "in Christ" in order to describe the new life of deliverance from the old bondage (2 Corinthians 5:17) or he can speak of Christ being in the Christian ("Christ lives in me" Galatians 2:20). Indeed, the relationship between Christ and the Spirit after the resurrection is so close that one can almost interchange the ideas of the Spirit's indwelling (Romans 8:9) and Christ's indwelling in the Christian (8:10).[7] Similarly one can speak either of being "in Christ" (6:1, 8:10) or "in the Spirit" (Galatians 5:22f.) to describe the new life. When Paul describes the work of the Spirit in leading us to understand the deep things of God, he says that we received the Spirit from God in order that we might know the things freely given by God to us (1 Corinthians 2:12). These things are "the wisdom of God in a mystery hidden . . . before the ages for our glory" (2:7). That wisdom and mystery, as the word *charisthenta* (v. 12) suggests, is nothing other than the word of the cross (1:18). The word that is taught by the Spirit in comparing "spiritual things with spiritual" (2:13) is thus the gospel of the crucified Lord (2:2). Small wonder that Paul concludes this section on the mystery with the triumphant claim "but we have the mind of Christ" (2:16)![8] That does indeed lead one to know the mind of the Lord (Isaiah 40:13), if not to be his counselor.

The bridge between Christ and the Spirit is the proclamation of the gospel. It is the "hearing of faith" (Galatians 3:2, 5) that brought the Spirit to the Galatians. The Thessalonians were selected as first fruits for salvation "in the sanctification of Spirit and faith that is true"; God called them into it through Paul's gospel (2 Thessalonians 2:13-14). Paul hawked the gospel of God to the Gentiles that the offering of the Gentiles might be acceptable, sanctified by the Holy Spirit (Romans 15:16). The false message of the super apostles is described by Paul as the reception of "another Jesus," "another Spirit," and "another gospel" (2 Corinthians 11:4). Indeed the Spirit that comes with the gospel and his mighty deeds is all that is needed to ratify the gospel, to show that it really is the gospel of God. The gospel does not depend on persuasive arguments of wisdom; in that way confidence will rest in the power of God (1 Corinthians 2:4-5).

Because the Spirit is tied to Christ and the gospel, he also cannot be separated from faith. The Galatians received the Spirit *ex akoēs pisteōs* (Galatians 3:2, 5). The Spirit and true faith are the means by which God chose the Thessalonians (2 Thessalonians 2:13). The promise of the Spirit comes through faith (Galatians 3:13-14). Paul blesses the Romans: But the God of hope fill you with all joy and peace in believing that you may abound in hope by the power of the Holy Spirit (Romans 15:13).

[Handwritten marginal note: What brings the Spirit to people is the proclamation of Christ]

There is in Paul no speculation about the role of the Spirit in cosmology.[9] There had been in Judaism. Nor is there any hint of the enthusiasm (in the literal sense) of Philo. The Spirit does not come or work apart from Christ, the gospel, and faith. There is thus no room in Paul's thought for a kind of independent possession of the Christian by the Spirit operating alone and for itself.

This does not mean that the Spirit does not do deeds of power. As the life-giving Spirit of the resurrected Christ he is accompanied by power and its effects. *Dynamis* is frequently found in tandem with Spirit, for example in Romans 1:3 of Christ's resurrection, in 1 Thessalonians 1:5 of the signs accompanying the Spirit in preaching, in Galatians 3:5 of the powerful ratification of the presence of the Spirit through the proclamation of the cross. (See also 1 Corinthians 2:4 and Romans 15:18f.) [10]

As the eschatological presence of Christ, the Spirit produces eschatological "results." He produces in Christians the acclamation that demonstrates that they are "sons" of the Father (Galatians 4:6; Romans 8:15-16). He gives the certain conviction of the gospel to the Thessalonians that leads them to joy, the mark of eschatological life (1 Thessalonians 1:5-6). That joy is called a "fruit of the Spirit" in Galatians 5:22, and gives pride of place only to love. Joy is accompanied by righteousness and peace in the Holy Spirit as demonstrations of the kingdom of God (Romans 14:17). The blessing of Romans 15:13 similarly calls for joy and peace through faith. As Rudolf Bultmann [11] has pointed out, peace in such phrases is the equivalent of salvation, an eschatological phenomenon (cf. Romans 2:10; 8:6; 15:33; Philippians 4:7, 9; 1 Thessalonians 5:23). The Spirit brings a renewal of the mind as he teaches men the "mind of Christ" (1 Corinthians 2:16);[12] now Christians can think the things of the Spirit (8:5) and now they can know that the Spirit brings peace and life (8:6). As eschatological force the Spirit brings to the Christian the phenomena of the eschaton. To be "boiling with the Spirit" (Romans 12:12) is thus also to be "rejoicing in hope."

As eschatological force the Spirit also points to the future consummation of the work of Christ. He is himself only the first fruits (Romans 8:23), the down payment or earnest money on the future (2 Corinthians 1:22; 5:5). In the middle of the groaning of this world in labor pains as it waits for its own adoption as sons, the Spirit prays for our spirit and with our spirit (Romans 8:23, 26). That prayer produces the conviction that nothing can keep God from carrying out his plan of love in the future. He is the God who raised Jesus from the dead (8:32-34); that resurrection is the assurance that we also shall be made alive "through the Spirit that inhabits our mortal bodies" (8:11). Life by the Spirit is the way to resurrection (8:13). The Spirit is the one who makes alive (2 Corinthians 3:6; cf. 1 Corinthians 15:45). Just as the old covenant written on stone was a covenant of death, so the new covenant written by the Spirit of the living God (2 Corinthians 3:3) on fleshly hearts is a covenant for life. Even though the events of the world about us shout that we are in a world of destruction, transitoriness, and death (1 Corinthians 4:1ff.), still we know that we are being transformed from glory to glory (3:18). We see that glory in the face of Christ, the image of God (2 Corinthians 4:4-6), "who raised the Lord Jesus and will raise us with Jesus and set us before himself with him" (4:14). Our conviction is effected, says Paul, and comes from having the "same Spirit of faith" (4:13). Therefore we know that life is active among you.

The Spirit is thus "the eschatological guarantee in the present," and he will not disappoint us.[13] "Hope will not make us ashamed" because the Spirit given to us pours out the love of God in our hearts (Romans 5:5). By the Spirit from faith we have "hope of righteousness"; our conviction comes from him who called us (Galatians 5:6-8). The Christian who sows to the Spirit will reap eternal life from the Spirit (Galatians 6:8). Paul can face an uncertain future with confidence because he has been equipped with the Spirit of Jesus Christ (Philippians 1:19); therefore, all will turn out *eis sōtērian.*

W. D. Davies is thus correct when he describes the Spirit as the one through which Paul expresses the ". . . redemptive and eschatological aspects of his faith, that newness of life now and in the future that had come through Christ."[14] For Paul can only speak of the Spirit in terms of Jesus Christ.[15]

B. The Community Dimension

What has been said up to this point might suggest that Paul has a strongly individualistic Spirit in his theology. The Spirit then is conceived of as that dynamic power of God that actualizes in the heart of the individual the achievement of the work of Christ. And that is, of course, true. But it is scarcely the whole truth. The Spirit in Paul has strongly communal character.[16] He has been given primarily to the community.[17] The individual Christian discovers that the Spirit does not lead to individual spiritualism, but rather to the life of loving service in the community of faith that edifies the neighbor. The Spirit sustains Christian life through the gifts he gives to the community (1 Corinthians 12:4ff.).

The unity of the Church is inferred by Paul both from the unity of Christ and from the one Spirit. Over against the schisms in the church of Corinth Paul pleads the fact that Christ cannot be divided (1:13). The church should have the same mind and the same opinion (knowledge), i.e., the word of the cross. The evaluation placed on the brother is given to him by the fact that Christ died for him; therefore even the weakest brother has the value of Christ (8:11). The sin of individualism is a sin against Christ.

But the unity of the Christian church is just as easily inferred by Paul from the fact that the church is the one temple of the true God. In 1 Corinthians 3, Paul argues that while he and Apollos both worked in the garden of the church, it was God who caused increase. While he and others worked at erecting the building, only Christ is the foundation. The building metaphor leads Paul to describe the church as God's temple (3:16, 17).

R. J. McKelvey has pointed out that it is the church and not the individual Christian that is the temple here (contrary to 1 Corinthians 6:17). God no longer lives in a building located on a specific piece of land. No, the church as corporate entity *(hymeis!)* is the temple of God because (explicative *kai* in v. 16) the Spirit of God inhabits it. The church is numinous; like the temple in the Old Testament (cf. Numbers 16:3; Zechariah 14:20), and it must also be holy.[18]

In 1 Corinthians 12, Paul brings the two bases for the unity of the church together. The one Spirit leads to the confession of the one Lord (v. 3). That common confession thus triumphs over the variety of gifts present in the one church. They come from the one Spirit, the one Lord, and the one God who works all things in all people. As the first gifts are mentioned (vv. 8-10) Paul emphasizes that they are given by "one and the selfsame Spirit," who works in each as he (sovereignly) wills (v. 11). The variety of gifts, however, does not lead to a variety of communities, as Paul illustrates by the metaphor of the body. "For just as the body is one and has many members, but all the members of the body being many are one body, so also is— Christ" (v. 12). The conclusion is a surprise. One expects to hear "so also is the church." But the purpose is made clear in verse 13. The Spirit was active in baptism to incorporate all Christians, varied as they are, into one body—Christ's. Thus Spirit and Christ come together in working the unity of the Christian community. You are Christ's body and members part by part (v. 27). The one Spirit and the one Christ are the base from which to argue the one church.

Schisms and divisions contradict this essential unity of the church. The division between Jew and Gentile is irrelevant. Those far off are now together with those who were near. Both are in one body and have access to the Father by the one Spirit (Ephesians 2:15-18). The unity of the church is founded by the sevenfold variation: one body, one Spirit, one hope, one Lord, one faith, one baptism, one God and Father (Ephesians 4:4-6). There is no longer Jew or Greek, slave or free, male or female; in Christ all are one, because of the promise (Galatians 3:28-29). Schisms and offenses are contrary to the gospel Paul taught; those who make them offend against the one Christ (Romans 16:17-18).

C. The Liberating Dimension

The Spirit is both eschatological and social in his effects. He transfers men to the community of sons who are heirs of the promise and sons of God. They are joined in the body of Christ; they are those who by the Spirit confess *Kyrios Iēsous*. The Christian is one who has a new Lord—and thereby is set free from all other lords "to serve as slave in the newness of the Spirit, not the antiquity of the letter" (Romans 7:6). He is no longer under the slavery to sin (5:12-20), but set free to serve righteousness and God (6:18, 22). He is delivered from the law (Romans 7:6; Galatians 3:13, 25; 4:4, 5) into sonship by the Spirit through the gospel (cf. 1 Corinthians 6:11). Death too is on the way out, for the life-giving Spirit (1 Corinthians 15:45; 2 Corinthians 3:6; cf. Galatians 3:21) already knows that the song of victory can be sung over death (1 Corinthians 15:54, 55). "The goad of death is sin, and the power of sin is the law" (1 Corinthians 15:56). But the "law of the Spirit of life in Christ Jesus has freed us from the law of sin and

death" (Romans 8:2). The victory over the unholy three is shown by
the fact that the law cannot bring the Spirit, but the Spirit is present.[19]

This freedom calls the Christian to a thoughtful and careful testing
of the spirits. There are other spirits abroad in the world, the rulers of
this age (1 Corinthians 2:8). "There are many gods and many lords"
(8:5). It is a spirit, though not the Spirit of God, that calls forth the
acclamation *Anathema Iēsous* (12:2). The *diakrisis pneumaton*, the
distinguishing of spirits, is the counterpart to the confession of one
God and one Lord (12:7; 8:6). While one should not extinguish the
Spirit or despise prophecy, he should put all to the test (1 Thessalonians 5:19-21). Liberty in the Spirit that is given by Christ can be
lost by individualism (1 Corinthians 12), by not recognizing the work
of the one Spirit. It can be lost by moving from the Spirit back to the
law (Galatians 3:1-5; 5:1-4), or by living according to flesh (one's own
individualistic selfish self) and not Spirit (5:13, 16).

D. *The Parenetic Element*

The free community of sons is the temple of the Spirit called to
holiness (1 Corinthians 6:11), an "active holiness" that is realized in
life according to the eschatological standard.[20] The Spirit is not the
giver of formless freedom; rather the life of the Spirit is formed and
normed by the Spirit of Christ.[21] "Only carry on your life in a way
worthy of the gospel of Christ, that whether coming and seeing you or
being absent I hear about your affairs, that you stand fast in one Spirit,
with one mind contesting for the faith of the gospel . . ." (Philippians 1:27). "If there is then an exhortation in Christ, if any encouragement of love, if any fellowship of the Spirit, if any mercies and
pities, fulfill my joy. . . ." (Philippians 2:1). If holiness is not the character of Christian life, then one is setting aside the God who gave us
the Holy Spirit (1 Thessalonians 4:7). Holiness, actively lived, is the
hallmark of life in the Spirit.

Parenesis in the age of sonship by the Spirit is and must be eschatological parenesis. Life is to be lived as holy in body and in spirit
(1 Corinthians 7:34). That can only be achieved by living in the
world "as if not. . . ." (7:29-31). The time is compressed and the fashion of this world passes away; therefore one must live as if he is not
in this world. That means a liberation from the standards of this world,
from conformity to men and their standards (cf. 7:17-24), and a living

"before God." The Spirit as the power of the present Lord is the one who makes such life in the face of God possible.

The Christian is to be led by the Spirit (Romans 8:14; Galatians 5:18). The Spirit is the source of power for the new life, for he brings newness with him (Romans 7:6). The love of the Spirit is poured out in our hearts, and therefore we can pray for one another (cf. Romans 15:30). That love produced in Paul (1 Corinthians 4:21) and in the Christian community in general a spirit of meekness (Galatians 6:1). The Spirit in our hearts makes the new life possible.

But he is also its norm. To be led by the Spirit means to walk according to Spirit *(kata pneuma)* and not some other standard (Galatians 5:16; Romans 8:4). The Christian walks by the Spirit (Galatians 5:16) and guides his steps *(stoichein)* by the Spirit (5:25). The Spirit is not a power that drags the Christian along as an unwilling slave. That is the attitude of the Stoic who prays:

> Lead thou me on, O Zeus and Destiny,
> To that goal long ago to me assigned.
> I'll follow and not falter; if my will
> Prove weak and craven, still I'll follow on.[22]

To which Seneca added the Latin line:

> *Ducunt volentem fata, nolentem trahunt.*[23]

Rather the Spirit creates in man a new will. He enters into the heart of man (Galatians 4:6), so that the Spirit there "lusts against the flesh" (5:17). The Spirit has a thought *(phronēma)* that is life and peace (Romans 8:6); that thought is a power and a guide for the Christian. It leads him to seek the higher gifts of grace (1 Corinthians 12:31).

The Spirit gives the Christian a guide to life in a number of ways. By the Spirit Paul gives ethical directives (cf., for example, Galatians 6:1-10). When he discusses the spiritual gifts in 1 Corinthians, he stresses that these gifts are given for the upbuilding of the body (12:7); every action does not build up (6:16, 10:23). Paul therefore has no hesitation or reserve about giving specific directives to his congregations about specific actions. However, the Spirit also provides a more general guide that fits all situations: the entire law is comprehended in the word love *(agapē,* Galatians 5:13, 14), which the Galatians are to use in serving as slaves to one another. The same "law" is urged in Romans 12:8-10 from Leviticus 19:18; its importance is underscored by setting it into an eschatological context (Romans 12:11-14). This *agapē* is stressed as the "more excellent way" (1 Corinthians 12:31) and exemplified in 1 Corinthians 13. In Galatians Paul stresses that the Spirit produces fruit and gives a long list of the effects it has (5:22-24). The list is composed of "social" virtues; these are the results of the crucifixion of the flesh and the walking according to the Spirit (5:24, 25).

The Spirit is a Spirit of power. It produces the ministrations of *agapē*. But it also produces the "strange" events that accompany the proclamation and support it. These occur in word and deed, "in the power of signs and marvels, in the power of the Spirit." (Romans 15:18, 19). But such deeds pale before the great miracle of the Spirit taking residence in us, becoming immanent and producing the good fruit of love (cf. Romans 8:9, 11; 1 Corinthians 6:19).

E. The Doxological Dimension

The Spirit is the one prerequisite for worship in the New Testament.[24] He is the source of all *charismata*, all spiritual gifts (1 Corinthians 12:7-13); to every Christian some such gift is given (v. 11). In these gifts the exalted Lord (15:45) and the Spirit (1 Corinthians 12) are at work for the community. That work includes the production of the visible wonders of ecstasy, glossolalia, visions, and miracles. The reality of such wonders is not contested; indeed, Paul himself sees visions in ecstasy (2 Corinthians 12:1ff.) and also speaks in tongues (1 Corinthians 14:18). He knows too that the Spirit is the revealer of the "deep things of God" (2:6-16). The Spirit does wonders.

But Paul knows that such wonders in worship need a criterion to prevent them from dividing the community of the one Spirit. The unity of the Spirit itself becomes such a criterion for Paul. Every gift of the Spirit must serve the common good in edification (1 Corinthians 12:7). That is especially true of these gifts that are more spectacular, such as speaking in tongues (1 Corinthians 14:4, 12, 17). If a gift can be used in the service of the community, it is of the Spirit. For *every* Christian is pneumatic, since by the Spirit he confesses Christ (12:3).[25] The Spirit is not more present in the more spectacular works; the "better way" includes faith, hope, and above all love (1 Corinthians

13). That is why the list of *charismata* in 1 Corinthians 12:8-10 includes such down-to-earth gifts as helpers and administrators. The one who speaks in tongues is to have an interpreter there to make all know what has been said (14:27).

The list of *charismata* (1 Corinthians 12:8-10, 12:28, 12:29-30; Romans 12:6; Ephesians 4:11) all include the gift of prophecy.[26] (Only Galatians 5:22, 23 is an exception.) The Spirit is a revealer of the mysteries of God (1 Corinthians 2:6-16). Paul supports this gift of revelation. But he stresses that prophecy, which is "the proclamation of salvation through the operation of the Spirit," must be both lucid and rational. To know the mystery of the cross is to have "the mind of Christ" (1 Corinthians 2:16). The proclamation of that mystery must appeal to the mind as well as the Spirit; it must speak to understanding (14:14-19). Then two vital goals are accomplished. Those in the Spirit can pronounce their "amen" to your words as evidence that they are built up (14:16). The non-Christian who wanders into the Christian assembly will be put to examination by all and will recognize that God is truly present among the worshiping congregation (14:24, 25). The Spirit is thus an eminently rational and lucid force. Glossolalia, regarded by the Corinthians as *the* charisma, is put into its proper, i.e., secondary, place.

And thereby the Spirit is revealed as a Spirit of propriety and order (14:40). Events take place in the doxological assembly in an order that respects the gift of the Spirit to each Christian. The gift to each Christian is recognized without there being a stifling of the Spirit. ". . . the Spirit and order are no more mutually exclusive than are Spirit and (church) law."

The Spirit is the dynamic power of Christ at work in the church and each Christian. He calls, forms, and norms the faith and life of the church. His presence by gospel and baptism is the indispensable prerequisite for the existence of the church which he mightily endows with his gifts.

II. The Spirit in John

A. *Jesus, Disciple, and Spirit in John*

The Gospel of John fascinates; its thought is like quicksilver, bright and glittering. But like quicksilver it often slips away from one's grasp just as one seems to have firm hold on it. Its thought does not move as does much of earlier New Testament thought. Earliest Christians at times thought of the death of Jesus as an evil that needed to be set right by the resurrection (cf. Acts 2:36; Philippians 2:6-11; Acts 3:13-15). But John puts the whole of Jesus' life, death, and resurrection under the category of "glory." His entry into our flesh shows forth glory (1:14), his miracles manifest his glory (2:11), his cross is his exaltation and glorification (3:14, 12:32, 17:1-2, etc.).[27] John's thought spirals around this theme, not in logically structured progression, but in cumulative meditation.

Indeed, John has so meditated on, prayed, and preached the words of Jesus that it is hard to tell where Jesus leaves off and John's own words begin in this Gospel. The parade example is the discourse with Nicodemus in John, chapter three; commentators differ widely as to where the change in speaker is made (v. 13, v. 16, or no change at all).[28] John talks like Jesus; Jesus talks the author's own language and style. The Gospel bears the imprint of this speech from beginning to end. Thus there is no point in trying to distinguish Jesus' and the author's words about the Spirit. They cohere.[29] For our purposes we shall treat John 1-20 as a unity.

B. *The Spirit and Jesus*

John's Christology is a unified one, set under the heading "glorification." So too is his conception of the manner in which salvation is accomplished. Salvation is a unity, achieved by the *acta salvifica*. These include Jesus' entry into the world from above, the deeds and words of Jesus, his exaltation on the cross, his resurrection, and the coming of the Spirit. Indeed, these are all united under the heading of glorification. The gift of the Spirit is the final, completing act of salvation. The full significance of Jesus' work and the full interpretation of his words are given only by the Spirit. Thus the gift of the Spirit is not an incidental addendum to the work of Christ, but the capstone to the saving act.[30] One is not surprised to find that the Spirit is mentioned early and, by contrast to the Synoptics, frequently; the Spirit is also regarded as present throughout Jesus' ministry.

Scholars have frequently pointed out that the Spirit in John is not an independent entity, but rather is tied closely to the work and words of Jesus. The Spirit descends on Jesus and remains on him

(1:32); he is thus present with Jesus during his entire ministry. He does not act independently during Jesus' ministry. He will be given to the disciples only after Jesus goes away (7:39), or is glorified. Thus the Spirit is tied to the incarnate Christ and works "apart from him" only after Jesus' glorification. The Spirit is evidence that God is with Jesus, just as later his presence is evidence that God is present with the believers (1 John 3:24; 4:13).[31] Jesus has the full Spirit; for the Spirit is not given "in part" *(ek metrou)*. Thus the Spirit does not lead to a truth later on that is different from or superior to what the Son knows and says, for the Father has given all things into his hands (3:34, 35).[32]

Thus the Spirit does not really exist in and for the disciples until Jesus is glorified. Jesus is prior to the Spirit (cf. 16:13), who can offer only what belongs to Jesus; in a sense Jesus is the canon of the Spirit, whom the disciples will receive "in the name of Jesus" (14:26).[33] But until Jesus' glorification the Spirit is tied to him. When Jesus is himself with them, the disciples in fact do not need the Spirit. For the Spirit says only what Christ says and does only what he does. Indeed, Ignace de la Potterie suggests that there is no need for the Spirit prior to the glorification of Christ, for his task is to call to faith in Christ via the word of Christ—a task that Jesus carries on himself before his glorification.[34]

The Spirit's close tie to Jesus is emphasized by the way in which the Spirit after the exaltation of Jesus parallels Jesus in his incarnation. Günther Bornkamm, J. Louis Martyn, C. K. Barrett, and Raymond Brown are only representative of many scholars,[35] when they say that the origin (16:27 equals 15:26; 8:42 equals 14:26), coming into the world (14:18, 28 equals 15:26), relation to world (8:19 equals 14:17; 15:18 equals 14:17; 3:18, 19 equals 16:8ff.), authoritative teaching of all they are told (7:16 equals 16:13, 3:32-34 equals 16:13), witness (8:14 equals 15:26), and final return to the Father (8:21 equals 16:5ff.) of Son and Spirit are described in similar terms. And the parallels could be extended! The paraclete is, to use Martyn's phrase, "the return of Jesus to his own." [36] In that way the disciples are in him and he in them (14:20). The Spirit takes Jesus' own and declares it to the disciples (16:14). Thus the Spirit is *"functionally* as well as *essentially* Christ's Spirit." [37]

The relationship is underscored by the fact that the Spirit is called

"another comforter" *(allos paraklētos)* in John 14:16. This other paraclete is entirely in the service of Jesus. Jesus promises to come again
himself (14:18), and that promise is kept by the coming of the Spirit
in his name (14:15, 16). That promise is kept when Jesus himself puts
his own breath *(pneuma)* on them and tells them to "receive holy
Spirit" *(pneuma* 20:22). It is understandable that James Dunn should
argue that the Spirit is the Spirit of Jesus, though John never uses
the phrase.[38]

Jesus was marked off by the abiding presence of the Spirit as more
than a prophet of the Old Testament; prophets possessed the Spirit
from time to time. But Jesus' words are words of God because he has
the Spirit (3:33, 34); Jesus has come from above *(anōthen)* and thus is
filled with Spirit, just as Nicodemus was to be born from above, of
the Spirit. Thus Jesus was equipped to know all things that belonged
to the Father, for God is Spirit. "Like comes through like" *(homoia di'*
homoiōn) is an old Greek principle. Jesus, endowed with Spirit, can
speak words that are Spirit, and thus faith in him brings waters of
life that conquer death (7:38, 39).

That clarifies why Jesus had to leave before the paraclete could
come (16:7). Jesus is himself a paraclete, the prior one (cf. *allos*
paraklētos in 14:16). As the heavenly man present in the world (cf.
3:13, 31; 6:62; 8:23), Jesus has (and keeps) the Spirit abiding on
him (1:32). There cannot be two concurrent paracletes in the world
at the same time. Therefore Jesus must go away in order that the paraclete might come *to the disciples* (16:7). His exaltation via the cross
is the necessary condition for the giving of the paraclete Spirit in
John.[39] One can also understand why John makes no mention of Jesus
as baptizing with Spirit in the fourth Gospel.

C. The Spirit and the Disciples

John 20:22 has the exalted Jesus give the Holy Spirit to the disciples.
What does this gift mean to the disciples? Dunn phrases it well: the
Spirit "affords *an immediate and direct continuity between believers*
and Jesus." [40] He does it by teaching and reminding the disciples of all
things that Jesus said to them (14:26). He is not independent. The
Father sends him "in my name" (14:26). If men ask anything "in his
name" (14:13), then Jesus will ask the Father and he will send the
paraclete (16:16), the Spirit of truth. That Spirit will witness to Jesus

(15:26). The Spirit is thus the teacher who repeats Jesus' teaching, who guarantees the gospel teaching to the disciples. He is not independent of Jesus' teaching or opposed to Jesus.[41] Just as Jesus did not speak on his own authority in John, but spoke the words of God, who had put all things into his hand (3:34, 35), so the Spirit speaks not his own words but Jesus' words. The Spirit is not a free-wheeling spirit. He is not an alternative to the tradition, to the *paradosis.* Rather the tradition controls the Spirit, who says nothing of himself.[42] He guides into all truth (16:13), but not on his own authority; he will only speak what he has heard, what is "mine." [43]

But the Spirit also marks an advance over the pre-glorification relation of Jesus to the disciples. He marks the fulfillment of what is in Jesus, prior to his glorification, partial and incomplete. Jesus lives in a time that is a "not-yet." He is on the way to the hour of glorification (cf. John 17:1ff.). The paraclete is quite otherwise. He gives or leads into the "full truth," into "all truth" that remains forever. Therefore the paraclete is not a temporary resident in the disciple community: the Father gives him that he may "be with you forever" (14:16)! And the disciples know him as the world does not, "because he stays with you and will be in you" (14:17). This almost makes Jesus a kind of "forerunner" of the paraclete, as Bornkamm strikingly formulates it.[44] John here strikes a unique note in early Christianity. The Spirit, while bound to the teaching of Jesus, will also complete it (16:12-13). He will teach "all things" (14:26). Sent by the glorified Jesus the Spirit "will glorify" Jesus, a formulation that is both strikingly Johannine and singularly impressive (16:14). The Spirit will define and confirm the words that he will not speak of himself (16:13). He will continue, complete, and perfect the words of Jesus; he has no independent function, no separate *raison d'être.*[45] As Ulrich Müller puts it on the basis of a study of "farewell speeches," the paraclete will legitimate the church by providing a continuing presence of the absent one.[46]

The Spirit performs another function: he also defends Christ.[47] He reminds one of Jesus (14:26), makes him understandable (cf. 2:22 and 12:16), and so testifies to him. His testimony will also be a defense of Jesus (15:26) through the testimony which the church gives. For the Spirit enables confession to Jesus. He is the Spirit of truth, the truth that Jesus is the Christ, the Son of God (cf. 16:13; 1 John 4:2, 13). As the advocate of Christ he does not add to the confession or revelation; rather he enables the confession by assuring men that they are indeed in God (1 John 3:24).[48]

Because the Spirit witnesses to Jesus, he also forms and teaches the disciple community. John never uses the word church, but stresses the community in various ways. One is by holding that the Spirit has "altogether ecclesiastical and eschatological nature," to use Alf Corell's trenchant (if non-Johannine) phrase.[49] The Spirit is the giver of life also in John (6:63), the source of living water that comes via Jesus' words (7:39, 3:34, 35; cf. 4:10). The Spirit, who comes in baptism (3:5; 1 John 2:20), is thus the common possession of all Christians. He continues to come in the words of Jesus (6:63), words that "are spirit and life." Baptism enables one to hear and believe heavenly things (3:12), because it endows with Spirit from above. After the glorification of Jesus, the Spirit is present (7:39) and men who have the Spirit know and believe *(homoia di' homoiōn)*. The life-giving Spirit works via the words of Jesus.[50]

And so he enables the "greater works" of John 14:12. He announces the "things that are coming" and so leads into all truth (16:13). What are these greater works? Jesus' work was not ended or completed with his death. He goes to the Father (7:33) and leaves behind a work to be done. He is to work while it is day (9:4), but now that he is gone this work must be carried on by the Spirit in the disciples. That work is continued in the witness of the disciples (9:8-41).[51] The Spirit is throughout John related to the words of Jesus. After the exaltation of Jesus, "the Spirit is nothing else but the continual possibility and reality of the new encounter with Jesus in the post-Easter situation as the one who is revealing his Word to his own and through them to the world." [52] John does not know anything of an ecstatic Spirit who gives unusual gifts. The Spirit does not come now and then in extraordinary ways. He inspires no miraculous deeds. Neither Jesus nor his disciples are pneumatic.[53] Rather the Spirit is given as the power to forgive or retain sins (20:22-23). And that is done by the Word. The Spirit does no other work in or through the disciples.

D. The Spirit and the Cosmos

Thereby we come to the worldly and cosmic function of the Spirit. The Spirit convicts the world of sin, righteousness, and judgment (16:8-11). Thus John applies the well-known, earlier motif of the cosmic, life-producing power of the Spirit to the religious motif of life. The Spirit becomes the world's accuser because it does not know Jesus (14:17). Thereby the world is shown to be from below and condemned, because it does not believe on the name of the Son of God (3:17-18). Thus and thus alone the Spirit carries out its cosmic function by the Word.

When Jesus had taken the sour wine, he said, "It is finished," bowed his head and handed over the spirit (*paredōken to pneuma*, 19:30). To whom? The conclusion corresponds to the Johannine interpretation of Jesus' death as exaltation. There are no mockers at the cross in John. His mother and the disciple he loved stood close at hand. His glorification means the release of the Spirit into the church and through her into the world. That Spirit ties the disciple community to the Jesus who died, keeps it fixed to the tradition in the Word, and calls it to confession. John 20:22 makes it formal. The paraclete is come.

Notes

1. The literature is immense. For the earlier literature see E. Schweizer, *pneuma, pneumatikos, Theological Dictionary of the New Testament,* tr. by G. W. Bromiley (Grand Rapids: Eerdmans, 1968), vol. 6, pp. 389-455, especially pp. 415-437, and the bibliography on pp. 332-334.
2. E. Krentz, "Freedom in Christ—Gift and Demand," *Concordia Theological Monthly,* vol. 40 (1969), pp. 356-361.
3. See Hans Conzelmann, *An Outline of the Theology of the New Testament* (New York and Evanston: Harper & Row, 1969), p. 205.
4. *Ibid.,* p. 211.
5. Dieter Lührmann, *Das Offenbarungsverständnis bei Paulus* (Neukirchen, 1965), pp. 28-29.
6. W. D. Davies, *Paul and Rabbinic Judaism* (New York: Arno Press, 1955), 2nd edition, p. 201; Ferdinand Hahn, *The Worship of the Early Church* (Philadelphia: Fortress Press, 1973), p. 66.
7. Davies, *op. cit.,* pp. 177-178.
8. Schweizer, *op. cit.,* p. 425.
9. Davies, *op. cit.,* p. 188.
10. E. Earle Ellis, "Christ and Spirit in 1 Corinthians," *Christ and Spirit in the New Testament,* edited by Barnabas Lindars and Stephen S. Smalley in honor of C. F. D. Moule (Cambridge, 1973), pp. 270-271.
11. Rudolf Bultmann, *Theology of the New Testament* (New York: Scribner, 1951), vol. 1, p. 339.
12. Günther Bornkamm, *Paul* (New York and Evanston: Harper & Row, 1969), pp. 162-164, points out that the Spirit makes true wisdom avail-

able. See also G. Bornkamm, "Faith and Reason in Paul," *Early Christian Experience* (New York and Evanston: Harper & Row, 1969), pp. 35-42.

13. Bultmann, *op. cit.*, p. 348.
14. Davies, *op. cit.*, p. 177.
15. Bornkamm, *Paul*, p. 156.
16. Hahn, *op. cit.*, p. 62; Davies, *op. cit.*, p. 200.
17. Conzelmann, *op. cit.*, p. 258.
18. R. J. McKelvey, *The New Temple. The Church in the New Testament* (London, 1969), pp. 98-102.
19. F. D. Bruner, *A Theology of the Holy Spirit* (Grand Rapids: Eerdmans, 1970), p. 229.
20. Bultmann, *op. cit.*, p. 338.
21. Hahn, *op. cit.*, p. 63.
22. Epictetus, *Encheiridion*, 53.1.
23. *Epistulae Morales*, 107.11.
24. Hahn, *op. cit.*, pp. 33-34.
25. Lührmann, *op. cit.*, pp. 27-29.
26. On the *charismata* see A. C. Piepkorn, "Charisma in the New Testament and the Apostolic Fathers," *Concordia Theological Monthly*, vol. 42 (1971), pp. 369-389; E. Earle Ellis, "Spiritual Gifts in the Pauline Community," *New Testament Studies*, vol. 20 (1973-74), pp. 128-144, with rich bibliography.
27. Ernst Käsemann, *The Testament of Jesus* (Philadelphia: Fortress Press, 1968), pp. 6ff.; R. Bultmann, *Theology of the New Testament* (New York: Scribners, 1955), vol. 2, p. 48ff.
28. Raymond Brown, *The Gospel According to John* (Garden City, New York: Doubleday, 1966), vol. 1, p. 149.
29. I am aware that there is much discussion of the integrity of John and of the paraclete sayings. That discussion is not of significance for the purposes of this paper.
30. James D. G. Dunn, *Baptism in the Holy Spirit* (London, 1970), pp. 173-174.
31. F. Büchsel, *Der Begriff der Wahrheit in dem Evangelium und den Briefen des Johannes* (Gütersloh, 1911), p. 100.
32. Franz Mussner, *Zōē* (München, 1952), pp. 115-116.
33. Büchsel, *op. cit.*, p. 102.
34. I. de la Potterie, "L'Esprit dans l'Evangile de Jean," *New Testament Studies*, vol. 18 (1972), pp. 448-449.
35. G. Bornkamm, "Der Paraklet im Johannes-Evangelium," *Geschichte und Glaube* (München, 1968), vol. 1, pp. 77-79; J. Louis Martyn, *History and Theology in the Fourth Gospel* (New York and Evanston: Harper & Row, 1968), pp. 140-141; C. K. Barrett, *The Gospel According to St. John* (New York: Macmillan, 1955), p. 402; R. Brown, "The Paraclete in the Fourth Gospel," *New Testament Studies*, vol. 13 (1966-67), pp. 126-128.

36. Martyn, *op. cit.*, p. 141.
37. James Boice, *Witness and Revelation in the Gospel of John* (Grand Rapids: Zondervan, 1970), p. 152. The term "essential" in this quote is, I think, unjustified.
38. James D. G. Dunn, *Jesus and the Spirit* (Philadelphia: Westminster, 1975), pp. 350-351; Hans Windisch, *The Spirit-Paraclete in the Fourth Gospel* (Philadelphia: Fortress, 1968), p. 2, does not agree; Bornkamm, *Geschichte und Glaube*, pp. 80-83, calls attention to the fact that the Spirit is given messianic functions in John (teacher, prophet, judge) and compares it to the Son of Man in 1 Enoch.
39. W. F. Howard, *Christianity According to St. John* (Philadelphia: Westminster, 1946), p. 76; Windisch, *op. cit.*, p. 10.
40. Dunn, *Jesus and the Spirit*, p. 361; Ulrich B. Müller, "Die Parakletenvorstellung im Johannesevangelium," *Zeitschrift für Theologie und Kirche*, vol. 71 (1974), p. 60.
41. Windisch, *op. cit.*, pp. 6-8.
42. Käsemann, *op. cit.*, p. 37.
43. Bultmann, *Theology of the New Testament*, vol. 2, p. 89.
44. Bornkamm, *Geschichte und Glaube*, p. 69.
45. Martyn, *op. cit.*, p. 136.
46. Müller, *op. cit.*, p. 60.
47. Brown, "The Paraclete in the Fourth Gospel," p. 116.
48. Boice, *op. cit.*, pp. 153, 154.
49. Alf Corell, *Consummatum Est* (New York: Macmillan, 1958), p. 89.
50. George Johnson, *The Spirit-Paraclete in the Gospel of John* (Cambridge, 1970), p. 22.
51. Martyn, *op. cit.*, pp. 7-9.
52. Käsemann, *op. cit.*, pp. 45-46.
53. E. Schweizer, "Pneuma," *Theological Dictionary of the New Testament*, vol. 6, p. 438; Büchsel, *op. cit.*, p. 100; Werner Georg Kümmel, *The Theology of New Testament* (New York: Abingdon, 1973), p. 213.

William G. Rusch

The Doctrine of the Holy Spirit in the Patristic and Medieval Church

Actually our title is somewhat misleading, for it implies that in the extensive corpus of writings produced by the church of the patristic and medieval periods there was one belief, teaching, and confession about the Holy Spirit.[1] The impression could be given that like Athena from Zeus' head, *a* doctrine of the Holy Spirit emerged from the biblical material which experienced no vicissitudes from the close of the New Testament until the Reformation of the sixteenth century. As the following survey will clearly indicate, nothing could be farther from the truth. There is a considerable divergence of views about the Holy Spirit in the early history of the church. While it is accurate to acknowledge that by the time of scholasticism such dissimilitude has sharply decreased, homogeneity did not result. In fact, down to our own day, churches of the East and West retain different points of view about the third person of the Trinity.

An examination of the understanding of the Holy Spirit from the second to sixteenth centuries will reflect at times considerable unclarity, if not confusion, on the part of the church, as well as a certain progression. Such a progression is apparent in comparing the doctrine of the Holy Spirit in the second and fifth centuries. It might be tempting to suggest that these circumstances occurred because theologians of the church were engaging in an intellectual pastime of speculative imagination. Such a temptation would be a serious misreading of history. A more precise explanation of the formulation of doctrine to be reviewed here is to see it as the end process of four factors at work on the conscience of the church.

First, the role of Scripture in the church. Christianity is a religion of the book, actually two books, Old and New Testaments. While there is not a great deal in the text of the Bible to force belief in a third co-equal person of the godhead, the presence of the Spirit in the biblical text is admittedly a fact the church cannot ignore.

Second, the influence of heresy. Some Christians claim to be able to define an aspect of faith more fully than the church has done up to that point, but they do so in a way that proves unacceptable to the main body of the church. In rejecting such views church leaders are forced to give a more detailed definition than the church has done up to that time.

Third, the worship of the church. It is often forgotten that the church is hopefully not only a thinking community but a worshiping one. The practice of worship was an effective means for passing aspects of the church's message from place to place and generation to generation. Besides this conservative function, worship could also aid more exact doctrinal definition, in that the terms of definition would be commensurate with the function of worship. One key reason for the acceptance of the full divinity of the Spirit was that baptism was regularly administered in the threefold name of Father, Son, and Holy Spirit.

Fourth, soteriology. Christianity is not merely a way of worship; it is a way of salvation. Soteriological concerns were of extreme importance in all the doctrinal disputes of the church. The Holy Spirit's work of sanctification, in baptism and elsewhere, involved making men sharers of the divine nature. If the Spirit was not himself of a fully divine nature, how could he make men partakers of it? Such thinking shows the effects of soteriology on the church's understanding of the Holy Spirit.

The development of the doctrine of the Holy Spirit which resulted from the interplay of these four factors is the subject of this chapter. Whether this particular development has been wholly good, true, or necessary would result in a treatment of questions which are fascinating but outside the scope of this endeavor.[2] Because of the complexity of the subject and the sheer bulk of primary and secondary materials, only the most significant aspects will be treated here. The reader interested in fuller accounts is advised to consult the standard works on the topic.[3]

The church's reflection about the Holy Spirit in the patristic and medieval ages can be divided into three periods which are able to be distinguished by certain preoccupations and limited to specific spans of time. While the device is artificial and may lead to an oversimplification of our subject, it is still an accurate gauge of how and when the church's attention was brought to bear on first one and then another aspect of its belief, teaching, and confession about the Holy Spirit. The first period may be called a time of "benign neglect." It extended from the end of the first century until the fourth. As the title suggests, concern about the Holy Spirit was not a priority item for the church during those centuries. The second period may be described as a "preoccupation with person." The overriding question of pneumatology at this time was a discussion of the Holy Spirit—is the Holy Spirit a person of the godhead or a creature?[4] This debate was one of the issues of the fourth century. The third period may be pictured as an "engrossment with the mode of origin." It was a time devoted to a consideration of the relationship within the godhead of the Spirit to the Father and the Son. What was the mode of origin of the Spirit and how did it differ from that of the Son? These questions taxed the ingenuity of ecclesiastical thinkers from Augustine to the Council of Florence (approximately fifth century until fifteenth).

I. Benign Neglect

It is fair to state that the church up to the year 300 was aware of the Holy Spirit, but it did not think out the implications of that awareness. The reasons for this situation are not as startling as might be imagined at the outset. For one thing, the earliest Christians had a higher agenda item: to think through and defend the person and work of the Son. This task had become urgent because of the pressures from paganism and Gnosticism. If in this process the church proclaimed that God was not unitary, it was as simple a matter to conceive of three persons as two. Also the biblical witness to the Spirit was not as comprehensive as that pertaining to the Son and did not require the same type of immediate apologetic. These factors contributed to a "benign neglect." For Christians of the first three centuries the Holy Spirit was real,

experienced in the life of the church, but the Spirit's status and relation to the Father and Son were not scientifically formulated. The
compulsion for such steps simply did not occur in the first three centuries of church history.

Nevertheless, if these years were not a time of profound thinking
about the Spirit, the Holy Spirit was not ignored. This period preserved the biblical references to Father, Son, and Spirit. Admittedly
there are statements about the Spirit which are obscure or imply a
subordination of his being to created or impersonal forces, but clearly
the Holy Spirit is an object of adoration and faith. In spite of the fact
that there is extreme reluctance to address the Spirit as God *(theos* or
deus), the Spirit in the mind of these early writers belongs to the
godhead.

The Apostolic Fathers, a varied group of Christian writers of the first
and early second centuries, present no formal theology of the Holy
Spirit, although references to the Spirit can be found in their writings.
1 Clement speaks of Father, Son, and Holy Spirit together (42.3 and
46.6); he coordinates them in an oath (58.2). Ignatius of Antioch
refers to Mary's conception by the Holy Spirit (Eph. 18.2). In some
passages he joins together Father, Son, and Spirit (Magn. 13.2, Eph.
9.1), although he does not cite the Matthean baptismal formula. The
Spirit spoke through Ignatius (Phil. 7.1). The Shepherd of Hermas
confuses the Son and Holy Spirit (Sim. 9.1, Sim. 5.6.5-7). The exact
views of this book are difficult to determine. Its author may well have
been a binitarian who posited only two pre-existent persons. In the
Didache the Holy Spirit as a divine agent is only found in the trinitarian formulas (7.1.3). In the Martyrdom of Polycarp there is a
trinitarian doxology put in the mouth of the martyr (14.3). No passages in the Epistle of Barnabas unambiguously refer to the Spirit as
a divine person, although the Spirit has the function of inspiration
and prophecy (12.2). 2 Clement may well have confused Christ and
the Holy Spirit (9 and 14); it is not clear. Thus the Apostolic Fathers
do not call the Holy Spirit God, although most appear to indicate the
Spirit's personality and divinity by coordination in oaths and baptismal
formula and ascription to the Spirit of the divine task of inspiration.

The Apologists were writers of the second century who sought to
vindicate Christianity against the claims of pagans and Jews. They
emphasized points of contact between Christianity and reason in order

to show Christianity as a form of wisdom superior to the Greek philosophy. In this process they employed the terminology and philosophy of their day to set forth Christian truths. They were almost exclusively preoccupied with the question of the relation of Christ to God the Father. Understandably what they have to say about the Spirit suffers in comparison. JUSTIN MARTYR is the most important of these apologists. His references to the Holy Spirit are numerous, if not clear. Possibly for Justin *logos* and "spirit" were two names for the same conception. For example, in speaking of the annunciation Justin appears to use "spirit" and *logos* for the same person (1 Apol. 33.6). On other occasions he coordinates the Father, Son, and Holy Spirit (1 Apol. 61.3-12; 65.3) Justin may have subordinated the Son to the Father and the Spirit to the Son, at least in function, if not essence (1 Apol. 13.3). For Justin the Holy Spirit is responsible for the inspiration of the prophets (Dial. 1-7). Among the effects of baptism were reception of the Spirit (1 Apol. 1.6), but apparently the Spirit played no role in the incarnation (Dial. 100.5). Yet the Spirit is described as the power of God (1 Apol. 33.6). TATIAN, a disciple of Justin hardly mentions the Holy Spirit. Tatian does not see the Spirit in all believers but in some of the just (Orat. 13). For Tatian the Spirit is God's ambassador or deputy (Orat. 15). Such language may well imply a subordination of the Spirit, but Tatian never directly addressed this question. THEOPHILUS OF ANTIOCH is the first Christian author to apply the word "trinity" *(trias)* to the godhead. It is for Theophilus a trinity of God, his Word and his Wisdom (Autol. 2.15). In this connection the Spirit is not named. Theophilus speaks of the Spirit as the Spirit of prophecy (Autol. 1.14) and identified wisdom with the Spirit. This Spirit or wisdom came forth from God before creation, as did the Word. (Autol. 2.10) Athenagoras, an Athenian Christian philosopher, also conceived of the Holy Spirit as inspiring the prophets (Supp. 7.2; 9:1). He defined the Spirit as "an effluence of God, flowing forth and returning to God like a ray of the sun" (Supp. 10). Athenagoras teaches, at least by implication, a doctrine of essential procession. Although there is no use of the terms "essence" or "person," clearly Athenagoras has thought deeply about the relation of Father, Son, and Spirit. His writings have several trinitarian passages (Supp. 6; 10; 24) which show Athenagoras was much ahead of his day. In spite of such contributions, the apologists are vague about the Spirit's function in salvation and even less clear about the Spirit's relation to the Father and Son. They are aware of a unity based on the fact that both Son and Spirit somehow have their origin from the Father, and not by creation, but such awareness is not developed. The Spirit is viewed primarily as the inspirer of the prophets. At times the "Spirit" is used to express the pre-existent nature of Christ as well as the name of the third person. But none of the Apologists refers to the Spirit as a creature.

IRENAEUS OF LYONS (d.c. 202) is one of the most important thinkers of the second century. Born in the East, he wrote in Greek, but carried on his work in Lyons where he was bishop and defender of the faith against the Gnostics. Irenaeus' chief interest is the incarnation of the Son. Nevertheless he gives attention to the Spirit beyond that of his predecessors. He holds there is one God, Lord and Creator, who formed all things by his Son and Spirit who were always with him (Haer. II. 2.2; IV. 20.1). The Spirit is never called "God," but Irenaeus quite clearly regarded him divine (Haer. V. 12.2). The Spirit is God's Wisdom and with him from eternity (Haer. IV. 20.3-4). The Spirit is also considered the source of prophecy (Haer. I. 10.1). Irenaeus makes much of the Spirit's work in the hearts and minds of men. The Spirit works the Father's will (Haer. III. 17.2); brings fellowship and union between God and men (Haer. V. 1.2); cleanses men for life with God (Haer. V. 9.1). Without the Holy Spirit, God's Word is not able to be seen (Dem. 7). On occasion Irenaeus spoke of the Son and the Spirit as God's hands (Haer. IV. pref. 4; V. 6.1.; IV. 20.1). He also called them the Father's ministers (Haer. IV. 7.4.). Such language in Irenaeus is not to convey subordinationism; its background is probably biblical. Irenaeus is a child of the second century. He does not make use of the image of three co-equal persons. No technical language was developed by him to express the Trinity. He did, however, defend the traditional view of one sole God who eternally was Father, Son, and Spirit.

TERTULLIAN of North Africa (d.c. 220) is probably the greatest of the early Latin fathers. It is in Tertullian's writings that an apology against Monarchianism (a view in the West that denied the distinction of Father, Son, and Spirit or which rejected the divinity of Christ and the personality of the Spirit) can be found as well as a gradual acceptance of Montanism. Both Monarchianism and Montanism are significant to understand Tertuallian's teaching about the Holy Spirit.

Montanism was essentially a movement of the Spirit in the second and third centuries. In a church that was already becoming institutionalized, Montanism called for a renewed witness to the immanence of the Spirit within the living church. It lived in the expectation of a speedy outpouring of the Spirit on the church and saw the first manifestations of this outpouring in its own prophets. Montanism proclaimed as the work of the Spirit the establishment of a new discipline within the church that was growing lax. Its primary stress was not on a new teaching. Tertullian's own acceptance of Montanism had little affect on his Christian beliefs, although it may have been one factor in his more personal view of the Spirit.[5] Quite possibly at its outset Montanism accepted a doctrine of the Trinity expressed as Word, Spirit, and power. Such a formulation could have been understood in an orthodox manner in the third century. Possibly at a later stage in its development Montanism accepted a doctrine that the Father, Son, and Holy Spirit were successive modes of manifestation of the godhead. If the movement did take such a step, it was quickly branded as heretical by the church. More important is the shift in the conception of the role of the Spirit in the church caused by Montanism. Montanism claimed that the supernatural inspiration by the Spirit was the source of prophecy and that the church in its laxity was losing this charisma. Orthodox writers in the second and third centuries insisted that the church had such inspiration. But gradually another answer to Montanism developed: that prophecy had ceased. The church now found its assurance of the presence and work of the Spirit in the threefold apostolic authority of canon, creed, and ecclesiastical office. A significant alteration in the understanding of the Spirit's activity occurred. Now to substantiate its existence the church looked not to the future and Christ's return, not to the present and the Spirit's extraordinary gifts, but to the past, canon and creed, preserved by an officer of the church. Such are the circumstances that form a backdrop to Tertullian's writings.

Tertullian is the first father before the fourth century to teach the Holy Spirit's divinity in a clear and precise fashion. As a Montanist, Tertullian writes in *Against Praxeas* that the Spirit is closely joined with the Father in substance, proceeds from the Father through the Son, is third with God and the Son, is one God with the Father and Son, and is God. For Tertullian, Father, Son, and Holy Spirit are three, not, however, in quality but in sequence, not in substance but in aspect, not in power but in manifestation, yet of one substance, one quality, and one power (Adv. Prax. 3, 4, 8, 12, 13). In two of his pre-Montanist works, *On Repentance* and *On Baptism,* he teaches the same trinitarian coordination of the Spirit with the Father and the Son, the same belief in the Holy Spirit as the third in the godhead (De Paen: 10, De Bap. 6). Tertullian's language can be crude. He speaks of God having a body *(corpus)* and of the origin of the Spirit in material analogies, e.g., as fruit of the shoot is third from the root (Adv. Prax. 7, 8; Apol. 21), but he clearly goes beyond Irenaeus in teaching the divinity of the Holy Spirit.

CLEMENT, one of the pioneers in the Christian school at Alexandria (d.c. 215), often speaks of the Spirit, although his trinitarian thought is far from finished. At times there are hints of subordinationism. The Spirit is the light from the Word that enlightens the faithful; the Spirit is the power of the Word and third in order after the Father and the Son (Str. 6.138. 1-3; 7.9.4.). The Spirit inspires Scripture so that in Old and New Testament the voice of the Spirit is heard (Paed. 1.5.15; Str 7.16.99). The true gnostic is united to the Spirit through boundless love. (Paed. 2.2.20; Str. 7.7.44).

ORIGEN of Alexandria (185-c.254) is the most influential theologian of the Alexandrian school. His greatest writing *On First Principles* has been correctly seen as the first *summa* composed in the church. Like Clement before him, Origen was deeply influenced by the Platonism of his day. In regard to the status and origin of the Holy Spirit, Origen was puzzled. He believes that the church has not answered these questions, and he is at a loss to resolve them because of the lack of guidance from the Bible and tradition. On occasions Origen teaches the divinity of the Holy Spirit, for he states that everything was made except the nature of the Father, Son, and Spirit (Princ. 1.33; 2.2.1). The Spirit is always with the Father and Son, and always was, is and will be (Ep. ad Rom. 6.7). In order and dignity the Spirit is associated with the Father and the Son (Princ. praef. 4). Elsewhere Origen definitely sees the Spirit as inferior to the Son (Jo. 2.6.). This inferiority and Origen's debt to Platonism are clear when he writes that the Father's action extends to all reality, the Son's is limited to rational beings, and the Holy Spirit to those being sanctified (Princ. 1.3.1-8). But the most disturbing question for Origen was that of the Spirit's origin. Was the Spirit born like the Son or created (Princ. praef. 4.3.)? On occasion Origen thinks the Spirit must be a work of the Word, since the Word made all things (Jo. 2.6). At other points Origen expresses the view that the origin of the Holy Spirit is a process from the Father (Princ. 1.2.13). Elsewhere he sees only two possibilities: the Spirit was born or was made. Origen decides he cannot accept generation for the Spirit's origination, and so he is left with the conclusion that the Spirit was made by the Father through the Son (Jo. 2.6). Origen's thought is close to orthodox Catholic faith; yet because he did not have the necessary technical language, some of his comments were later employed by the Arians to support their own views. Origen was to some extent a subordinationist, but he was not an Arian subordinationist, making the Son and Spirit creatures.

Several facts emerge from this survey of the first three centuries. Even in this period of benign neglect there is abundant reference to the Holy Spirit, but admittedly less than there is to the Son. The emphasis is on the Spirit's work rather than nature. The Spirit is acknowledged primarily as the inspirer of Scripture and the sanctifer of believers. No writer considers the Spirit a creature, yet the Spirit is rarely called God. The influence of the Bible and worship has kept the Spirit in the experience and thinking of the church. The absence of the pressure of heresy about the Spirit and the lack of exploration of the Spirit's role in soteriology have resulted in little reflection on the Spirit's person or origin. The disputes of the fourth century will change this.

II. Preoccupation with Person

No better documentation for the notion of benign neglect up to the year 300 can be found than the Nicene Creed of 325. As Jaroslav Pelikan has put it so well, "At Nicea the doctrine of the Holy Spirit had been disposed of in lapidary brevity: 'And we believe in the Holy Spirit.'"[6] This succinctness discloses that even in the early phases of the Arian controversy attention was so fixed on the Son that little reference was made to the Spirit, apart from affirming the traditional work of the Spirit. This is true for creeds as late as the year 360. This is not strange since ARIUS himself (d.c. 336), a priest at Alexandria, was mainly concerned with the Son. He began to teach his views about the nature of Christ around the year 318. His basic premise was simple. God is uncreated and unbegotten. Since the Son is begotten by the Father, he is not God but only a creature, although the instrument of creation. It is likely that Arius had some notion of the consequences of such teaching for the Holy Spirit. According to Athanasius, Arius in his *Thalia* declared that the essences of the Father, Son, and Holy Spirit were of their nature distinct, alien, diverse (Thal. in Ath. De Syn. 15) and also that the essences were incapable of participating in each other (Thal. in Ath. C. Ar. Or. 1:5-6). But it is not around such opinions that the early disputes of the Arian struggle took place.

CYRIL OF JERUSALEM (d.c. 386) is an excellent illustration of this last point. This bishop, sometime between the years 347 and 350, delivered his *Catechetical Lectures*. Part of this material (Cat. 16 and 17) is especially concerned with the Holy Spirit. Cyril begins these lectures to adults about to be baptized with reference to the Bible as the sole source for teaching about the Holy Spirit. He refrains from describing the Spirit's being. For salvation the believer need only to know there is one God, the Father; one Lord, the Son; one Holy Spirit, the Comforter. It is enough to know to acknowledge the identity of the gifts of the Father and of the Holy Spirit. The nature and the substance of that Holy Spirit are not proper subjects of inquiry (Cat. 16.24). Most of the contents of Lectures 16 and 17 is devoted to the Holy Spirit as the inspirer of Scripture and the sanctifer of believers. The Spirit is not called "God," but is clearly associated with the Father and the Son (Cat. 17.11). Cyril of Jerusalem indicates that the pressures of Arianism had not yet in 350 forced the church to think through with greater precision the doctrine of the Holy Spirit.

However, Cyril's position was ultimately untenable. The logical conclusions of Arius' teaching began to assert themselves among such late Arians as AETIUS and EUNOMIUS who regard the Spirit as the noblest of creatures, produced by the Son at the Father's bidding (Eunomius, Apol. 25, 28 and Basil, C. Eunom. 2.33). A group in Egypt known as the "Tropici" taught the deity of the Son along with the view that the Spirit was a creature, in fact, an angel of different substance from the Father and Son. Serapion, bishop of Thmuis, brought the attention of this local sect to Athanasius, the great defender of the Nicene faith and bishop of Alexandria (d. 373). In his *Letters to Serapion*, written in 360, Athanasius put forth his own doctrine of the Holy Spirit against the "Tropici." These letters, composed a mere ten years after Cyril's

Catechetical Lectures, disclose how the influence of heresy moved theologians of the church to a further exactness of definition than their predecessors felt was required.

ATHANASIUS insisted that the Holy Spirit is not a creature but belongs to the indivisible Holy Trinity and that the entire Triad is one God (Ep. Serap. 1.17). Athanasius argues that, as the Father and the Son, the Holy Spirit must be fully divine because the Spirit is no creature and comes from God; the Spirit is immutable, omnipresent, the one who sanctifies, vivifies; and deifies men (Ep. Serap. 1.22-27). The Spirit is also one with the Son, as the Son is with the Father, and is active in the works which the Father works through the Son (Ep. Serap. 1.31.). Therefore, the Spirit must be proper to God who is one and consubstantial with him (Ep. Serap. 1.27). Here is the soteriological argument coming to the fore. Since what the Holy Spirit did what is appropriate only to the divine, the Spirit must be fully divine. If creatures were objects of the Spirit's renewing, creating, and sanctifying work, the Holy Spirit could not belong to the same class of being. Athanasius claims that Scripture teaches that the Holy Spirit belongs to the Triad (Ep. Serap. 1.21). Thus Athanasius goes considerably beyond the Nicene formula of 325 in stating explicitly the full divinity and consubstantiality of the Holy Spirit. Nevertheless, he never applies to the Spirit the title "God." This omission may be nothing more than deference to the convention of even Athanasius' day. Although Athanasius clearly defended the divinity of the Spirit, his views on the Spirit's origin are left largely unanswered. He was not a speculative theologian and was willing to leave the inner aspect of the Trinity a mystery (C. Ar. Or. 2.36). Athanasius did state that the Spirit proceeds from the Father (Ep. Serap. 1.2). He nowhere explicitly teaches that the Spirit proceeds from the Son, but scholars of his letters have seen a procession of the Spirit from the Father through the Son as a necessary corollary of his entire argument.[7]

It is the Cappadocians, BASIL THE GREAT (d. 379), his brother GREGORY OF NYSSA (d. 394), and GREGORY OF NAZIANZUS (d.c. 390) who followed and built on Athanasius' efforts to combat Arianism. In so doing they made greater use of philosophy than Athanasius had done. The issues raised by Athanasius in his correspondence with Serapion received additional treatment by the Cappadocians. For in spite of the fact that Athanasius had insisted on the full divinity and consubstantiality of the Holy Spirit, this teaching was not accepted throughout the church. As late as the year 380 Gregory of Nazianzus declared in a sermon (Or. 31.5) that some consider the Holy Spirit a force, others a creature, others divine but less so than the Father and the Son. And of this latter group some believed the divinity of the Spirit was a private opinion; others felt it should be preached publicly. In such a context of continuing uncertainty all three Cappadocians maintain the full divinity of the Holy Spirit. They base their argument on the inseparability of the Spirit from the Father and the Son in the creeds, on the Spirit's coequal adoration with the Father and the Son, and on the Spirit's divine work.

Basil's work *On the Holy Spirit*, written in 375, is the first work so entitled in Christian literature. The title itself reflects the growing concern in the church about the third person of the Trinity. The immediate occasion for this treatise was interestingly enough the context of worship and the correct form of doxology. In *On the Holy Spirit* Basil does not explicitly call the Spirit "God" nor state the Spirit's consubstantiality with the Father. He does show the divinity of the Spirit who is completely coordinate with the Father and the Son, completes the Trinity and is adored with the Father and the Son (De.Sp.S. 41-47; 58-64; 71-75).

Gregory of Nyssa in his *Catechical Oration* repeats the views of Basil. He too refrains from calling the Holy Spirit "God" but he stresses the oneness of the nature of the three (Or. Cat. 1-4). When attention is turned to Gregory of Nazianzus a somewhat different picture presents itself. He explicitly affirms that the Holy Spirit is God and consubstantial (Or. 31.10). He defends this opinion on the divine work of the Spirit in baptism and the adoration accorded the Spirit. Both indicated for Gregory that the Spirit is God (Or. 31.28, 10).

But Gregory of Nazianzus reflects a certain embarrassment with his views. He is aware of the paucity of Scripture to support his conclusions and also that most of the earlier tradition did not make so bold a conclusion. Therefore Gregory is forced to develop a special doctrine of development. He admits that Scripture does not explicitly indicate the divinity of the Spirit. This he explains as a progression of development. The Old Testament revealed the Father and hinted at the Son. The New Testament disclosed the Son and suggested the Spirit. In the church the Spirit was active and revealed his true nature (Or. 31.26).

However, the teaching of the divinity of the Spirit confronted the Cappadocians with still another problem. If the Holy Spirit is consubstantial with the Son, must the Spirit not then be a "Son"? The Cappadocians rejected such a view as not in keeping with the biblical and Nicene teaching of an only begotten Son. Now the dilemma was how to differentiate the origin of the Holy Spirit from that of the Son. Gregory of Nazianzus answered that the Holy Spirit comes forth from the Father, but not in the manner of the Son, not by generation, but by procession which is a word Gregory admits he coined (Or. 39.12). But what this "procession" was Gregory could not explain. Basil simply indicated that the Holy Spirit comes forth as a breath from the mouth of the Father (De.Sp.S. 46). Gregory of Nyssa noted that the Spirit proceeds from the Father and receives from the Son, but the exact nature of this procession puzzled him (C. Maced. 2, 10, 12, 24). The Cappadocians nowhere stated that the Holy Spirit proceeds from the Son, but they did acknowledge that the Son has some role in the origination of the Spirit. Basil said goodness, holiness, dignity extended from the Father through the Son to the Spirit (De.Sp.S. 47, 45, 43). Gregory of Nyssa compared the Father, Son, and Holy Spirit to three torches which pass their light from one to another (C. Maced. 2, 5). At times Gregory of Nyssa seems to indicate that the Spirit is caused by the Son (Eun. 1.42) or that the Son has a functional role without this being a detriment to the role of the Father (Quod non sint; ad fin.). The contribution of the Cappadocians was significant. They asserted the Holy Spirit's full divinity, and Gregory Nazianzus called the Spirit God. They attempted to differentiate the Son's origination from the Spirit's by generation and procession. Although they were not totally successful, they laid the foundation of later procession theology.

HILARY OF POITIERS (d.c. 367) is one of the leading theologians of the West in this period, but his achievement is not as great as that of the Cappadocians. Hilary in many ways affirms the Spirit's divinity. In his summaries of faith he coordinates Father, Son, and Spirit (Trin. 2.1; 12.57; 4.1; 3.27; 4.28). He names the three in doxologies (Ps. 143.23). The Holy Spirit is not called "God," but Hilary denies that the Spirit is a creature (Trin. 12.55). The Spirit receives from the Son and proceeds from the Father (Trin. 8.20). Hilary clearly implies the Holy Spirit receives the divine nature from the Father and Son (Trin.

9.73). The origination of the Spirit Hilary admits he does not know how to explain (Trin. 12.56). At times Hilary appears to deny that the Holy Spirit is *homoousion* or *homoiousion* with the Father and Son (Syn. 32), but such passages must be taken in the light of all of Hilary's teaching. Occasionally Hilary applies the term "Holy Spirit" to the Father or to the Son (Trin. 8.23). In such usage "Holy Spirit" becomes a synonym of "divine nature." Yet Hilary also assigns the Spirit personal functions to divinize the faithful (Trin. 1.36; 2.29), to enlighten the patriarchs and prophets (Trin. 2.32), to teach the faithful (Trin. 2.23) and to dwell in believers' hearts (Trin. 8.26). Thus Hilary considers the Holy Spirit divine, assigns the Spirit personal functions, and regards the Spirit a third in divinity, although he never calls him a "person."

AMBROSE (d. 397), the great bishop of Milan, like Hilary fought against Arianism. His *On the Holy Spirit* is the first separate work on the Spirit of any importance in the West. In composing it Ambrose borrowed from Athanasius and Basil. The treatise teaches that the Holy Spirit is consubstantial with the Father and the Son. The Spirit is Light, Life, Creator, and Lord just as the Father and Son (De.Sp.S. 1.171; 2.32; 3.96). The Spirit is also eternal, infinite, omniscient, and omnipotent (De.Sp.S. 1.99; 1.82; 2.115; 3.169). The Spirit, for Ambrose, is God. (De.Sp.S. 3.112; 1.8; 3.90-91). Sometimes Ambrose regards the Spirit's procession from the Father, through the Son, at other times from the Father and the Son (De.Sp.S. 2.134; 1.120). It is not always clear whether Ambrose, when he uses "procession," does not actually mean "mission." [8] But if Ambrose's teaching about the Spirit's procession is not exact, there is no doubt that he presented a picture of the Holy Spirit coequal and coeternal with the Father and the Son (De.Sp.S. 3.158; De Fide 4.147).

The Council of Constantinople convened by the emperor Theodosius I in 381 set itself to resolve the questions debated since Nicea fifty-six years earlier. Although the pope was not invited nor were any Western bishops present, the council was later accepted as ecumenical in the West. It appears it promulgated a creed, which came to be known as the Nicene-Constantinopolitan Creed. The Nicene Creed of 325 had merely affirmed "We believe in the Holy Spirit." The symbol of Constantinople went further. It added to "the Holy Spirit": "the Lord and Giver of life, who proceeds from the Father, who together with the Father and Son, is adored and glorified, who spoke through the prophets." Thus this creed ascribed to the Holy Spirit divine names and functions. It coordinated the Holy Spirit with the Father and the Son as object of the same faith and worship. Thus it put the Spirit on the same divine level as the Father and Son. It affirmed the Spirit's divinity, but it did not give the Spirit the title "God." [9]

The fourth century, which we have identified with a "preoccupation with person," was a time of particularly rich theological thought. The influence of Scripture and worship in the life of the church guaranteed that attention would continue to be given to the Holy Spirit. But in addition various heretical views of the Spirit (e.g., those held by the Arians and the Tropici among others) along with soteriological implications of the Spirit's work compelled orthodox leaders to give ever-increasing precision to the Spirit's status. The result was that by the end of the fourth century the church in council could declare the Spirit not a creature but divine. It implied the Spirit was God but did not say it! As the fifth century was to dawn, the status of the Spirit was fixed. The question of the Spirit's origination remained open. And this brings us to the time we have characterized as "an engrossment with the mode of origin."

III. Engrossment with the Mode of Origin

The Council of Constantinople in 381 proclaimed the triune personality of God-one God existing permanently and eternally in three spheres of consciousness and activity, three modes, three persons in the inner relationships of the godhead as well as in the relations of God to the world. The factors that urged the church to take this action were noted in the above section. In so doing the church resolved the question of the Spirit's status but it also raised another issue: the Spirit's mode of origin, what was it, and how did it differ from the Son's? Some of the theologians already mentioned confronted this question but found it impossible to settle. In this third division of our subject we shall observe how theologians from Augustine until the Council of Florence attempted to explain the origin of the Spirit. To some this may appear to be among the most pedantic of enterprises. Actually it is a topic that is directly related to an understanding of God and had immense effects in the practical life of the church. The different "answers" to this question of the mode of the Holy Spirit's origin were contributing causes of a schism between the churches of the East and West for ten centuries.

AUGUSTINE OF HIPPO (d. 430) must be placed among the greatest Christian thinkers of all ages. His influence upon the thought and life of the church for all subsequent time defies calculation. Here an attempt will be made to describe briefly Augustine's teaching on the Holy Spirit. Augustine stressed the divine unity (Trin. 5.9). The three constitute a divine oneness of one and the same substance (Trin. 1.4.7). The three have the same eternity, immutability, majesty, and power (De doctr. christ. 1.5). For Augustine each person of the Trinity is God and all together are one God. This stress on the unity was new and would influence later Western theology, but its assertions of the full divinity of the Spirit repeated the conclusions of other orthodox writers in their struggle with Arianism.

Where Augustine broke new ground was his teaching about the process of the Spirit and his understanding of the Spirit as a gift and love, the sanctifying inhabitant of the just soul. Augustine teaches that the Holy Spirit proceeds from the Father and the Son, but principally from the Father (Trin. 15.29). He states that just as the Father has in himself that the Holy Spirit should proceed from him, so he has given to the Son that the same Holy Spirit should proceed from him and both apart from time (Trin. 15.47). Yes Augustine is careful to add that since the Father and Son are one God, there is one principle and not two (Trin. 5.15). This brings the question, why should not the Spirit be a son if he proceeds from the Father? The answer of Augustine is that the Spirit came forth, not born, but given (Trin. 5.15). This statement indicates clearly Augustine's contribution to the debate about the mode of the Spirit's origin. The Spirit proceeds timelessly and simultaneously from Father and Son (filioque) as one principle. The Son's power to principiate the Spirit was given to him by the Father in his generation. Therefore, the Spirit's process from the Son did not deny the Father's primordiality.

Augustine also often sees the Holy Spirit as the bond, the common gift, of the Father and the Son (Serm. 71). This gift is eternal, although given in time (Trin. 5.17). There is no subordination of the gift to the givers (Trin. 15.36). The Spirit is a gift, because the Spirit is love (Trin. 15.32). Augustine recognizes that this title of love is not given to the Spirit by Scripture, but he believes that as the Spirit of both Father and Son, the Spirit grants us that common love by which the Father and the Son love each other. Thus the Spirit should be called love (Trin. 15.27-29). The Spirit is then the love from God and is God, through whom the Trinity dwells in believers. According to Augustine the spiritual life thus depends upon the Holy Spirit, this love, this gift (Ep. 194.18, Serm. 71 & 267). Augustine was to return repeatedly to this divine indwelling in believers, which is the basis of the spiritual life. The indwelling is of the Trinity, but the Holy Spirit has a special introductory role (Ep. 187. esp. 16): it begins with baptism (Ep. 187.21, 27, 29).

Augustine's teaching of a double procession is an obvious advance over his precursors, although he owed them a debt, especially Origen. He did not, however, answer all questions as he himself realized (Trin. 9.17). Still unresolved were the questions: what is the nature of the two processions and how do they differ? Also, why are there only two processions in the godhead and thus only three persons?

CYRIL OF ALEXANDRIA (d. 444) is remembered in Christian thought chiefly for his role in the Christological disputes, but there are numerous references to the Holy Spirit in his writings. He acknowledges that the Holy Spirit is God, of and in God (Thesaur. 34.592) and of the same essence as the Father and the Son (Thesaur. 34.577 and 581). His statements about the Spirit's origination are less clear. In one passage Cyril speaks of the Holy Spirit flowing from the Father through the Son (De Trin. Dial. II. 721). Regularly he declares the Spirit proceeds from the Father (Thesaur. 34.589). Whether such passages mean that the Father is the exclusive or only primordial cause is not explained. On the other hand, there are passages which appear to imply the Son also has a role in the production of the Spirit (Thesaur. 34.585, 608; De Ador. 1.147; In Jo. XI. 1.449). It is difficult not to see in such passages a relationship of causal origination between the Son and the Spirit. Cyril also has much to say about the activity of the Spirit in the believer's soul. At baptism the Spirit is given to believers to make them sons of God. Although the entire Trinity inhabits the just, the Spirit is stressed (De Trin. Dial. VIII. 1093; In Jo. XI. 561). This work of the third person includes deification, vivification, and regeneration (Thesaur. 34.592, 660, 661, 664). The believer's return to the Father is effected through Christ by means of the Spirit. The

Spirit elevates believers to the Son and unites them with God. Through the Holy Spirit the faithful become sharers of the divine nature. But the Spirit is received through the Son, and in the Son the Father is received (In Jo. XI. 545). Some have concluded that Cyril's doctrine of sanctification results in a collective incarnation of all believers, but such conclusions are probably a misreading of his intentions. Whether the special role in sanctification given to the Spirit by Cyril is only one of appropriation because of the unity of the three persons or implies a division of sanctification to the Spirit, paternity to the Father, and filiation to Son, is a question that cannot be answered here.

The years immediately after the mid-fifth century were generally barren of great theological development. In the West, Augustine's influence exerts a powerful force, less so in the East. It is a time in both West and East of compilers and transmitters of the biblical and patristic traditions, not creative giants. In this period belongs POPE LEO I (d. 461) who taught that the Spirit was a coequal, coeternal person of the Trinity, fully divine (Serm. 75). In the same sermon Leo declares the Spirit is the inspirer of faith, the teacher of knowledge, the fount of love, the one who sanctifies the entire church (Serm. 75.5). Leo teaches the double procession of the Spirit (Ep. 15.2).

FULGENTIUS of Ruspe in North Africa (d.c. 533) follows in the thought of Augustine. The Holy Spirit is God as the Father and Son, of one nature with them (De Trin. 2). Although sent by the Father and Son, the Spirit is in no way inferior (De Trin. 6). The Spirit proceeds from the Father and the Son (De Incarn. Filii 3; Ep. 14.28). Fulgentius accepts the *filioque* as a traditional teaching of the church. He gives, however, no thought to the character of this procession or how it differs from the origination of the Son. He is content to repeat the Augustinian view. Fulgentius speaks of two ways of coming by the Spirit, one visible, one invisible (De Trin. 6; C. Fabian. 30). In this distinction he does not seem to be indebted to Augustine.

The Athanasian Creed, or *Quicunque vult,* probably dates close to the year 500. Surrounded with much uncertainty, one can confidently state that the document is neither a creed in the classic definition of that word nor is it a product of Athanasius' pen. Nevertheless its influence was pervasive.[10] The creed proclaims the Father, Son, and Holy Spirit are three distinct persons who have one identical godhead. Each of the three is uncreated, eternal, omnipotent God. Unlike the Nicene-

Constantinopolitan Creed, the *Quicunque* explicitly gives the Spirit the title God. Tritheism is excluded, for the three are one God. The distinction of the three persons is explained by the fact that the Father originates from no one but generates the Son, the Son is generated by the Father alone but with him produces the Holy Spirit, and the Holy Spirit proceeds from the Father and the Son. The double procession, the *filioque*, is merely presented as a fact and an object of orthodox faith.

Boethius (d.c. 525) continued in the Augustinian tradition but applied Aristotelian philosophy to theological problems. He states that Father, Son, and Holy Spirit are one God (Trin. 1.7). The Holy Spirit proceeds from the Father and the Son but it is not possible to understand this with human mind (Fid. 25-28). For Boethius the relation of Father to Son, and of both to the Holy Spirit, is a relation of identicals, but this relationship is unique, not to be found in other things (Trin. 6.20-23).

The creed ascribed to, and possibly expanded, at the Eleventh Council of Toledo in 675 was one of the most developed formulas produced by the Western church. It spoke of the Holy Spirit as the third person of the Trinity, one God coequal and consubstantial with the Father and Son, not begotten nor created by proceeding from the Father and the Son, and the Spirit of both, sent by both Father and Son. The creed teaches: although the Father, Son, and Holy Spirit are one God, they are three persons inseparable in existence and operation but distinct in personal properties. The Father has eternity without birth, the Son eternity with birth, the Holy Spirit eternity without birth but with procession.

For our purposes only two writers of the eighth century need to be mentioned: Alcuin in the West and John of Damascus in the East. Alcuin (d. 804), who was of the Bishop's school in York and then head of the Palatine school for Charlemagne, repeated those features of the church's teaching about the Spirit that had become traditional by his day. The Father's distinctive property is that he alone is not from another (De Fide 1.11), the Son's that he alone is generated from the Father alone, the Holy Spirit's that he proceeds equally from the Father and the Son and is the consubstantial and eternal Spirit of both (De Fide 1.11). However, the Spirit's relation to the Father and Son lacks the reciprocal convertibility of the relation of Father and Son, for while the Holy Spirit is the Spirit of the Father and of the

Son, the Father is not the Father nor is the Son the Son of the Holy Spirit. For this difference Alcuin provides no explanation. In *Libellus de Processione Spiritus Sancti,* written for Charlemagne, Alcuin defends on the basis of Scripture and the fathers the double procession, *filioque.*

JOHN OF DAMASCUS (d.c. 750) produced a *summa* of Greek theology entitled *The Source of Knowledge.* The work is clearly indebted to earlier Greek fathers, especially the Cappadocians. John describes the Holy Spirit as the Lord and Giver of life, who proceeds from the Father and rests in the Son. The Spirit is of equal adoration and glorification with the Father and Son, Lord of creation, deifying, sanctifying, proceeding from the Father, derived from the Father but not by generation, rather by procession (De Fide Orth. I.8). Thus John notes a difference between generation and procession but he claims he is unable to understand it (De Fide Orth. I.8). Probably for the Damasene the Son has no causal role in the origination of the Spirit. Only the Father is called the producer of the Spirit. In this opinion John of Damascus will be followed in the next century by Photius, Patriarch of Constantinople, and it is then that different approaches by West and East to the mode of the Spirit's origin will lead to schism.

The creed of the Council of Constantinople of 381 had affirmed belief in the Holy Spirit who proceeds from the Father. Possibly as early as the Third Council of Toledo in 589 the interpolation, "who proceeds from the Father and the Son" *(filioque),* was made. Certainly by the year 796 and the Synod of Friuli the addition of *filioque* was in the Western recension of the creed. In so doing the West was following the lead of its theologians such as Tertullian and Augustine. It was believed in the West that the insertion of the *filioque* was decisive against Arianism. Initially the Western church seems genuinely unaware that the doctrine of the double procession was an advance on, certainly a clarification of, earlier teaching. While the West held to the double procession from at least the seventh century, it was the emperor Charlemagne who paraded it before the East.

The issue came to a head at the time of PHOTIUS (d.c. 897), but the writings of John of Damascus and Alcuin among others show the problem was there earlier. Several other concerns became attached to the *filioque* debate as it proceeded: the right of the Pope to fix and revise the norm of orthodoxy, the Eastern definition of antiquity as the standard of tradition and the dominance of Augustine in Latin theology. But a theological issue was also involved. It can be discerned in Photius' *Mystagogia Spiritus Sancti*. Photius' basic thesis is that just as the Son is born of the Father alone, the Holy Spirit proceeds from the Father alone. But this Spirit is called the Spirit of the Son because he is sent by the Son and is consubstantial with the Son (Myst. Sp. S., inscr.). The biblical support for this argument is chiefly based on Johannine texts (Myst. Sp. S. 2). Photius turns to the fathers for additional argumentation. To the objection that Ambrose and Augustine taught double procession, Photius answered they were fallible (Myst. Sp. S. 66-72).

Some of Photius' other concerns are raised when he asks, if the Son produces the Spirit, must it not also be said the Spirit produces the Son (Mys. Sp. S. 3)? If the Spirit exists by double procession, Photius wonders, must there not be composition in the Trinity (Myst. Sp. S. 4)? Also what can the Spirit receive by proceeding from the Son that he does not already have from the Father (Myst. Sp. S. 7)? Photius is also concerned if double procession does not imply a Sabellian confusion of Father and Son or the destruction of the monarchy and the introduction of polytheism (Myst. Sp. S. 9, 11). Photius' writings became an arsenal for later Greek polemicists. While many of Photius' worries are valid, the controversy became out of all proportion. Both East and West were striving to say the same thing from different starting points. The East began with the difference of persons. It affirms the Father is the origin of the two divine persons. It does not deny that the Father and the Son are one as principle of the Holy Spirit. The West emphasizes that the Father and Son form a single principle, but it does not mean that the Son did not receive from the Father his propriety as the origin of the Spirit as, indeed, he ceaselessly receives it. Unfortunately, besides different theological methods, other issues were joined in the *filioque* debate. The schism that resulted was more than theological differences would warrant. But the mode of the Spirit's origin divided East and West and remained the unresolved agenda item of the church's thinking about the Spirit as the Middle Ages drew near.

The ninth century in the West saw the production of numerous works to defend the *filioque*. At the request of POPE NICHOLAS I, RATRAMNUS (d. 868) maintained the *filioque* was based on the teaching of Christ and handed down from the Apostles to the Fathers. He quoted Scripture from Luke, Paul, and especially John and the fathers, mostly Augustine but also Athanasius, Gregory of Nazianzus, and Didymus (C. Graec. App.). A considerably more significant figure of the time was JOHN SCOTUS ERIUGENA (d.c. 877) who attempted to relate reason and authority. Eriugena created a synthesis of philosophy and theology indebted to Neoplatonism. His doctrine of God (Div. Nat. I.72) was accused of being pantheistic, but a consideration of all he taught on the subject may reveal this conclusion as unfounded. Eriugena tends not to use the Latin *filioque;* he prefers the Greek *dia hyiou.* He appears not to employ the Augustinian teaching that Father and Son are not two principles of the Spirit but only one. The reader of Eriugena is uncertain at times whether he teaches that the Father alone is the cause of the Spirit or the Father and Son. In one passage he does say the Spirit proceeds from the Father through the Son and this means the Spirit does not have two causes but one, the Father of the generated Son and of the Spirit proceeding from him through the Son (Div. Nat. II.32). But is this his final solution?

PETER DAMIAN (d. 1072), as opposed to Eriugena, rejected the use of reason in matters of faith. For him there is a coeternal, coequal, consubstantial Trinity of Father, Son, and Holy Spirit who differ from one another by their originational properties but are one essence (Op. 1.1, 5; 1, 2). Damian teaches that the *filioque* must be believed, for it is taught by Scripture and the fathers (Op. 1.10). Using the words of the creed of the Eleventh Council of Toledo, Damian says the Spirit proceeds from the Father and the Son, but adds simultaneously from both for the sanctification of creatures (Op. 1.1).

With the eleventh century, Western Europe enters the Middle Ages, a time of intense theological creativity. In pneumatology western authors continue to defend the double procession and work toward a solution to the very vexing question of the precise difference between the origin of the Son and the Spirit. The first theologian of this period to be noted is ANSELM OF CANTERBURY (d. 1109). An Augustinian in thought, most widely known for his ontological proof of God's existence, Anselm also wrote on the Holy Spirit. His *De Processione Spiritus Sancti contra Graecos* is a defense of double procession based on the Bible and reason. Of the biblical authors Anselm is most indebted to the Johannine books. On the basis of reason Anselm teaches everything in God is identical except where there are opposed relations of origin, as in the case of the Father, Son, and Holy Spirit. This answers the dilemma of how unity and plurality can be reconciled. For Anselm unity does not lose its consequence unless some opposition of relation stands in the way (De Proc. Sp. S. 2). Only where one proceeds from the other can there be two, for then there is a relation of opposition. Accordingly Anselm states the Holy Spirit must proceed from the Son as well as the Father. Thus the Son cannot be the Father because he proceeds from the Father; the Holy Spirit cannot be the Father because he proceeds from the Father.

But are the Son and the Spirit distinct? To this Anselm answers only if one proceeds from the other. Since it is apparent from the faith that the Son is not from the Spirit, it follows by reason that the Spirit is from the Son as the Spirit is from the Father. For just as the Spirit cannot really be distinct from Father unless he proceeds from the Father, thus the Spirit cannot be really distinct from the Son (De Proc. Sp. S. 4). Because of the relationship of the Father and Son, if the Spirit proceeds from one then he proceeds from both (De Proc. Sp. S. 7). But the Father and Son are not two principles of the Spirit but one (De Proc. Sp. S. 18). In spite of his debt to Augustine, Anselm disapproves of the Augustinian view that the Spirit proceeds principally from the Father (De Proc. Sp. S. 24). Anselm himself wrote that he believed the Trinity was a mystery beyond the human intellect. There have been those who have read the Archbishop of Canterbury and have come to the conclusion that he ascribed to reason more competence than it ever possessed.

In his early career PETER ABELARD (d. 1142) agreed with the high place assigned to reason by Anselm, but later this opinion was rejected. This shift in position is one of the causes of difficulty in learning exactly what Abelard really taught. For example, under the influence of Bernard of Clairvaux (d. 1153), the Council of Sens condemned a series of propositions as heretical and identified Abelard with them. Pope Innocent II confirmed the action of the council, but the sentence was not carried out. Questions remain concerning Abelard's relation to these *capitula* and if they are all heretical. Several of these propositions treat the Holy Spirit. Proposition 1 rejects the omnipotence of the Son and the Holy Spirit; 2a denies the consubstantiality of the Holy Spirit with the Father; 2b denies the coequality of the Holy

Spirit with the Father and the Son; 14 denies the Father's coequality with the Son and Holy Spirit in wisdom. Apparently these views are not found in Abelard's writings in the exact wording presented at Sens. Yet teachings close to the meaning of these *capitula* have been located in the Abelardian corpus. *Capitula* 1 is taught in Theol. IV, 1288-89, 1299; 2a in Theol. IV, 1299-1300; 2b in Theol. IV, 1307, Introd. II, 1080-82; and 14 in Theol. 1, 1131. Final judgment cannot be determined here whether or not Abelard's final and total teaching was heretical. Individual passages as they stand appear to point in that direction.

RICHARD OF ST. VICTOR (d.c. 1173) believed that the Trinity could be demonstrated by means of reason as well as the existence of a second and third person. In regard to proof of the latter, he turned to charity. In God there must be a plenitude of charity. To be charity, love must tend to another, for charity cannot exist as private love of self. Since a divine person must have supreme charity—and this cannot be had for a creature—there must be in God a plurality of persons. From this conclusion Richard moves to prove that there can only be three persons in God, not more, not less. He says that in mutual love that is fervent nothing is rarer or more excellent than you wish another to be equally loved by him whom you love supremely and by whom you are loved supremely (De Trin. III, esp. III, 11). Needless to say, such proof will not convince all.

PETER LOMBARD (d. 1160) in his *Book of Sentences* created a systematic and traditional summary of the Christian faith that was studied and used throughout the Middle Ages. Lombard built his doctrine of the Trinity on the witness of Scripture, quoting many texts from both Testaments (Sent. I d.2, c.4-5). He believed that in accord with the Bible the Father, Son, and Holy Spirit are of one substance and equality. There is a unity in essence and a plurality in persons (Sent. I, d.2, c.1-2). He states that Scripture proves the procession of the Holy Spirit from the Father and the Son (Sent. I, d.11, c.1), and says that many Greek fathers taught the *filioque* (Sent. I, d.11, c.2). Lombard does not explore the nature of the Spirit's origination nor its difference from the Son's generation on the ground that it is impossible for men in this life to know such things (Sent. I, d.13, c.3). For Lombard the Holy Spirit is the love by which men love God and neighbor (Sent. I, d.17, c.1). The Spirit operates acts of faith and love through the medium of virtues of faith and hope. The Spirit operates the act of loving by himself without the medium of any virtue (Sent. I, d.17, c.6).

JOACHIM OF FLORA (d. 1202) attacked Peter Lombard's teaching of the Trinity and taught a theory of three ages of history. These three epochs are called by one name in accord with the image of him who is three in persons, one in essence (Conc. III, 1, c.1). The first state is attributed to the Father, the second to the Son, the third to the Holy Spirit. In each of these ages the respective person reveals his glory (Conc. II, 1, c.8). The Father has the time under the Law, the Son the time under the gospel, and the Spirit the time of spiritual intelligence (In Apoc. Introd., c.5). In this third age the Spirit will make human nature divine so that all people can participate in his fullness (Psalt. II, 260 rB). Joachim's system required a substantial distinction of the divine persons. This is why he so strongly opposed Peter Lombard. But to avoid Quaternianism, which Joachim believed Lombard taught, and Sabellianism, Joachim fell into Tritheism. This he did by insisting the three persons were three really distinct but completely like substances. He called them one substance (Psalt. I, d.1, 233 rA); the unity was assimilative and collective (In Apoc., Introd. c.12). This teaching was to be condemned shortly after Joachim's death by a council of the Western church.

The Fourth Lateran Council was convoked by Pope Innocent III in 1215. It condemned Joachim's views of the Trinity and proclaimed its own trinitarian doctrine in greater detail than any other council to that time. This council was the first ecumenical synod (at least in Western eyes) that stated the Holy Spirit proceeds from the Father and the Son. In setting forth its views the council identified itself with the teaching of Peter Lombard. There is a Trinity, not a quaternity, because each of the three persons is that reality which is the principle of all things. It is the Father who generates, the Son who is generated, and the Holy Spirit who preceeds. There are distinctions in the persons, unity in the nature. What this distinction is in the final analysis the council refused to say. But the council did go beyond Nicea of 325 and Constantinople of 381. It declared the consubstantiality, coeternity, coequality, coomnipotence of the three persons, their distinction from one another, their unity of nature, the procession of the Father from no one, of the Son from only the Father and of the Holy Spirit from both. It condemned a quaternity in God and a collective unity of the three persons. Because of such efforts it represents a high point in the medieval church.

ALBERT THE GREAT (d. 1280), teacher of Thomas Aquinas, led the way for Aquinas by realizing Aristotle could be used to explain the Christian faith. In Albert's *Commentary on the Sentences,* he said that divinity can be communicated in only two ways: by intellect and will, not by nature. Communication by intellect is generation (In I Sent. d.10, a.12). In his *Summa Theologiae* Albert said procession of a word from the intellect did not make the Son, but the Son's substantial emanation from the Father brings it about that he is the Son (S. Th. tr. 7, g 30, m.2). Because the Holy Spirit does not proceed by nature, as the Son, but by love, the Spirit is not generated (S. Th. tr. 7, g 31, m.2, Sol). Thus Albert touches on the difference between generation and procession, for he notes that to be generated means not merely to be produced in likeness of nature (as the Spirit is) but in likeness of nature by means of a likeness-producing operation (as the Son is, but the Spirit is not). Albert also teaches that the Father and Son spirate the Spirit as one spirative principle, although there are two spirators (S. Th. m.3, ad g.1). He realized that only relations of origin distinguished divine persons, but he could not come to an adequate definition of person. His famous pupil will continue and advance his work.

THOMAS AQUINAS (d. 1274) undertook to bring about a combination of Christian faith and Aristotelian philosophy which would be faithful to the two elements that comprised it. How successfully Thomas accomplished his goal is a question beyond the scope of the present effort. But few would deny him a place of extreme importance in Christian thought. In his impressive system Thomas dealt with the Trinity on many occasions. For Thomas it was clear that while natural reason may know something of the unity of the divine essence, it cannot know the distinctions of persons. The Trinity cannot be demonstrated nor known by reason (ST 1.a, 32.1; ad.1, ad.2). Within the Trinity there can only be two processions (ST 1.a, 27). These two origins, generation and procession, Thomas described in terms of intellectual nature: acts of understanding and willing. It follows that no other procession is possible in God but the process of the Word and of love (ST 1.a, 27.5). For Thomas, there is no need to go on to infinity in divine processions, for the procession which is accomplished within the agent in an intellectual nature terminates in the procession of will

(ST 1.a, 27.3). This is why for Thomas there are only three persons within the godhead.

Thomas also addressed the problem that had been confronting theologians for centuries: the nature of the generation of the Son and its differentiation from the process of the Holy Spirit. As we have seen, one answer suggested was that the Holy Spirit was not generated because the Spirit proceeded from two, as given and gift not through nature but through will. Yet such a suggestion was not satisfactory. For if to be generated means that a living being originates from a living being in likeness of nature, then it appears the Spirit was generated. Thomas sought to answer the problem by an analogy from the area of intellectual activity. He believed that the answer must be found in an examination of generation and procession by way of intellect and will. There must be some element in generation that is not found in procession (C. Gent. 4.11). Thomas' answer is that the generative act is essentially a likeness-producing act. In God the intelligible operation that produces the Word is such a likeness-producing act. Thus it is called generation. But in God the operation of the will that is love is not a likeness-producing act but rather an impulse-producing act. Thus it is not called generation (ST 1.a, 27.2 and 4). This is the first time we have seen a clear differentiation of generation and procession in terms of the inner life of the triune God. It certainly moves beyond the efforts of Augustine and John of Damascus, but it cannot be regarded as proof of the Son's generation by intellect and the Spirit's procession by will. Thomas also teaches the gift of sanctification belongs to the Holy Spirit who proceeds by will, love. The Holy Spirit is the sign of sanctification; the Son its author (ST 1.a, 43.7). There is little doubt that in Aquinas a high point of speculative theology was reached. Various judgments could be given to Thomas' work, but it could not be ignored.

ALEXANDER OF HALES (d. 1245) is the first great thinker of the Franciscan order. There are differences of opinion whether or not a *Summa Theologica* attributed to him is actually his. For our purposes it is enough to state that if the treatise is not Alexander's, it reflects thirteenth century Franciscan theology. Alexander makes his fundamental principle *bonum est diffusivum sui.* The diffusion of divine goodness is twofold: personal within the godhead and essential in communication of divine goodness to creatures (ST 1.n 330 ad 4). On the part of divine

goodness there is intrinsic influence of goodness in the eternal emanation of the Son from the Father and of the Spirit from the Father and
Son (ST 1.n. 64 ad 4). This fundamental principle explains not only
why there is a divine procession but a trinity of persons. For the nature
of supreme goodness demands there be one person in which there is
the term of diffusion, as there is one which is the principle of diffusion
and a third which is the so-called medium of diffusion (ST 1.n. 319
ad 4). For Alexander there is generation in God, and the second person is the Son. To generate is to give to another the nature one has.
This communication of good by nature is generation (ST 1.n. 297 ad
25; n. 319 So.). Alexander further defines generation as the univocal
production of one like in nature from the whole substance according to
the principal mode (ST 1.n. 296 Sol.). Alexander on the basis of dif-
fusive good declares the second procession in God is not generation
by nature, but by will or affection, thus a process of the Holy Spirit
by way of love from the Father and the Son (ST 1.n. 317 Sol.; n. 306).
This love, or perfect charity, requires three persons—no more or less
(ST 1.n. 317 ad 1). Alexander more than most other scholastics stressed
the connective relation of the three persons of God. He laid the ground-
work for his celebrated successor, Bonaventure, another Franciscan.

BONAVENTURE (d. 1274) constructed a system that in some ways
rivaled Aquinas. Like Aquinas, Bonaventure believed that the Trinity
cannot be known by reason. But faith teaches a plurality of persons
in God and then reason gives confirmation based on divine simplicity
which is able to be communicable to several (In Sent. 1, d.2, a.1, q.2).
In God there is then simplicity, beatitude, perfection, etc. In God this
must be supreme simplicity, beatitude, perfection, etc. If there is
supreme perfection, then the producing person produces perfectly in
regard to the mode of producing and the one produced. There are
only two ways of producing perfectly: by nature and will. Therefore
it is necessary that there be only two emanating persons and the one
from whom they emanate. According to Bonaventure's reasoning there
can only be three persons (In Sent. 1.d, 2.a, 1.q. 4). Bonaventure states
the first person is innascible and unspirable, he generates and spirates;
because the second person is unspirable but generate, he does not
generate but he does spirate; because the third person is spirated and
proceeds from one who generates, he neither generates nor spirates
(In Sent. 1, d. 2, a.1, q.4). Faith tells Bonaventure that the Holy Spirit

proceeds from the Father and Son and that the Spirit is neither a son nor generated. But reason indicates that there are two modes of producing in God, by generation and will, and that the Spirit is by will (In Sent. 1, d. 13, a.1, q.2). It is not hard to see why Bonaventure has received extreme praise and blame for his system.

The Second Council of Lyons, which was called together in May, 1274, by Pope Gregory X, had as one of its main goals the reuniting of the Western and Eastern churches. Because one of the causes of schism was disagreements about the Holy Spirit, the council addressed itself to the question of the Spirit's procession. This council decidedly went beyond Lateran IV in its teaching about the Holy Spirit. As will be recalled, Lateran IV had declared that the Holy Spirit is from both the Father and the Son equally; the Holy Spirit proceeds from both. Lyons II moved beyond this by affirming explicitly several other items. It stated that the Holy Spirit proceeds from the Father and the Son not as from two principles but as from one; not by two spirations but by one. The council also insisted that the Roman church always taught this, and that this is the position of Greek and Latin fathers. It condemned all who deny the *filioque* or who assert the Spirit proceeds from the Father and the Son as from two principles or by two spirations. The question of whether the Greek delegation was present when these articles on the Spirit were debated and the subsequent reaction to the council in the East are interesting points but beyond the present limits of inquiry. For our purpose it is important to see Lyons II ratifying several elements of western teaching about the Spirit that were formulated in the thirteenth century.

Duns Scotus (d. 1308), a Franciscan theologian, produced a synthesis of the teachings of Alexander of Hales and Bonaventure with sufficient scope for Aristotelian thought. There are, for Scotus, only two processions in God because there are only two ways of producing: by nature and will. These two are different because they have opposite ways of principating, determinately and freely (Oxon. 1, d.2, q.7, n.18). The first productive principle constituted by the divine essence and by the divine intellect is called memory. This memory has an operative and a productive aspect. In its operative aspect it operates intellection. This intellection is common to the three persons. In its productive aspect, it produces diction and is proper to the Father (Oxon. 2, d. 1, q.1, n.9, 13). The second productive principle is constituted by the divine essence as lovable object and by the divine will as loving power. There is an operative and productive aspect to this will. In its operative aspect it operates dilection and is common to the three persons. In its productive aspect it produces an infinite love and is proper to the Father and Son and is the productive principle of the Holy Spirit (Oxon. 2, d. 1, q.1, n.9, 13). The production of the Word is generation because it is a natural production (Oxon. 1, d. 13, n.20). The Father and the Son are one principle in spirating the Holy Spirit (Oxon. 1, d. 12, q.1, n.2). The spiration of the Holy Spirit is not generation because it is not a production by way of nature, but by way of will. It is both necessary and free (Oxon. 1, d. 2, q.7, n.18). The Thomists insisted that only opposed relations distinguish divine persons and thus if the Spirit did not proceed from the Son, the Spirit would not be distinct from the Son. Scotus denied this and maintained that even if the Spirit did not proceed from the Son the two would be distinct by virtue of their constitution and procession (Oxon. 1, d.11, q.2, n.6).

WILLIAM OF OCKHAM (d.c. 1349), who was accused of heresy for his views, was a leading figure of the nominalist school. He was excommunicated by Pope John XXII. Although Ockham saw the appropriate place of reason, he greatly limited its capacity to know of things divine. For Ockham reason is unable to show that God is one or that there are three persons in God (Sent. 1, d.3, q.2, M and 1, d.30, q.1 B). He believes both because they are in the Bible (Sent. 1, d.2, q.1, F). Ockham denied the formal distinction of Scotus for creatures and between divine attributes (Sent. 1 d.2, q.6, E and 1, d. 2, q.1, F). But he recognized such distinction in the Trinity, saying that the essence and the three persons are distinguished formally. This is not to say anything else than essence is three persons, and a person is not three persons (Summa Logic, p.2, c.2). As opposed to Scotus, Ockham denied that the Holy Spirit would be distinct from the Son even if the Spirit did not proceed from the Son (Sent. 1, d. 11, q.2). Ockham's work can properly be regarded as a reaction against the systems of Christian Aristotelians.

Pope Eugene IV summoned the Council of Florence (1438-45) for the purpose of restoring unity between the Eastern and Western churches. Thus its goal was similar to that of the Second Council of Lyons. This also meant that the *filioque* question was once again on a council agenda. All of the arguments, Eastern and Western, were raised in the lengthy debate. Finally the council produced a *Decree for the Greeks.* While in large measure this decree repeated the statements of Lyons II, in some ways it went beyond. It stated that the Holy Spirit's essence and subsistent being are from the Father and Son simultaneously, that the teaching of the fathers which declares the Spirit proceeds from the Father through the Son is to be interpreted to mean that the Son as well as the Father is the cause of the Spirit. In effect this means "through the Son" is viewed as equivalent to *filioque.* In addition the Council of Florence affirmed that the *filioque* had been lawfully and reasonably added to the creed for good and sufficient reasons. Besides these statements in the *Decree to the Greeks,* there are some additional points made in the *Decree for the Jacobites.* This decree also built on the work of Lateran IV and Lyons II, but it put forth more clearly than before that the Father and Son are but one principle of the Holy Spirit as Father, Son, and Spirit one principle of creation; that Father and Son and Spirit mutually exist in one another because of their unity of essence; that in God everything is one where opposition of relation does not intervene. This last point was the acceptance and approval by the council of the teaching of Anselm of Canterbury that unity does not lose its consequence unless some opposition of relation stands in the way.

According to this teaching everything in God is identical except where opposed relations (as in Father, Son, and Holy Spirit) stand in the way of identity. Here there is a real distinction, but where there is no such opposition as between the divine persons and the divine essence, there is real identity and thus the three persons are one essence. The Council of Florence had brief success. When the Greek delegation returned to the East, it at once repudiated the union that had been forced upon them at Florence. But Florence does mark the close of a chapter. It was the last statement of the Western medieval church on the Trinity and the Holy Spirit. The next significant expression of views on the Holy Spirit in the West would be those of the reformers.

The period we have characterized as "engrossment with the mode of origin" lasted almost exactly ten centuries. Augustine died in 430, and the Council of Florence finished its work in 1445. In this span of time a substantial amount of movement can be perceived on the question of the Spirit's origination. For all of Augustine's genius, he was unable to solve all the problems connected with the Spirit's procession. These unanswered aspects of the Spirit's origin continued to fascinate theologians. The "mode of origin" question may well have first appeared on the church's agenda as the result of the influence of heresy, but it is hard to escape the conclusion that the dogged pursuit of answers to the Spirit's mode of origin is evidence of a determination in the medieval church to think through the full implications of the faith for its own sake. The Western church finally attained "answers" from the pen of Thomas Aquinas who found his resources in the rarefied metaphysical world of Aristotelian philosophy. When the Council of Florence adjourned, the medieval church had uttered its final statements about the third person of the Trinity. In purely intellectual terms the achievement was of note. Yet it had been purchased at the price of schism between East and West (at least partially caused by the *filioque* issue) and in the currency of a philosophical speculation that some would find less than compatible with the Christian faith. However, an evaluation of the truth and necessity of all the developments we have been tracing in this chapter must be left to others. Chronologically the first individuals to give serious reflection on the medieval synthesis of teaching about the Holy Spirit were the reformers, and this brings us to another chapter.

Notes

In order to reduce the number of footnotes, references to primary texts of the fathers and medieval theologians are incorporated within the narrative. Standard abbreviations are employed. References are to the *editio princeps* as listed in the *Oxford Dictionary of the Christian Church,* 2nd edition, edited by F. L. Cross and E. A. Livingston (Oxford, 1974).

1. Jaroslav Pelikan defines "doctrine" as "what the church of Jesus Christ believes, teaches, and confesses on the basis of the word of God," in this case about the Holy Spirit. See J. Pelikan, *The Christian Tradition, Vol. I: The Emergence of the Catholic Tradition* (Chicago: University of Chicago Press, 1971), p. 1.
2. See M. Wiles, *The Making of Christian Doctrine* (Cambridge, 1967), esp. chapter 1, and J. Pelikan, *Development of Christian Doctrine: Some Historical Prolegomena* (New Haven: Yale University Press, 1969).
3. Older but still valuable discussions are H. B. Swete, *The Holy Spirit in the Ancient Church* (London, 1912) and H. Watkin-Jones, *The Holy Spirit in the Medieval Church* (London, 1922). See also A. Palmieri,

"Espirit-Saint," *Dictionnaire de Theologie Catholique,* ed. A. Vacant, E. Mangenot and E. Amann, V (1913), 679-829; P. Galtier, *Le Saint-Espirit en nous d'apres les Peres grecs* (Rome, 1946); T. Rüsch, *Die Entstehung der Lehre vom Heiligen Geist* (Zurich, 1952); Wolf-Dieter Hauschild, *Gottes Geist und der Mensch: Studien zur frühchristlichen Pneumatologie (Beiträge zur evangelischen Theologie, 63)* (München, 1972). For bibliography see Pelikan, *The Christian Tradition,* Vol. I, pp. 369-371.

4. "Person" is not to be understood here in the modern sense of possessing oneself as subject in consciousness. "Person" in this discussion is the aspect of the divine plenitude of being and life which possesses an ultimate inalienability through its relative opposition to other "persons" and thus allows the identical plenitude of life to exist in unique and mutually opposite ways. The use of the language of three persons in the Trinity does not posit the same thing three times but indicates that which makes the Father, Son, and Spirit absolutely different, i.e., relatively opposed to each other. When this second period declared the Spirit as the third person in the godhead, it did not mean that there are in God three active subjects.

5. See E. Evans, Tertullian's *Treatise Against Praxeas* (London, 1948), p. 4.

6. Pelikan, *op. cit.,* Vol. I, p. 211.

7. C. R. B. Shapland, *The Letters of Athanasius Concerning the Holy Spirit* (London, 1951), p. 42, and J. Quasten, *Patrology,* Vol. III (Westminster, MD: The Newman Press, 1960), p. 77.

8. See Swete, *op. cit.,* p. 322.

9. On the detailed questions of the origin of the Nicene-Constantinopolitan Creed, see J. N. D. Kelly, *Early Christian Creeds* (London, 1960), pp. 296-331; pp. 297-298 for text of creed.

10. See J. N. D. Kelly, *The Athanasian Creed* (London, 1964).

Bernard Holm

The Work of the Spirit: The Reformation to the Present

Introduction

A hundred years ago Albrecht Ritschl complained that there existed as yet no adequate history or systematic formulation of the doctrine of the Spirit.[1] The three great German historians of dogma who came after him—Adolf von Harnack, Friedrich Loofs, and Reinhold Seeberg—did not trace this doctrine beyond the fourth century.[2] There have been partial English studies of later developments by Henry Barclay Swete and H. Watkin-Jones.[3] The only comprehensive German history of the Spirit came from Karl F. Nösgen.[4] Wilhelm Stählin expressed regret that Evangelicals and Roman Catholics alike have not yet articulated an adequate doctrine of the Spirit.[5]

This essay sets itself a limited task. Leaving aside the history of religious movements and awakenings, it pursues only the doctrine of the work or the effects of the Spirit, with a view to determining to what extent, and in what ways, the Holy Spirit was a truly significant, integral part of theology in the centuries from Luther onward. Without taking note of the Spirit's participation in creation or providence, we shall consider the questions: How have theologians interpreted his soteriological work, namely, his activity in effecting our salvation? And how have they construed his relation to the Second Person of the Trinity?

We suggest that (1) the Middle Ages largely displaced the Spirit by emphasizing the role of the visible church as mediator of salvation,

99

and that the scholastics taught salvation by "infused grace-love" in tandem with man's meritorious works; [6]

2) in their recovery of the gospel and "Christ alone" *(solus Christus)*, both Luther and Calvin underscored the indispensable role of the Holy Spirit in the event of justification;

3) seventeenth century Protestant Orthodoxy again lost sight of the Spirit by lapsing into a neo-scholasticism which threatened to displace him by "applied grace" and an elaborate "order of salvation" *(ordo salutis)*;

4) during the eighteenth century, Pietists and such religious leaders as August Hermann Francke, Nicolas von Zinzendorf, and John Wesley became preoccupied with sanctification and "holy living," moving in Wesley's case to the verge of perfectionism and the notion of a second baptism;

5) with F.D.E. Schleiermacher and other nineteenth century theologians, there came a perilous depreciation of the theological concept of the Spirit;

6) in the twentieth century there has been a new surge of interest in the Holy Spirit, above all in the "gifts of the Spirit," or special *charismata,* extolled by Pentecostal and other groups. This development may well have something important to say about long-overlooked powers and operations of the Holy Spirit.

I. The Reformation: A New Impetus to Pneumatology

As one of the church's foremost biblical interpreters, MARTIN LUTHER was preeminently concerned that Scripture be apprehended in its powerful divine dynamic. Central is the gospel: the message concerning Christ must ring out; the touchstone for theology is "what preaches Christ" *(was Christum treibet)*. Scholars have analyzed Luther's theology in amazing detail.[7] Luther is much lauded for his originality and massive concentration on Christ. Yet when discussion shifts to the Trinity, the usual judgment is that here he was only "traditional" in following the ancient creeds—and that the Holy Spirit does *not* play a decisive role in his revolutionary, i.e., evangelical theology. Experts like Albrecht Ritschl, Rudolf Otto, Karl Holl, Adolf von Harnack, Reinhold Seeberg, and Paul Althaus have seen no compelling reason to stress Luther's pneumatology.

It has been the special merit of the Danish scholar Regin Prenter to demonstrate that Luther, throughout virtually the whole of his theology, has accorded the Holy Spirit that attention, weight, and active role which can unite a living pneumatology with a no less vital soteriology and with Christ. Luther's soteriological approach to the Spirit's work, and his conviction of the Spirit's absolute centrality, at last fills out what the fourth century fathers had only begun.[8]

Luther discovered through agonizing experience that salvation involves an utterly different mode of divine working than represented in the Augustinian-scholastic notion of an "infused *caritas*" (grace-love) which enables us to perform meritorious works and so attain final approbation before God. Of ourselves we are helpless and saved only by the gracious action of the Holy Spirit himself upon our hearts through the twofold proclamation of law and gospel.

Luther already depicted this law-gospel dialectic in his early lectures on Romans (1515-16). When, under the impact of God's law, a person renounces self-love, when he appropriates God's just sentence of condemnation over himself, he enters into terrible distress *(Anfechtung)*, the dark night of tribulation and inner conflict. In such assaults a person is beset by every demonic and divine power, including the wrath of God. Even the Son seems to turn against him! In this fiery trial, when almost consumed and cast down to the very gates of hell, the Paraclete is at hand. No one else is near then save the compassionate Spirit of Romans 8:26 (Luther's key verse). The Comforter makes groanings unutterable for us. He intercedes and sustains in the midst of *Anfechtung*. By this "strange work" the Spirit conforms us to the pattern of Jesus Christ. We too are brought to obloquy and rejection, convicted and led out to execution of sentence. The Old Man is mortified, and in accord with biblical realism we are "buried into Christ's death." This is the necessary *mortificatio* of the sinner. But all this the Spirit does (via the law in its "second use") only that he may powerfully intercede, rescue, and carry the dying over into a new life *(vivificatio)*. God desires not the death of the sinner, but repentance and life. So the Spirit is quick, as he strikes the soul with remorse through the law, to apply the balm of healing through the gospel. To the heart in anguish he brings Christ "crucified and risen again" as fulfillment of all righteousness in our stead. He awakens in the stricken sinner the assurance that this Christ is present, stands at his side forever, and will share with him his divine grace, purity, and power.

Christ is thus really present in and for faith—but for Luther it is precisely the Spirit who makes Christ present so effectually. The Spirit creates faith, unites us with Christ, and thereby effects our justification through Christ's alien righteousness. All this is the work of the Spirit.[9] From first to last justification is God's own act. So in Luther's profoundly existential or experiential view the Holy Spirit is the divine compassionate Counselor who works mightily upon our heart, conveys us from contrition and pain to that other side of repentance and conversion we call "faith." I am sure that Christ is my righteousness, even as I am his sin; he is now my Lord, and I am called to live in his kingdom forever. Thus the Spirit imparts, in the same moment with justification (divisible only in logic, but simultaneous), the beginning of total renewal.

Sanctification in Luther's view is an ongoing process which is only consummated at the time of death. Our progress in holiness may never be visible to others or even to ourselves. Yet once believers have been laid hold of by the Spirit, they struggle mightily against sin. Christians, however, always remain at one and the same time righteous persons and sinners *(simul justi et peccatores)*. (Luther could not countenance any empirical notion of perfection such as John Wesley later maintained.) As we lapse into new sin and new pains of contrition, the Spirit fills us again and again with the peace that comes from daily forgiveness and a hope stayed on Christ's own righteousness. He who has begun his good work in us will also perfect it unto the day of Jesus Christ.[10]

By what means does the Spirit do this? The Spirit is indeed God, the sovereign Lord of life; he works upon us "where and when he pleases." [11] But he always comes via the divinely instituted external signs. These are the Word (which for Luther is above all spoken or preached, but also written in the Bible) and the visible elements and action in Baptism and the Lord's Supper. The Spirit never works redemptively without these "means of grace" which our senses can perceive. God stoops to us through such vehicles.

Though the Spirit is never found without the outward means of grace, he is their master and, for Luther, the full soteriological partner of the Second Person, Jesus Christ. His work is to make Christ present to the believer. Justification actually occurs through Christ's real presence in the believer: "Believe, and you have!" Thus the Spirit's redemptive role is to effect justification and sanctification by uniting into "one person" Christ and the Christian. And when the Spirit actually makes the Son present to a person as Savior, the Son, in turn, makes the Father present also. The Holy Trinity begins to dwell in that person; rather, the believer is swept into the "force field" of the almighty Trinity confessed in the Athanasian Creed.

For Luther, therefore, if Prenter is right, salvation involves a fully active Trinity: God the Father justifies the sinner for Christ's sake through the power of the Spirit. Hence the Spirit is indispensable for this event of salvation.[12] In justice to those Luther scholars who have not found the Spirit so prominent, it must be conceded that Luther does not always speak explicitly of the Spirit. Yet he is always implicitly present in Luther's thought. Especially in his catechisms, he assigns to the Spirit (after the neglect of the Middle Ages) a crucially central role in partnership with Christ. He is the Spirit *of Christ,* operative since Pentecost in every believer, the *Spiritus creator* or "Lord of Life" who once spoke by the prophets. Now the Spirit uses the words of Christ and of the apostles to summon people to repentance and to gather the church, to create faith in the faithless, to justify them and begin the life "hid with Christ in God." In this fellowship of believers the same Spirit will richly and daily forgive our sins, and in time bring us all to the resurrection and present us sinless before the throne.

Martin Luther, in sum, believed, taught and confessed the Holy Spirit for the sake of justification. The Spirit makes Christ and his atoning sacrifice and righteousness present to every believer, that in faith the believer might be sheltered against the wrath of God and rendered acceptable to the Father. But "where there is forgiveness of sins, there is also life and salvation!" [13] Hence sanctification necessarily follows justification, and both are works of God the Holy Spirit. One can also say that Luther construed justification quite broadly, as including regeneration no less than forgiveness. When Luther, therefore, speaks of God's "grace," or ever and only of Christ *(solus Christus),* he sees the whole Trinity involved. If one studies Luther's works carefully one will find the Spirit unobtrusively but potently there. The Spirit, not the pastor, presides over the two functions of God's Word, law-and-gospel, and he alone applies them as a saving and not a shattering combination. In this intimate partnership of the Spirit and the Son, Luther offered massive resources for a splendid pneumatology, and provided strong indirect support for the Western *filioque* of the Nicene Creed, the procession of the Spirit from the Father and the Son.

Luther's closest associate was the brilliant humanist PHILIP MELANCHTHON, who in 1521 issued the first Protestant dogmatics, the *Loci communes*. Melanchthon eliminated the traditional first section on "theology" (doctrine of God) characteristic of the standard medieval textbooks. In thus making his *Loci* a biblical treatise on salvation, he returned to Augustine's preoccupation with sin and grace, while giving his readers both Paul and Luther. What is man's sinful and helpless condition?; what is his terrible need?; what has Christ provided?; and how does one receive release from sin and every blessing? Melanchthon further articulated these soteriological themes in the Augsburg Confession of 1530. It is striking, however, that nowhere in the *Loci* or in any of the Lutheran Confessions does one find a special article "Concerning the Holy Spirit." Why? Because the Spirit is assumed throughout, even as the treasured Scriptures are accorded no specific article, although they underlie all evangelical theology.

As regards the functions and significance of the Spirit, Melanchthon agrees with Luther, his spiritual father. To be sure, in later years Melanchthon was charged with the error of synergism (Formula of Concord, Art. II) because he had come to speak of three "causes" of conversion: the Word of God, the Holy Spirit, and man's assenting will. Putting the best construction on this, as did Chemnitz, one sees that Melanchthon only asserted that the Holy Spirit, via the Word, draws a person and then involves his newly created will.[14]

JOHN CALVIN was a second generation Reformer. French legal training and humanistic scholarship made him precise in definitions, strong in argument, and a scrupulous exegete. His *Institutes of the Christian Religion* are perhaps the finest dogmatics produced in the Reformation century.[15] His views accord largely with Luther's although the two men did not have close contact. Calvin confessed the Trinity no less firmly than Luther, and bowed reverently before every word of Scripture. Yet Calvin absolutized the Scriptures in a way that is foreign to

Luther, but akin to later Lutheran Orthodoxy. The biblical writers are the docile "amanuenses of the Holy Spirit," making the Scriptures the very voice of God. There is also the inner testimony of the Spirit convincing us that we must listen obediently to this book of revelation. Calvin does not quite say like Luther that the external Word is given first, and that the Spirit then applies it internally.[16] He seems to reverse the emphasis: the divine Word lies like a holy lawbook before us, and the Spirit within testifies to it.

Calvin, like Anselm, emphasized God's high majesty, though John McNeill reminds us that the term "sovereignty of God" does not occur in the original texts. Calvin's account of eternal election appears only in Book III, ch. xxi. It is, therefore, not the foundation stone of the *Institutes*. Calvin even admitted that it is a "horrible decree." Calvin denied the efficacy of Christ's death for any save the elect. Presumably the Spirit is the executor of this eternal decree. Upon the elect his ministrations would be happy and irresistible. But how could his work on the non-elect be "happy"? Either the Spirit does not truly approach them in a gracious manner, or he even hardens them in sin and unbelief. Calvin did not elaborate this point.

Doctrinal differences, especially over the Lord's Supper, separated the Lutheran and the Reformed churches. The several Reformed confessions, however, include strong statements on the Trinity, clearly teach that we are justified solely through faith in Christ, and devote considerable attention to the Holy Spirit.[17] In any case, it is clear that all the mainline Reformers regarded the Spirit as essential in appropriating Christ's saving work. One might also contend that this understanding of the Spirit informed their revolution in ecclesiology. They abolished the medieval concept of the church as a salvatory institution presided over by a priestly hierarchy. The church is the assembly of believers called into existence by the Spirit through the gospel and empowered by the same Spirit, through the same gospel, to know and follow its one true Shepherd, Jesus Christ.[18] The sixteenth century Reformers, in short, articulated a clear and compelling pneumatology.

Far less disciplined was the thinking of the Enthusiasts, Anabaptists, and other groups who loudly hailed the advent of the Holy Spirit. The Zwickau prophets who came to Wittenberg in 1521-22 resembled in part the ancient Montanists. In criticism of Luther they declared that one does not need an "external word," even the Bible. The Spirit

enters directly into some hearts, evoking prophecy and conveying pre-
scriptions for Christian living. Thomas Müntzer and Sebastian Franck
were notable exponents of the primacy of this "inner word." Luther
stormed against these "heavenly prophets" who presumed to think they
had captured the Spirit, and against his erstwhile colleague, Karlstadt, who had "swallowed the Holy Ghost, feathers and all!" The
Spirit as God is free. He does not give himself into human hands, and
certainly does not speak through persons drunk with pride. The Spirit
comes only through his chosen, sober ways, through the external means
of Word and sacrament. Luther lumped the Enthusiasts with the
Roman papacy: both believed that they possessed the Holy Spirit en-
shrined in the treasure chest of their own heart. Both also asserted
that the Spirit had *new* things to offer. Here was another chief ground
for Luther's scathing attacks on the Enthusiasts and Romanists: revelation, he taught, had reached its climax and conclusion with Christ
and the New Testament.[19]

II. The Seventeenth Century: A New Period of Obscuration

After the great springtime and summer of the Reformation, a kind
of theological autumn set in marked by Orthodoxy, prodigious scholarship, fierce polemics, and devastating religious wars. In a time of
great courage and industry, why should the doctrine of the Holy
Spirit have lost ground? Perhaps, despite veritable arsenals of doctrine,
what happened to these late scions of the Reformation was something
unavoidable. Faith as a personal relationship has a glorious and vital
center: for Paul and Luther and Calvin it is Christ. But when professional theology comes along to explain and codify "faith," it becomes
propositional and even admonitory (cf. the opening phrases of the
Athanasian Creed). In moving away from the living center to map
the scattered periphery, theology often loses its appeal and value for
the majority of humanity in direct ratio to its sublety.

Thus the seventeenth century became a great age of the dogmaticians.[20] Each confession was embattled but determined to give no
ground. The leading theological combatants in the university faculties
buttressed their arguments and distilled their materials, reintroducing
an Aristotelian-scholastic methodology. In an age of proof passages
(*dicta probantia*) the Scriptures were plowed and furrowed for more

and more "impregnable" texts. Roman Catholics like the able Robert Bellarmine were equally busy documenting the canons and decrees of the Council of Trent. The disputants were determined to prove their own party right, rather than humbly asking if biblical exegesis really supported a cherished view. One of the first things lost among Evangelicals was Luther's obedient freedom with the Bible, his retention of the Apocrypha, his understanding of the Bible's human side, and his emphasis on its self-authenticating dynamic center: the gospel of free forgiveness for Christ's sake. To be crushingly authoritative, the systematicians now reached for a Bible which their lengthy Prolegomena described as plenarily inspired, infallible, and formally "perfect." In this heightened emphasis on a supernatural book its divine Author was relegated to the background and the Holy Spirit's role was diminished.[21] Doubtless this was never intended, but perhaps one remembered too well Luther's criticism of the Enthusiasts, and leaned the more heavily on the external Word: "It is written . . . "

Likewise salvation was dissected into a detailed process or sequence of steps hard to distinguish. After Philip Melanchthon, Martin Chemnitz, and Aegidius Hunnius came a score of dedicated thinkers. They range from Leonhard Hutter, determined to be right (he once trampled on a picture of Melanchthon), to the warm and noble Johann Gerhard, to John Andrew Quenstedt, "the bookkeeper of Orthodoxy," to the militant Abraham Calovius. They gradually defined soteriology with an astoundingly minimal mention of the Spirit. The believer's "appropriation" of Christ's benefits is unfolded in a series of phases or operations called the order of salvation *(ordo salutis)*. This order, to be sure, is controlled by grace, and is sometimes linked with the Spirit. But grace as such is the applicator, rather than the living Spirit who, as in medieval theology, again seems to have been removed to a distance. The Spirit's gifts are separated from their sovereign Giver.

Each writer sought to explicate more completely all the theological (hardly psychological) steps in man's transition from sinner to saint: vocation, illumination, conversion, justification, regeneration, renovation, sanctification, and finally mystical union! To be sure, the impersonal grace which regulates this process is not the infused and cooperating grace of the medieval scholastics, poured into the soul by the sacraments. It is now the unmerited mercy of God. It is the divine pardon which acquits sinners and cancels their sin for Christ's sake.

Still, justification has become a strictly judicial verdict; it and its sequel processes are completely forensic or logical.

This "objectivizing" trend of seventeenth century dogmatics is well illustrated in works such as those by Heinrich Heppe and Heinrich Schmid. The Holy Spirit is rarely accorded a distinct topic of his own. He is the Third Person of the Trinity who inspired the Scriptures. But any discussion of his personal work or effects is ordinarily limited to brief remarks following the treatment of Christ's person and work, and as a transition to consideration of the church and the means of grace. The lengthy sections on justification, conversion, sanctification, etc., purport to identify and codify what is often submerged, unconscious, or concurrently present in the believer's experience.[22] The Holy Spirit, who is the Prime Mover, is rarely or never mentioned.

Yet this Protestant *ordo salutis* was far sounder than the medieval approach; at least it was clearly seen that salvation involves "passive" changes, i.e., that it is God's work alone. Here one finds unmistakable affirmation of Christ, of grace alone and not of works. But why so little positive, explicit stress on the Spirit? Even the challenge posed by the *Racovian Catechism* (1605) of the Polish Socinians hardly altered things. The Socinians expressly denied the orthodox Trinitarian doctrine, acknowledged Jesus as at most God's Son by adoption, and rejected a unique and distinctly "personal" Holy Spirit. Lutherans and Calvinists did not engineer a full-orbed defense of the Spirit and his essential role in salvation; they were content to reaffirm the traditional teaching that the Trinity consists of "three coequal and consubstantial persons in one Godhead."

Reformed theology underwent a development akin to that of Lutheran Orthodoxy. Calvin's successors guarded and cultivated his great legacy, redemption through Christ, but also took seriously God's eternal will as manifested in double predestination. The elect were bidden to prove their election by decorous living and proper piety. Here may have been one source of the Calvinistic work ethic. Max Weber and R. A. Tawney have argued that much of the world view that engendered modern capitalism ultimately derived from Genevan religion.

The conservative Calvinist emphasis on God's twofold eternal decree inevitably evoked a reaction: witness the young Arminius in the Low Countries. This assault on double predestination was the work of the so-called Remonstrants. It occasioned the Synod of Dort (1618-19) which repudiated the "Arminian heresy" that God willed to save many, not the chosen few, and that the call *(vocatio)* should be interpreted as universal.[23] Dort defined election more cautiously, in a sublapsarian sense. Yet the issue had now been posed which would prompt Methodism in the next century to preach Christ to the unconverted multitude, rather than limit the Spirit's work to a relative few. One recalls that orthodox Calvinism did not stress foreign missions; the latter first came to the fore with eighteenth century Pietism.

England witnessed the rise of the Quakers, and their doctrine of the "Inner Light," in the wake of Puritanism and the Civil War. Quakers believed that God has equipped the human heart with a special receptivity. Divine light would illumine heart and mind if one waited in quietness and patience. The Quakers were a living, visible criticism of the established church: they rejected all sacraments, had no need of priests or pastors, and to some extent even bypassed the Bible. Their adherence to the language of "thee and thou" indicated a stubborn intention to live, not discuss, their faith. Their honest endeavor in this direction antedates the heightened interest in "sanctification" which would characterize Wesleyan Methodism in eighteenth century England.[24]

Despite their unyielding confessional loyalties, and erudite dogmatic systems, all camps in the seventeenth century—whether Lutheran, Reformed, or Roman Catholic—must have grieved the Holy Spirit. While trumpets sounded the call to bloody battle, and pulpits declaimed propositional theology and denounced human depravity, countless hearts missed what is also in Scripture: the love of God and the neighbor, daily impulses toward a more joyous life, walking together in the zeal of the Lord. When Orthodoxy turned the message of life into fundamental, non-fundamental, and mixed articles of faith, corollaries and consequences, hearts were not always warmed and consoled.

How could it happen that such devout religious establishments thrust the Spirit somewhat aside? The answer might be that he was frozen in the surrogate of the inspired Bible. The theory of the plenary inspiration of Scripture is a seventeenth century elaboration of reverent but much vaguer notions of former times.[25] One must reject as simplistic the alternatives still often heard: "The Bible *is*, versus *contains*, the Word of God." Both Luther and Calvin insist that "the Bible *speaks* the Word of God," i.e., it is above all God's Word of *address* (law and gospel). For Luther and Calvin the Bible or external Word is an instrument, a two-edged sword which the Spirit uses to confront the human heart and conscience with the twofold message of God's judgment and mercy. But the seventeenth century men proceeded to absolutize the Bible, to give the book autopistic force. It carried self-evident authority as a supernatural book. It possessed an intrinsic, formal efficacy in working salvation, certainly among the elect, while it would rouse unrepentant folk to resistance and further hardness of heart. For pastor and professor the Bible was now an open reference book, a legal code with verse numbers. Men possessed the plain *printed* truth. The determined age of Orthodoxy could not fully comprehend that the Spirit must work with that book, not as its bounden servant but forever as its free Master, even as he is the ultimate Author.

III. The Eighteenth Century: A New Emphasis on the Work of the Spirit

In the century following Orthodoxy, traditional Christianity was strongly challenged by two diverse yet not unrelated movements: Pietism and Rationalism. Both movements favored a new individualism and the quest for religious autonomy. In the Early and High Middle Ages everyone had been included *de facto* in the universal religious community of Christendom. The Late Middle Ages and the Reformation introduced several "state" or "folk" churches. Sixteenth and seventeenth century England witnessed the rejection of the Anglican "establishment" by the Puritans and Dissenters. Now, with the rise and spread of Pietism and English Wesleyanism, serious tensions developed not only between the claims of personal religion and the traditional patterns of belief and behavior in the state churches, but no less between the "true" Christian and his "once-born" neighbors. These tensions show themselves, for example, in Spener's idea of *ecclesiolae in ecclesia*—small assemblies of genuine believers separated from the unconverted in the territorial church.[26]

German Pietism may be said to have been launched with the publication in 1675 of PHILIP SPENER's *Pia Desideria*.[27] In this beautiful little book of "pious wishes" Spener expressed great admiration for Luther. He stated his intention not to depart from Reformation doctrine, although he was sharply critical of Lutheran Orthodoxy. He demanded that sermons edify, instead of sounding harsh calls for controversy. Theological students should be spiritually formed, not merely trained to be academics. Spener advocated devotional exercises and provided some noble examples. As a conscientious pastor and *Seelsorger*, Spener was concerned to imbue his entire congregation with Christian ideals. Recognizing that this was a task impossible of realization, he gathered select groups from his Frankfurt congregation for devotional meetings twice weekly in his home *(Collegia Pietatis)*. The existence of these "little churches within the church" meant in practice that the Pietists were inclined to dissociate themselves from those persons who were only formally church members. This development led to the insistence on a conversion experience, the earnest struggle for a spiritual breakthrough. Salvation now came to be psychologized or interiorized in a new way.

AUGUST HERMANN FRANCKE, who was attracted to Pietism through the influence of Spener, possessed rare organizational ability and a practical sense. Having passed through a profound conversion experience, he was especially concerned, while a young professor at Leipzig, that his students devote more attention to prayer than to assimilation of quantities of dogma. Driven from Leipzig in controversy with such Orthodox theologians as Johann Carpzov, he became the guiding spirit at the new university of Halle. There he founded his celebrated Institutes *(Franckesche Stiftungen)* or charitable institutions, including an orphanage, schools for boys and girls, a dispensary and a publishing house. He encouraged the printing of thousands of Bibles through the generosity of the Count of Canstein. Halle not only became the largest training school for German Lutheran pastors, but also sent the first missionaries to India and the Danish West Indies. It was from Halle that Henry Melchior Muhlenberg came to Pennsylvania Colony in 1742, labored prodigiously (in accord with his motto "The Church Must Be Planted!"), and took the lead in founding the first Lutheran Synod in the United States in 1748.

While the Holy Spirit is not constantly invoked in the theology of Spener and Francke, he was definitely included in their total theological perspective. For them the Spirit is, of course, that Person of the Trinity who, according to Luther's Small Catechism, presides over the blessed work of sanctification. Francke believed that everyone should pass through a conversion experience, an hour which the Christian should forever remember as the turning point of his life. Thus religion was no longer a mechanical matter of being born into a "folk church." True religion commenced with a dramatic rebirth directed by the Spirit.

The theology of German Pietism was by no means as learned or finely developed as that of Orthodoxy. Pietists were intent upon creating a devotional literature, including hymns, prayers, edifying sermons, pious narratives, and mission accounts, rather than producing sober exegetical works or lengthy dogmatic tomes. What occurred was a loosening, perhaps a weakening, of the theological mindset. Preaching appealed to the heart and sought to console. There was much talk of the love of Christ, and repeated admonitions to help the unfortunate. But Pietists penned no great classics on the Spirit or his work.

In its later stages Pietism sometimes degenerated into pretentiousness or even hypocrisy, and it was always beset by the temptation to legalism and moralism. It was censorious of secular pleasures, including the theater and the arts, and inhibited creative impulses in these latter areas. It engendered bitter controversy within the state church by engaging in prolonged quarrels with the representatives of Orthodoxy. Pietism could nourish smugness and its adherents fall into work-righteousness. The true believer might well harbor a spirit of superiority over against the unconverted. Yet in its nobler representatives Pietism had much to teach the church in the period after the religious wars and in the midst of confessional antagonisms. Likewise, in the lay preaching movement of Hans Nielsen Hauge, it played a major role in the nineteenth century religious awakening in the valleys of Norway.

One practical sphere in which Pietists were active—the development of Protestant foreign missions in the eighteenth century—could have stirred some new thinking about the Holy Spirit. The story of mission work in the modern period—chronicled so ably by Julius Richter, Gustav Warneck, and Kenneth Scott Latourette—offers a portrait gallery of many courageous and devout individuals who brought the message of Pentecost to many shores. Hendrikus Berkhof has recently provided the salutary reminder that we still require a comprehensive theology of missions, which would at the same time be a theology of the Holy Spirit.[28]

JOHN WESLEY, the founder of Methodism, emerged as a leader during a time of great religious upheaval in England—the Evangelical Revival.[29] Theologically, the Anglican Church had been influenced by Reformed ideas and had retained much of Calvinism. In opposition to extreme Calvinism, Wesley became convinced of the Armenian principle that God had not limited the work of his Spirit to a few elect. He rejected the notion of predestination, since it gave a person no chance for salvation. In struggling against antinomianism, and drawing upon both Lutheran and Moravian resources, Wesley developed the concept of "scriptural holiness." He exhorted those who accepted the Savior to seek to live in newness of life. He did not want to place limits on what the grace of God could accomplish in people. The new relationship to God appropriated through faith makes good works and holiness not only possible but also necessary. Wesley could not conceive of those who are justified not being made righteous in deed by the Spirit of Christian sanctification. Holiness, sanctification, and perfection are terms Wesley related to "the ordering of Christian life to its full potential, assuming that persons have God-given powers to respond to God in faith, to grow in grace, and to attain to whatever *telos* God has in store for his children." [30]

IV. The Nineteenth Century: Loss and Recovery

By the dawn of the nineteenth century, the sea of European religious life was far from calm. Many new currents and crosstides had begun to run. Immanuel Kant, who had been the "destroyer" of many proud systems of speculative philosophy, died in 1804. He had represented the age of Enlightenment in its chastened form, incorporating into his thought strands of both Pietism and Rationalism. Tillich remarks that in some sense the Quakers, Pietists, and Rationalists were all akin: they "looked within a man" for ultimate guidance and the assurance of truth. The Quaker had the inner light; the Pietist relied on the inner testimony of the Holy Spirit; the Rationalist claimed an innate power of reason by which he could investigate and illuminate the secrets of nature, improve human society, and attain unending progress.[31] German Idealism, reaching back to Plato by way of Spinoza and climaxing in Hegel, conceived of God as decisively "immanent," as Absolute Spirit coming to self-realization in finite spirit. Likewise, natural science had achieved a number of significant discoveries (associated, for example, with the work of Laplace, Erasmus, Darwin, and Lamarck) and advanced new world views which would require major adjustments in theological thinking. In the midst of this intellectual and cultural ferment, the problem of tradition again came to the fore: what of the Christian heritage would be preserved, and what refashioned if not rejected?

FRIEDRICH SCHLEIERMACHER is that seminal genius from whom many theological movements in the nineteenth and twentieth centuries received their impetus. He was also a nodal point in whom many previous developments converged.[32] By family influence and early schooling he was reared in the Pietistic ethos of Herrnhut. He was a devoted student of Platonic philosophy and a friend of Romantic poets and dramatists. Original but disciplined, he possessed a synthesizing intellect which wove together in logical fabric things old and new, refashioning tradition in accord with new modes of sensibility.

When in 1810 Schleiermacher presented his "brief outline" for all theological disciplines at the recently founded university of Berlin, he proposed some startling changes. All theological data should be considered from the perspective of both philosophy (which meant critical reason) and history (which meant change and development, rather than stability). Dogmatics itself he regarded as an enterprise which changes from time to time, in accord with the altered needs, insights, and spiritual growth of each generation. What he proposed to offer, therefore, was a phenomenology or description of the Christian faith for his own day, rather than pretending to exhibit an eternally valid system of absolute truth. He recognized the limitations of our knowledge (Kant) and the permanent flux of things (Heraclitus).

Theologians had traditionally sought to erect their systems on the foundation of some external authority. For Roman Catholics this authority was the teaching office of the church; for orthodox Protestants the inspired Bible. Quakers, Pietists, and Rationalists looked within themselves. This turning inward was also the pattern which Schleiermacher, with considerable sophistication, offered his generation as a way of validating religious experience and undergirding theology. Hence Schleiermacher proposed to construct his dogmatics upon a systematic and critical examination of the religious experience of the

Christian community, insofar as everything in that experience is "related to the redemption accomplished by Jesus of Nazareth." [33] Schleiermacher also indicated that from this experiential perspective some traditional teachings, even pious beliefs once held dear, are not essential to Christian faith or should be entirely recast. He was the first bold "heretic" of the nineteenth century.

Schleiermacher replaced the old loosely concatenated series of theological topics *(loci)* with an internally coherent and tightly organized system. He grounded religion not on knowing (a la the older Rationalism), nor on doing (a la Kantian practical reason), but on feeling. By this latter construct he meant not emotion but modifications of the immediate self-consciousness, specifically the genuine religious feeling of being "posited," that is, the consciousness of being "utterly dependent" or, what is the same thing, of "being in relation with God." [34] Orthodox critics were shocked that this theology did not begin outside of man with the divinely revealed truths of Holy Scripture. Because Schleiermacher classified dogmatics as a historical and ethical (experiential) discipline, he was accused of having opened the door to a boundless relativism in theology: presumably Christian truth changes in step with changing historical contexts and with developing Christian experience. For Schleiermacher himself, however, authentic Christian faith must be determined at every point by reference to the historical appearance of Jesus of Nazareth and the redemption accomplished through him. And these historical givens, in turn, are to be interpreted through the medium of both the witness of Scripture and the confessions of the Evangelical Church.

Hence it is not fair to claim that Schleiermacher merely relativized the faith; one might more appropriately say that he historicized or psychologized Christian theology in a new and dramatic way. In any event, he broke decisively with the older propositional view of revelation as the impartation of timeless truths. In this respect Schleiermacher is properly designated the father of modern theology.

In his treatment of the Holy Spirit, Schleiermacher is especially dismaying and open to severe criticism. He has, at best, an attenuated doctrine of the Spirit. Apparently the Spirit is only that common spirit of religious trust in Jesus Christ which all believers share: a type of impersonal bond of kinship and similarity among the faithful. This is certainly not the Holy Spirit of the ancient creeds, or of the Reformers, or even of German Pietism. Schleiermacher, in short, effected a dissolution of the *person* of the Spirit. The classical Trinitarian dogma is relegated to an appendix at the close of *The Christian Faith* since, as Schleiermacher notes, the doctrine does not belong to "the immediate utterances of the religious self-consciousness." [35] One might claim, perhaps, that Schleiermacher replaced Trinitarian faith with "binitarianism": for him the Holy Spirit is no longer the Third Person of Trinity but is the divine power (Spirit of God) and the continuing presence within the community of the exalted Christ (Spirit of Christ). In this way pneumatology has been annexed to Christology.

In evaluating this reductionism characteristic of nineteenth century theology, however, one does well to remember that the Nicene Creed itself fails to relate the Spirit directly to Christ and to the church. Judged from the perspective of the New Testament, this latter omission is a serious failure. The insistence of Schleiermacher and his successors on the Spirit *of Christ* operative *in the church* is a valid emphasis and worthy of respectful attention. In this light, nineteenth century pneumatology, for all its glaring weaknesses, has a meaningful role to play in the construction of that comprehensive doctrine of the Holy Spirit which remains a desideratum of modern theological scholarship. [36]

Schleiermacher, to be sure, did not entirely dominate nineteenth century theology. In the welter of contemporary movements—religious awakenings, patriotic aspirations, political ventures—which filled the first half of the century, there were those theologians who stoutly resisted the Prussian Union of 1817 designed to bring Lutherans and Reformed together at the communion table. Reacting both to state coercion and to the still widespread Rationalism, they hewed to confessional lines and sought to recover again (repristinate) the theology of seventeenth century Orthodoxy. [37] Nevertheless, Schleiermacher's influence was clearly felt among those who sought to mediate between faith and knowledge, between the Christian tradition and the demands of modernity. This influence is also discernible in the well-known Erlangen school founded by Gottfried Thomasius and J. C. K. von Hofmann (the pioneer of *Heilsgeschichte*). [38]

For some thinkers Schleiermacher's mystical Pietism proved particularly appealing, for others his psychological probing of Christian experience: in either case his concentration on religious "inwardness" evoked cordial assent. On such a basis even conservative systematicians would be less likely to ponder the Holy Spirit as eternal God and Third Person of the Trinity, or as the prime mover in spiritual life and conduct. They were inclined, rather, to focus on the experience of the pious God-consciousness within the church, and thus to give primary attention to the congregation, the means of grace, and even to questions of church government and the ecclesiastical role of the consistory. Thus the church, the proper preaching of the Word, the correct doctrine and right administration of the sacraments were issues of deep concern to bishop, pastor, and ministerial candidate alike. One still paid reverence to the Spirit, of course. But ecclesiology and the practical tasks of ministry benefited, rather than formal pneumatology as such.

If for many writers of the earlier nineteenth century the person of the Spirit was not of signal importance, a gradual rise of interest can be discerned after 1860. In the Erlangen school, for example, Thomasius ventured a new approach in Christology *(kenosis)* and Frank sought to buttress theological espistemology (God as Absolute Being) against Albrecht Ritschl's neo-Kantian doubts. A more determined search for a rounded theological system meant that the Spirit had to be considered. But too often, after opening pages which assert that believers must relate to and rely on the Spirit, the systematicians shift their focus and become "concrete." Thus Lutherans would quickly concentrate on the law-gospel distinction, or on the nature of the church as visible-invisible, or on the proper understanding of the sacraments. Their discussions only noted in passing Luther's rich explanation of the Third Article.

After Schleiermacher, the second great figure of nineteenth century Protestant theology was ALBRECHT RITSCHL. His influence dates from about 1870 when he launched his magnum opus, *The Christian Doctrine of Justification and Reconciliation* (3 vols., 1870-74, and subsequent revisions). Over against Schleiermacher, Ritschl was allergic to Pietism, although he wrote a masterful *History of Pietism* (3 vols., 1880-86) which continues to be a major scholarly resource. Ritschl also broke with Schleiermacher by grounding dogmatics not on the testimony of the "religious affections" but on God's self-revelation in history through Jesus Christ, the church's Savior and Lord. Thus, in opposition to Schleiermacher's "subjectivism," Ritschl pictured Christianity as an ellipse with two foci: *redemption* through Christ's sacrifice of utter obedience to the will of the Father, and Christ's founding of the *kingdom of God* as the highest good of human existence (since this kingdom is at once God's own self-end and the ultimate goal for which God's entire spiritual creation has been created).

Working within this conceptual framework of the new covenant community established by God through the agency of his Son, Ritschl proceeded to reinterpret the cardinal Christian teachings. He rejected the traditional notion of God's wrath as "metaphysically" real, viewing it rather as a subjective misreading of God's true nature (pure love) owing to the sinner's consciousness of guilt. He replaced the Augustinian doctrine of original sin by the concept of a "kingdom of sin" which is built up by actual sins and the sway of evil habit. Above all, he concentrated massive attention on the religious and moral value of Christ's work of redemption for the Christian community, attributing to it both universal forgiveness of sin (= justification) and the believer's personal appropriation of a new life-style characterized by spiritual dominion over the world, fidelity in one's civic vocation, and love-prompted action in God's kingdom (= reconciliation).

From 1864 until his death in 1889, Ritschl was the leading professor in the Göttingen theological faculty. Both through the classroom and, more especially, through his weighty publications, he became the founder of a Ritschlian school that numbered among its adherents such influential figures as Adolf von Harnack, Wilhelm Herrmann, Julius Kaftan, Martin Rade, Ferdinand Kattenbusch, Friedrich Loofs, and, for a time, Ernst Troeltsch. The official organs of this school included the *Theologische Literaturzeitung* and the *Zeitschrift für Theologie und Kirche,* both of which survive as prestigious theological journals. Ritschl evoked vociferous and even violent reactions from friends and foes, and has been unjustly forgotten today (in large measure because of the harsh judgments passed on him by Karl Barth and the representatives of neo-orthodoxy). In spite of serious defects, Ritschl merits high commendation as a historical and constructive theologian who attempted to free the tradition of Reformation theology from the baneful effects of Hegelian speculation, Pietistic sectarianism, Enlightenment individualism, Orthodoxist intellectualism, etc. Not the least of his services was the impetus which he gave to modern Luther research through his programmatic return to the "young Luther" of the Reformation's formative years.

Nösgen is exceptionally severe on Ritschl and his school regarding the doctrine of the Holy Spirit.[39] True, there is a paucity of explicit statements about the Spirit in Ritschl's published works, although such statements are more frequent than one might initially expect (if one assumes, as is usually the case, that here Ritschl shares Schleiermacher's perspective).[40] One also does well to remember that Ritschl's magnum opus is not a full-blown "systematic theology" or dogmatics textbook, but an historical-biblical-constructive investigation of Evangelical Christianity's central tenet, the doctrine of justification. Furthermore, Ritschl regularly concluded his (unpublished) lectures on dogmatics with a discussion of the doctrine of the Trinity in which he is surprisingly orthodox, affirming the unity and consubstantiality of the Three Persons and their hypostatic distinction. Salient portions of these lectures have recently been published by Rolf Schäfer in his important book on Ritschl.[41]

Beyond these textual considerations, it is important to note that Ritschl's treatment of the Spirit is intimately bound up with his rejection of metaphysics in theology: one is not permitted to speak of the Spirit as he exists within the Godhead (although Ritschl does not deny the "immanent" Trinity), since God can only be spoken of properly in the light of his historical self-revelation. Hence we do not have authentic or saving knowledge of God-in-himself but only of God-in-action, God in his self-disclosure on the plane of history in the person and work of Jesus Christ. Likewise the Spirit is known not as a divine "substance" at rest *behind* his works, but is comprehended only *in* his effects. The following passage aptly sums up Ritschl's dominant perspective:

> We must give up the question—derived from Scholastic psychology, but insoluble—how man is laid hold of, or pervaded, or filled by the Holy Spirit. What we have to do is rather to verify life in the Holy Spirit by showing that believers know God's gracious gifts (1 Cor. 2:12), that they call on God as their Father (Rom. 8:15), that they act with love and joy, with meekness and self-control (Gal. 5:22), that they are on their guard above all against party spirit, and cherish rather a spirit of union (1 Cor. 3:1-4). In these statements the Holy Spirit is not denied, but recognized and understood.[42]

Certainly this listing of Pauline assertions is too brief, and Ritschl's own argument too elliptical, to serve as an adequate pneumatology. Yet the passage shows that Ritschl does more than merely posit the Holy Spirit as an impersonal "common spirit" *(Gemeingeist)* in the religious life, as Nösgen claimed. Nor does Nösgen take account of Ritschl's repeated assertion that the Holy Spirit is the very Spirit of God *in whom God knows himself.*[43]

This latter view entails the real "personality" of the Spirit and his co-eternity with the Father and the Son. Ritschl, however, in keeping with his epistemology, could not grant that we have knowledge of God's own intra-Trinitarian existence. We know the Holy Trinity only in the economy of salvation, in their saving works, not in their timeless being.

Ritschl, in short, did not follow Schleiermacher's precedent in treating the doctrine of the Trinity as a mere appendix to the Christian faith, as an artificial construct. At the same time, Ritschl did not effect a recovery of classical Trinitarian theology and its witness to the Spirit. In this respect he shared in that diminution of Trinitarian thought, and of the doctrine of the Holy Spirit, which is characteristic of nineteenth century Protestant theology.[44]

This failing only began to be put right in the period after the ascendancy of Schleiermacher and Ritschl, in the era of the "new orthodoxy." But the way for recovery was also prepared by the appearance, in the later nineteenth and early twentieth century, of new historical and theological investigations of the Holy Spirit.

V. The Twentieth Century: Renewed Interest and Theological Reconstruction

The first important monographs on the Spirit began to be published in the period between the death of Ritschl (1889) and the First World War. The Dutch theologian Abraham Kuyper published *The Work of the Holy Spirit* in 1888-89. John Owen's old Puritan classic on the Spirit was reprinted.[45] W. H. Griffith Thomas prepared a thorough and able book, *The Holy Spirit.*[46] H. Wheeler Robinson devoted fifteen years to the preparation of *The Christian Experience of the Holy Spirit.*[47] A pioneer in the history of the doctrine of the Holy Spirit was Henry Barclay Swete. In masterful fashion he surveyed first the ancient church and then the period up to the *filioque* controversy in the reign of Charlemagne. At Swete's urging the narrative was continued by Howard Watkin-Jones in two volumes, one on the medieval church (to the Counter-Reformation) in 1922, and a sequel on the Spirit from Arminius to Wesley in 1929. Nösgen's history was published in Germany in 1899, followed by his monograph on the nature and work of the Holy Spirit.[48]

Leaving aside literature on the history of Pentecostalism,[49] which usually does not antedate 1900, we shall review in this concluding section what a number of leading theologians of this century have said about the Spirit.

EMIL BRUNNER's well-known dogmatics, published in three volumes, shows the balance, comprehensive grasp, and biblical command which made it widely acceptable in Reformed circles.[50] His basic principle grew out of an earlier series of lectures on the divine-human encounter (*Wahrheit als Begegnung*). This encounter is the self-impartation of God to man: something far greater than simple revelation. Brunner's third volume begins with the Holy Spirit and treats "God's self-representation in us through the Holy Spirit." [51] Brunner frankly contends that one cannot construct a doctrine of the Holy Spirit by gathering utterances from the Old Testament, where his activity is only partially touched on. The Spirit inspires the language of the prophets, but "it is not His work to make men's hearts accessible to the prophetic Word" since "the Holy Ghost was not yet given." Nor will a concordance of New Testament passages suffice to erect a pneumatology. The concept of the Spirit does not occur in the Gospels of Matthew and Mark, in Hebrews, James, or the Pastoral Epistles, and the diverse statements which are made "could only with violence be brought to one common denominator. A doctrine of the Holy Spirit built on biblicist principles always rests therefore on a more or less unconscious self-deception," on our preconceptions.

Brunner no less rejects Rudolf Bultmann's tendency to regard the Holy Spirit as only one of the "mythical" elements of the New Testament, to be excluded as both unintelligible to modern man and even useless. We *must* speak of the Holy Spirit in speaking of the church and faith. Brunner first defines what he means by the person of the Spirit: "We mean that *mode* of God's being by which He is present

within us, and operates in our spirit and heart." [52] Brunner then
delineates the Spirit's work:

> His first and decisive activity is this, that He makes Christ
> Present to us . . . Faith is personal encounter. Thus we under-
> stand also why it was only in the New Testament, and not in
> the Old, that the Holy Spirit could be spoken of in this preg-
> nant sense. . . . He is the presence of God which bears wit-
> ness to, and makes effectual, the historical Christ as a living
> personal presence. The operation of the Holy Spirit is neces-
> sary for the Word about Christ to become the Word of Christ
> for us. . . . To be led by the Spirit of God is not to be pos-
> sessed. On the contrary, it is to be liberated from possession,
> from the alien domination of evil. Man only becomes himself
> through the operation of the Holy Spirit [53] . . . But the opera-
> tion of the Holy Spirit is not confined to bearing witness to
> us of Christ. Rather is He borne witness to by the Apostles
> as creative power, that produces new life, new feelings, new
> spiritual, psychological, and even physical powers. [54]

Like Barth, Brunner was deeply impressed by Johann Christoph
Blumhardt's experience of the power of the Holy Spirit, and echoed
Blumhardt's prayer for a new outpouring of the Spirit's powers and
gifts so much lacking in the church.

KARL BARTH was an even more strenuous exponent of the Holy
Spirit than Brunner. He was an heir of the liberal tradition through
his teachers in Berlin, Wilhelm Herrmann and Adolf von Harnack, but
his experience as a Swiss village pastor during the first World War
turned him into a biblical theologian. He first came to public notice
by a forceful exposition of Romans (1918). [55] Barth was convinced that
Schleiermacher was an erring signpost in theology. Religion as an
essentially human phenomenon is fruitless speculation, since one
cannot establish saving certainties out of the inner self, nor can God
be defined by raising man's noble qualities to a superlative degree.
As Kierkegaard said, God is "totally Other," and thus God's own self-
revelation is all-important. The church has nothing which has not
first been given to her. Dogmatics is simply the church's critical examination of her proclamation concerning God, and is an exercise of
obedient listening to Scripture and confessions: a *church* dogmatics.

After some false starts Barth launched the most extensive Protestant dogmatics of this century. Not quite a Summa, its volumes made theological history. Barth presents a powerful and often original kerygmatic theology.[56]

Volume I offers a "theology of the Word of God" which is already a complete dogmatics *in nuce*. It reverses Schleiermacher by involving the entire Trinity in this self-communication of God. God reveals himself as the Triune One: he is unimpaired unity but also unimpaired difference as "Revealer, Revelation, and Revealedness." God's Revealedness is his self-impartation as the Spirit of the Father and the Son, and thus he shows himself Lord in his freedom to become our God. Barth held that the Trinitarian dogma is not explicitly scriptural but is a work of the church, resulting necessarily from an analysis of the concept and total process of revelation. Barth repudiated the notion that the Spirit is a magical, mystical "indefinable whispering and compelling" within the human soul; nor is he a separate "person" who works in his own obscure way independent of the Father and the Son. The Spirit's share in the Trinity's divine work is discussed throughout the *Church Dogmatics:* in vol. II on God, in vol. III on creation, and especially in extensive sections in vol. IV on the reconciliation wrought by Jesus Christ. Since Barth redistributes dogmatic material originally, willfully, often with architectonic brilliance, and includes relevant ethical considerations at the end of each volume, the Spirit is treated at many points. This is fortunate since the planned vol. V was never written. This concluding volume was to have considered redemption and the final consummation worked *by the Spirit;* on the previous scale this discussion would have run to several thousand pages.

No greater influence in New Testament scholarship has been exercised in the present century than by RUDOLF BULTMANN. He wished to be a Lutheran in defending above all the Reformers' "faith alone," as well as a scrupulous modern scholar. He discusses spirit *(pneuma)* in his classic *Theology of the New Testament,* and in his commentary on John.[57] But as noted above, Bultmann really has no substantive role for the Holy Spirit. Here also he sought to demythologize the New Testament and especially Paul. Spirit is man's own genuine self. What Paul calls the gift of the Spirit, or walking in the Spirit, is best translated as saying: the believer has been given freedom from the power of sin and death.[58] The notion of the Spirit as an indwelling divine power would rob man of his capacity to make a free response to God. Demythologized, in terms of Bultmann's existentialism, the Spirit becomes "the possibility of a new life (authentic life) which must be appropriated by a constant deliberate resolve." Here as elsewhere his reduction has meant impoverishment rather than enrichment. Still, his soberness over against all texts teaches both exegete and systematician to use great caution in speculative statements.[59]

Perhaps the most unusual, suggestive, and problematic treatment accorded the Spirit by a modern systematic theologian is that found in the fourth part of PAUL TILLICH's *Systematic Theology*, entitled "Life and the Spirit." [60] Here Tillich kept to his method of "correlation," posing questions and problems from the human or cultural context, and proposing answers in his "apologetic" theology. Tillich maintains that human existence is filled with "ambiguities," the torment of uncertainties. It is the "spiritual presence" which speaks to the spirit of man, and imparts life within the dimensions of religion, culture, and morality. "Life" is universally present, not limited to the sanctuary or to religious and moral experience. The entire treatise is another Tillichian tour de force of abstract, symbolic thought. It is only in part traditional in its terminology, employing such novel constructs as structure and ecstasy, freedom and finitude, purpose and humanity, the spiritual presence as faith or as love.

Tillich faults Barth for reversing Schleiermacher and beginning with the Trinity, which properly should be "Postlegomena." On the matter of the *filioque* Tillich considers the East to be more correct than the West. "Christology is not complete without pneumatology, because 'the Christ is the Spirit' and the actualization of the New Being in history is the work of the Spirit." [61] He believes we require a radical revision of the Trinitarian doctrine and a new understanding of the divine life and the spiritual presence. "The doctrine of the Trinity is not closed. It can be neither discarded nor accepted in its traditional form. It must be kept open in order to fulfil its original function—to express in embracing symbols the self-manifestation of the Divine Life to man." [62] "Life and the Spirit" may be Tillich's finest contribution, and it may prove suggestive though unacceptable in detail.

Possibly the significance of the Spirit as "God bringing Christ," and Schleiermacher's legitimate concern for the "community spirit" or koinonia among Christians, might be held together in modern theology by following Dietrich Bonhoeffer's precedent in his treatise on the communion of saints. The author of this "dogmatic inquiry into the sociology of the church," and of *Life Together,* also spoke in his *Letters and Papers from Prison* of a return from New Testament individualism to the people-of-God concept of the Old Testament. The boundaries of the church as wrought by the Spirit are never narrowly ecclesiastical, or dare we say "religious"? [63]

One could add to this brief survey other important discussions of the Spirit, for example, those of Paul Althaus, Wolfgang Trillhaas, and John Macquarrie. In any event there can be no doubt that pneumatology had gained new attention among the leading systematicians by the middle of the twentieth century.[64] Perhaps no one has ventured so strong a statement as Werner Elert. After a beautiful and exquisitely chiseled summary of the "almost bewildering riches of ideas and viewpoints" contained in the New Testament's witness to the Spirit, including "glossolalia, baptism, and resurrection." Elert added:

> . . . All this is the work of the Holy Spirit. If one finally adds that we receive also the Gospel only through the Paraclete, then one could with good reasons not merely open the entire dogmatics with pneumatology, but even make the Work of the Spirit the theme of the whole.[65]

If Elert himself elected to go another route it was only to forestall the impression that God's relation to the world exhausts itself in the work of the Spirit.

By the 1970s the emergence and growth of Pentecostal and charismatic movements within the mainline Christian denominations have obliged even the reluctant to confront new questions and perhaps to acknowledge new evidence of the Spirit's presence in our times. Only the Spirit himself can guide us in mutual listening and understanding, in proper critical sifting, and in searching for those doctrinal formulations and churchly attitudes which will leave hearts open to his gracious and often surprising operations.

Veni, Creator Spiritus!

Notes

1. Albrecht Ritschl, *The Christian Doctrine of Justification and Reconciliation*, trs. and ed. by H. R. Mackintosh and A. B. Macaulay (Clifton, New Jersey: Reference Book Publishers, 1966), vol. III, pp. 533, 603-608.
2. Adolf von Harnack, *History of Dogma*, trs. from 3rd ed. (New York: Russell and Russell, 1958); Friedrich Loofs, *Leitfaden zum Studium der Dogmengeschichte*, 4th ed. (Halle, 1906), 1889 and later editions; Reinhold Seeberg, *Lehrbuch der Dogmengeschichte*, 5th ed. (Basel, 1960).
3. Henry Barclay Swete pursued the first thousand years in some excellent studies; cf. his article, "Holy Ghost," in *A Dictionary of Christian Biography* (London, 1882), vol. III, pp. 113-133, with bibliography. Swete persuaded Howard Watkin-Jones to undertake two very useful studies continuing his work after the early fathers: *The Holy Spirit in the Medieval Church. A Study of Christian Teaching Concerning the Holy Spirit and His Place in the Trinity from the Post-Patristic Age to the Counter-Reformation* (London, 1922); *The Holy Spirit from Arminius to Wesley. A Study of Christian Teaching Concerning the Holy Spirit and His Place in the Trinity in the Seventeenth and Eighteenth Centuries* (London, 1929).
4. Karl F. Nösgen, *Geschichte der Lehre vom heiligen Geiste in Zwei Büchern* (Gütersloh, 1899), see preface pp. iii-v. Nösgen has more on continental thinkers and runs to the end of the nineteenth century. In his view, Augustine, who merited so much by balancing sin with grace, was also responsible for shifting the attention subtly to grace and out of the area of the Holy Spirit. There is a historical section in W. H. Griffith Thomas, *The Holy Spirit of God* (Grand Rapids: Eerdmans, 1955); H. Wheeler Robinson, *The Christian Experience of the Holy Spirit*, reprinted (London, 1962), offers a historical chapter, pp. 246-266; T. Rees, *The Holy Spirit in Thought and Experience* (London, 1915), does a similar service in pp. 109-212, and his bibliography, pp. 213-216, shows what was available when he wrote. Most books on the Holy Spirit have even less on the history of the doctrine than the few items in Charles Caldwell Ryrie, *The Holy Spirit* (Chicago: Moody, 1965), pp. 111-120, or Henry P. Van Dusen, *Spirit, Son and Father* (New York: Scribners, 1958), pp. 70-85. Van Dusen notes, "A correct understanding of the Holy Spirit is the crucial issue in the Doctrine of the Church," on which the separated Christian churches have not yet been able to agree (p. 84).
5. Wilhelm Stählin, *Die Bitte um den heiligen Geist* (Stuttgart, 1969), see pp. 10-11.
6. Cf. William G. Rusch, "The Doctrine of the Holy Spirit in the Patristic and Medieval Church."
7. On Luther as biblical exegete see Karl Holl, "Luthers Bedeutung für

den Fortschritt der Auslegungskunst," in *Gesammelte Aufsätze zur Kirchengeschichte* 6th ed. (Tübingen, 1932), vol. I, pp. 544-582; and Jaroslav Pelikan, *Luther the Expositor* (St. Louis: Concordia, 1960). On Luther's new religious insights see Holl, *op. cit.*, pp. 155-287, "Der Neubau der Sittlichkeit," and pp. 111-154, "Die Rechtfertigungslehre in Luthers Vorlesung über den Römerbrief." The oft-quoted phrase "was Christum treibet" occurs in Luther's preface to the Epistle of James. For a list of his sayings about Scripture see the index of Buchwald in the Weimar edition, *Luthers Werke, Gesamtregister*, 58, i (1948), pp. 62-79.

8. Regin Prenter, *Spiritus Creator: Studies in Luther's Theology*, trs. John M. Jensen (Philadelphia: Muhlenberg, 1953). Scholars will want to work with the full German edition (1952) or the Danish original (1944, 1946). For comparison there is the recognized work of Paul Althaus, *The Theology of Martin Luther*, trs. Robert C. Schultz (Philadelphia: Fortress, 1966) and the sequel volume by the same author, translator and publisher, *The Ethics of Martin Luther* (1972); the older work of Reinhold Seeberg, *op. cit.*, IV, i; Nösgen, *op. cit.*, pp. 129-143. In its way, the riches and complexity of Luther's Explanation of the Third Article of the Creed match the eloquence and sweep of the Second Article; there has been nothing like it since the Nicaeno-Constantinopolitan Creed. Theodore G. Tappert, ed., *Book of Concord* (Philadelphia: Fortress, 1959), pp. 345, 415-420.

9. Prenter first describes the work of the Spirit, *op. cit.*, pp. 3-100, see esp. pp. 27-64; then takes up the means used by the Spirit, pp. 101-172; then centers on the Person of the Spirit, pp. 173-202. Typical of Luther's view is his statement on John 14:23-31 as quoted in *D. Martin Luthers Evangelien-Auslegung*, ed. by Erwin Mülhaupt, vol. IV, prepared by Eduard Ellwein, 2nd ed. (Göttingen, 1961), p. 418.

10. On the views of Prenter, Holl, and Althaus regarding Luther's concept of justification see Otto W. Heick, *A History of Christian Thought* (Fortress, 1966), vol. I. Cf. Erich Seeberg's idea of Luther on the Holy Spirit in his essay, "Der Gegensatz zwischen Zwingli, Schwenkfeld und Luther" in the *Reinhold Seeberg Festschrift*, vol. I (1929), pp. 43ff. What Kurt Dietrich Schmidt has gathered in "Luthers Lehre vom heiligen Geist," in the *Festschrift Simon Schoeffel* (1950) is summarized in his thoughtful *Grundriss der Kirchengeschichte* 5th ed. (Göttingen, 1967), pp. 305-307. Luther's pneumatology stands in a close inner connection with his Christology. What Christ once did in the past to win our salvation the Spirit bridges in time and makes salvation present to us. Without him we cannot have or reach Christ.

11. Augsburg Confession, Article V, in Tappert, *Book of Concord*, p. 31.

12. Prenter comes to a conclusion quite the opposite of that of Rudolf Otto's *Die Anschauung vom heiligen Geiste Bei Luther* (Göttingen, 1898). Prenter maintains, "Without the idea of the Holy Spirit all Luther's thoughts about Christ, about justification, about Word and sacrament,

about faith and love, are changed to a great ideology under the law. For only the real presence of the Spirit places the boundary between a Christ-like and *Christus ipse*, between gospel and law, between *littera* and *spiritus*, between sacrament and *sacrificium*, between faith and religion, between love and morality. Only the real presence of the Spirit leads from the domain of the law into that of the gospel," *op. cit.*, p. 202.

13. Small Catechism, in Tappert, *Book of Concord*, p. 352.
14. Nösgen, *op. cit.*, pp. 143-147. Literature on the controversial figure of Melanchthon has been multiplying. Cf. bibliographies such as F. L. Cross, *Oxford Dictionary of the Christian Church* (London, 1958) and *Die Religion in Geschichte und Gegenwart*, 3d ed. (Tübingen, 1957ff.). Also Kurt Dietrich Schmidt, *op. cit.*, pp. 354-359; Otto W. Heick and J. L. Neve, *A History of Christian Thought*, 2 vols. (Philadelphia: Fortress, 1965-66), vol. I, pp. 387-403; A. C. McGiffert, *Protestant Thought Before Kant* (New York: Harper Torchbooks, 1961), pp. 71-80. On the question of Melanchthon's synergism see George J. Fritschel, *The Formula of Concord* (Philadelphia: Lutheran Publication Society, 1916), pp. 142-143.
15. The Holy Spirit is treated in Book III, i ff. of Calvin's *Institutes of the Christian Religion*, see the edition by John T. McNeill, translated by Ford Lewis Battles, *Library of Christian Classics*, vols. XX-XXI (Philadelphia: Westminster, 1960), vol. I, pp. 537-542 fully, then sparsim to p. 587. See Wilhelm Niesel, *Calvin Bibliographia* 1901-1959 (Munich, 1961), pp. 82-90 for literature on the Spirit and his work; Nösgen, *op. cit.*, pp. 156-161 and on the "testimonium internum" of the Spirit, pp. 161-163; index in Watkin-Jones, *The Holy Spirit in the Medieval Church;* McGiffert, *op. cit.*, pp. 81-99. Benjamin B. Warfield, *Calvin and Calvinism* (Oxford, 1931), pp. 187-284, has a long chapter on Calvin's view of the Trinity, but virtually nothing on the Spirit's work. See Otto Ritschl, *Dogmengeschichte des Protestantismus*, vol. III (Göttingen, 1926), pp. 156-242 on Calvin's theological system.
16. For Luther, cf. the Smalcald Articles, in Tappert, *Book of Concord*, pp. 312-313.
17. For the Lutheran Confessions see Tappert, *Book of Concord;* cf. extensive literature in Edmund Schlink, *Theology of the Lutheran Confessions* (Philadelphia: Fortress, 1961); still useful Paul Tschackert, *Die Entstehung der lutherischen und der reformierten Kirchenlehre* (Göttingen, 1910); Watkin-Jones, *op. cit.*, and Nösgen, *op. cit.*, following their treatment of Luther and Calvin; for the Reformed churches see *Reformed Confessions of the 16th Century*, ed. with historical introductions by Arthur C. Cochrane (Philadelphia: Westminster, 1966); *The Heidelberg Catechism* with Commentary, 400th Anniversary ed. (Philadelphia: United Church Press, 1963), esp. pp. 94-104; George S. Hendry, *The Westminster Confession for Today* (Richmond, Va.: John Knox, 1960), pp. 116-120.
18. Smalcald Articles, in Tappert, *Book of Concord*, p. 315.

19. George H. Williams, *The Radical Reformation* (Philadelphia: Westminster, 1962); Otto W. Heick, *op. cit.*, vol. II, pp. 5-20 and bibliography, pp. 45-46; Paul Tschackert, *op. cit.*, pp. 121-162 for the spiritualist opponents of Luther, and pp. 162-200 for Luther's contrary principles; Prenter, *op. cit.*, part two, pp. 205-311 including bibliography. Luther's comments in "Against Heavenly Prophets," *Selected Writings of Martin Luther,* ed. Theodore G. Tappert (Philadelphia: Fortress, 1967), vol. III, pp. 150-301, on Karlstadt swallowing the Holy Spirit, p. 161; on enthusiasm in Smalcald Articles, Tappert, *Book of Concord,* pp. 312, 313. See also Mark U. Edwards, *Luther and the False Brethren* (Stanford: Stanford University Press, 1975).

20. For the age of Orthodoxy see accounts and bibliographies in Otto Ritschl, *op. cit.;* Emanuel Hirsch, *Geschichte der neuern evangelischen Theologie,* 5 vols., 3rd ed. (Gütersloh, 1964); Otto Heick, *op. cit.*, vol. I, pp. 468-484; more names in the older version of the same by J. L. Neve and Otto Heick, I (Philadelphia: Muhlenberg, 1946), pp. 313-326; Kurt Dietrich Schmidt, *op. cit.*, pp. 352-360; Heinrich Hermelink and Wilhelm Mauer, *Reformation und Gegenreformation,* 2d ed. (Tübingen, 1931), pp. 313-315 and 352-356; Werner Elert, *Morphologie des Luthertums* (Munich, 1958), mainly vol. I; Paul Tillich, *A History of Christian Thought,* ed. Carl E. Braaten (New York: Harper & Row, 1968), pp. 276-283.

21. McGiffert, *op. cit.*, pp. 141-154 on "Protestant Scholasticism"; Karl Heussi, *Kompendium der Kirchengeschichte,* 12th ed. (Tübingen, 1960), pp. 357-361. On the changes in pneumatology see Nösgen, *op. cit.*, pp. 163-189 for Germany, pp. 180-189 for Reformed theologians in Holland; Watkin-Jones, *The Holy Spirit from Arminius to Wesley,* pp. 11-54. Gustav Frank, *Geschichte der Protestantischen Theologie,* 2 vols. (Leipzig, 1862-65). Extracts from the dogmaticians gathered in Heinrich Schmid, *The Doctrinal Theology of the Evangelical Lutheran Church,* trs. by Charles A. Hay and Henry E. Jacobs, 1875, 1899. Reprinted by Augsburg, Minneapolis, see pp. 409-499 and appendix for brief sketches on a score of writers. Heinrich Heppe, *Dogmatik des deutschen Protestantismus im sechszehnten Jahrhundert,* 3 vols. (Gotha, 1857), in 28 "loci" none on the Holy Spirit as such, and Heppe, *Die Dogmatik der evangelischen reformirten Kirche, aus den Quellen belegt* (Elberfeld, 1861). Max Koch, *Der ordo salutis in der altlutherischen Dogmatik* (Berlin, 1899).

22. This seventeenth-century suppression of the Holy Spirit continued on into the nineteenth. If Karl Hase, famous in his own right and a grandfather of Dietrich Bonhoeffer, rationalized and revised in his pedagogically historical dogmatics *Hutterus redivivus* (Leonhard Hutterus of Wittenberg, 1563-1616, Jena, first ed. 1828, 12th 1882), he still carried p. 225 the heading "De Gratia Spiritus Sancti applicatrice," and passed immediately into Grace and then Faith. Very conservative seminaries in Europe and America in the nineteenth century would use Aegidius

Hunnius (reprinted by Friedrich Bauer of Neuendettelsau) or the Latin *Compendium theologiae positivae* of John William Baier (1647-1695).

23. Watkin-Jones, *op. cit.;* Otto Heick, *op. cit.,* vol. II, pp. 64-92.

24. For bibliography on the Quakers see F. L. Cross, *Oxford Dictionary of the Christian Church* (Oxford, 1974), under "Fox, George," p. 516, and "Friends, Society of," p. 529. Cf. Paul Tillich in his *History of Christian Thought,* pp. 40-41.

25. Two viewpoints may suffice: Robert Preus, *The Inspiration of Scripture, A Study of the Theology of the Seventeenth Century Lutheran Dogmaticians* (Edinburgh, 1955); Werner Elert, *Der christliche Glaube,* 3rd ed. (Hamburg, 1965), pp. 169-173 with bibliography. See also Elert's *Morphologie des Luthertums,* vol. I, pp. 157-176.

26. For various types of German Pietism and Wesleyan Evangelicalism in England see comments and bibliographies in Horst Stephan and Hans Leube, *Die Neuzeit,* in *Handbuch der Kirchengeschichte,* ed. Gustav Krüger, 2d ed. (Tübingen, 1931), vol. IV, pp. 39-77, 130-142; McGiffert, *op. cit.,* pp. 155-185; Heick, *op. cit.,* vol. II, pp. 20-46; Paul Tillich, *op. cit.,* pp. 276-293; Nösgen, *op. cit.,* pp. 205-232, and Watkin-Jones, *The Holy Spirit from Arminius to Wesley.*

27. English translation with introduction by Theodore G. Tappert (Philadelphia: Fortress, 1964).

28. Hendrikus Berkhof, *The Doctrine of the Holy Spirit* (Richmond, Va.: John Knox, 1964), esp. pp. 30-41. John A. Mackay in *Renewal and Advance, Christian Witness in A Revolutionary World* (London, 1948), pp. 148-161 on "The Holy Spirit in Proclamation."

29. On Wesley see the bibliography in Cross, *Oxford Dictionary,* p. 1446; Stephan and Leube, *op. cit.,* pp. 135-136; John T. McNeill, *Makers of the Christian Tradition* (New York: Harper Torchbooks, 1935), pp. 241-253, 273-274; the article in the New Schaff-Herzog *Encyclopedia of Religious Knowledge* (Grand Rapids: Baker, 1955); Watkin-Jones, *op. cit.;* extracts from his *Journal* give an instant flavor. H. Lindström, *Wesley and Sanctification: A Study in the Doctrine of Salvation* (Stockholm, 1946). The perfectionist or holiness movements rest on Wesley in Chester K. Lehman, *The Holy Spirit and the Holy Life* (Scottdale, Pa.: Herald, 1959), pp. 145-175; and Charles Webb Carter, *The Person and Ministry of the Holy Spirit, A Wesleyan Perspective* (Grand Rapids: Baker, 1974), with long bibliography on the Spirit, pp. 337-350.

30. Albert C. Outler, "Towards a Re-Appraisal of John Wesley as a Theologian," *Journal of Perkins School of Theology* (Winter, 1961), p. 11.

31. Paul Tillich, *Perspectives on 19th and 20th Century Protestant Theology,* ed. by Carl E. Braaten (New York: Harper & Row, 1967), p. 9, pp. 24-90 on the Enlightenment and its problems, and the Classic-Romantic reaction against it, then pp. 90-114 on Schleiermacher as "the classical theological synthesis." McGiffert, *op. cit.,* chapter X on Rationalism; Heick, *op. cit.,* vol. II, pp. 125-136 with bibliography.

32. For orientation on Schleiermacher and his age, and extensive bibliography see Stephan and Leube, *op. cit.*, vol. IV, pp. 110ff. but esp. pp. 121-124. John T. McNeill, *Makers of the Christian Tradition*, pp. 253-262; Heick, *op. cit.*, II, pp. 168-183; Hugh Mackintosh, *Types of Modern Theology* (New York: Scribners, 1937), pp. 31-100; Karl Barth, *Protestant Thought from Rousseau to Ritschl* (New York: Simon and Schuster, 1959), pp. 306-354; Otto Pfleiderer, *The Development of Theology in Germany Since Kant* (London, 1890), pp. 44-56 and 103-130; Ferdinand Kattenbusch, *Die deutsche evangelische Theologie seit Schleiermacher*, 6th ed. (Giessen, 1934), pp. 20-34; Fr. H. R. von Frank, *Geschichte und Kritik der neueren Theologie*, 4th ed. by R. H. Grutzmacher (Leipzig, 1908), pp. 56-168. From here on commentators are past counting. Concern over Schleiermacher's evaporation of Pneumatology (and the Trinity) is voiced by Nösgen, *op. cit.*, pp. 259-273.

33. Schleiermacher's *Des christliche Glaube*, often called his *Glaubenslehre*, was translated into English as *The Christian Faith* by H. R. Mackintosh and J. S. Stewart (Edinburgh, 1928). Quotation here is from § 11, 1. For other works see the bibliography in F. L. Cross, *Oxford Dictionary*, p. 1224. Schleiermacher deliberately placed consideration of the doctrine of the Trinity at the end of his dogmatics. Useful portions as a digest of his thought are in the *Textbuch zur deutschen systematischen Theologie und ihrer Geschichte*, 2 vols. by Richard H. Grützmacher, 4th ed. continued by Gerhard G. Muras (Bern and Tübingen, 1961), vol. I, pp. 61-77.

34. *The Christian Faith*, § 3, § 4.

35. *Ibid.*, p. 16.

36. There is no dearth of materials on theologians and movements in the 19th and 20th centuries. For general background cf. Hugh Mackintosh, *op. cit.;* Otto W. Heick, *op. cit.*, volume II; Otto Pfleiderer, *The Development of Theology in Germany Since Kant, and Its Progress in Great Britain Since 1825* (London, 1890); Karl Barth, *Die protestantische Theologie im 19. Jahrhundert* (Zollikon, 1947), rendered partially into English as *Protestant Thought from Rousseau to Ritschl* (New York: Simon and Schuster, 1959); Horst Stephan, *Geschichte der deutschen evangelischen Theologie seit dem deutschen Idealismus*, 2d edition revised by Martin Schmidt (Berlin, 1960); Paul Tillich, *Perspectives on 19th and 20th Century Protestant Theology* (New York: Harper & Row, 1967); F. Lichtenberger, *History of German Theology* (Edinburgh, 1889); and other titles in Heick, *op. cit.*, p. 156.

37. Nösgen, *op. cit.*, chapter ten, treats the pneumatology of conservative German confessional theologians, pp. 299-348. For F. A. Philippi see pp. 307-310, for A. von Oettingen, pp. 322-326.

38. For the Erlangen school see Nösgen, *op. cit.*, pp. 326-338; von Frank, *op. cit.*, pp. 259-299 (the last pages on Frank himself were added by his revisor Richard Grützmacher); Stephan-Schmidt, *op. cit.*, pp. 179-188. The last-named sees some members of this so-called school—after

all, they remained individuals—seeking less simple repristination, as a better relationship between faith, the biblical documents, and history (hence J. C. K. von Hofmann's "Heilsgeschichte").

39. Like many a great man, Ritschl came to times critical of him. Nösgen, *op. cit.*, pp. 349-356 on the master, and pp. 356-367 on his followers; Mackintosh, *Types of Modern Theology*, pp. 138-180; Karl Barth, *Die protestantische Theologie*, pp. 598-605; Heick, *op. cit.*, vol. II, pp. 234-246; Pfleiderer, *op. cit.*, pp. 183-195, and for his opponent Lipsius, pp. 195-204; von Frank, *op. cit.*, pp. 300-376 and 414-456 on his followers; Ferdinand Kattenbusch, *Die deutsche evangelische Theologie seit Schleiermacher*, 6th ed. (Giessen, 1934), part I, pp. 58-91, 100-110. There are signs that Ritschl is coming back, e.g., David W. Lotz, *Ritschl and Luther, A Fresh Perspective on Albrecht Ritschl's Theology in the Light of His Luther Study* (Nashville: Abingdon, 1974), with bibliography pp. 203-211.

40. Cf., e.g., *Unterricht in der christlichen Religion*, 2d ed. (Bonn, 1881), a textbook for schools and gymnasia. In the third part on the Christian Life, Ritschl speaks briefly of the Spirit "in the congregation *(Gemeinde)*," pp. 42-43. For this—which could or could not approximate Schleiermacher's common spirit—he gives a reference to Melanchthon's *Loci* of 1535, *Corpus Reformatorum* XXI, 366, 367.

41. See Rolf Schäfer, *Ritschl, Grundlinien eines fast verschollenen dogmatischen Systems* (Tübingen, 1968), pp. 186-206.

42. *The Work of the Holy Spirit*, trs. Henri De Vries (New York and London: Funk and Wagnalls, 1900).

43. Cf. *Justification and Reconciliation*, III, pp. 471-72.

44. On this entire topic, see Claude Welch, *In This Name: The Doctrine of the Trinity in Contemporary Theology* (New York: Scribners, 1952).

45. Cf. John Owen, *The Holy Spirit* (Grand Rapids: Kregel, 1954).

46. *The Holy Spirit of God* (Chicago: Bible Institute Colportage Association, 1913).

47. *The Christian Experience of the Holy Spirit* (New York and London: Harper, 1928).

48. For reference to Swete, Watkin-Jones, and Nösgen, see footnotes 3 and 4.

49. Frederick Dale Bruner, *A Theology of the Holy Spirit* (Grand Rapids: Eerdmans, 1970) in his first part discusses "the Holy Spirit in Pentecostal Experience," pp. 19-149, which is history and descriptive of the Pentecostals; his second part treats "the Holy Spirit in New Testament Witness," which is an examination of the biblical texts. His bibliography covers pp. 342-376, but cannot presume to match the enormous grasp of W. J. Hollenweger (see *ibid.*, p. 357), of whom we list only the following: *The Pentecostals, The Charismatic Movement in the Churches* (Minneapolis: Augsburg, 1972), with bibliography pp. 523-557; the German original entitled *Enthusiastisches Christentum, die Pfingstbewegung in Geschichte und Gegenwart* (Wuppertal and Zürich, 1969),

and *New Wine in Old Wineskins: Protestant and Catholic Neo-Pentecostalism* (Gloucester, 1973).

50. *Dogmatics,* trs. Olive Wyon, 3 vols. (Philadelphia: Westminster, 1950-62).

51. *Ibid.,* see pp. 7-18 for the nub of his view.

52. *Ibid.,* p. 12.

53. *Ibid.,* pp. 12, 13.

54. *Ibid.,* p. 15.

55. *The Epistle to the Romans,* trs. from the 6th ed., Edwyn C. Hoskyns (London and New York: Oxford University Press, 1968).

56. *Church Dogmatics* (Naperville, Illinois: Allenson, 1958ff). If Karl Barth has not been the most influential theologian of the twentieth century, he has certainly made the most waves. His output exceeded 500 titles, and there is as yet no definitive biography. See Mackintosh, *Types of Modern Theology,* pp. 263-319; Heick, *op. cit.,* vol. II, pp. 269-280 and 308-310; Stephan-Schmidt, *op. cit.,* index and pp. 356-364; Paul Tillich, *Perspectives on 19th and 20th Century Protestant Theology,* pp. 239-243; the article by William Hordern, "Karl Barth Today," in *Theologians of Our Time,* eds. A. W. and E. Hastings (Edinburgh, 1966), pp. 77-85; laudatory G. C. Berkouwer, *The Triumph of Grace in the Theology of Karl Barth* (Grand Rapids: Eerdmans, 1956), and critical Gustaf Wingren, *Theology in Conflict* (Philadelphia: Muhlenberg, 1959). Fine summary and foreign titles in F. L. Cross, *Oxford Dictionary of the Christian Church,* pp. 135-136. For Barth's frequent mention of the Holy Spirit see Otto Weber, *Karl Barth's Church Dogmatics, An Introductory Report* on Vols. I:i to III:4, trs. by Arthur C. Cochrane (Philadelphia: Westminster, 1953); Arnold B. Come, *An Introduction to Barth's Dogmatics for Preachers* (Philadelphia: Westminster, 1963), esp. the convenient list of section headings exhibited in tabular form pp. 84-85; and the imposing *Registerband* of the *Kirchliche Dogmatik,* ed. by Helmut Krause (Zurich, 1970), pp. 1-20 for all thetical headings and p. 237f. under "Geist, Heiliger," and p. 246 "Heiligung."—For twentieth century theology in Germany, there are two readable volumes, Eberhard Hübner, *Evangelische Theologie in unserer Zeit, ein Leitfaden,* 2d ed. (Bremen, 1966), and Heinz Zahrnt, *Die Sache mit Gott, Die protestantlische Theologie im 20. Jahrhundert* (München, 1967).

57. *Theology of the New Testament,* trs. Kendrick Grobel (New York: Scribners, 1965); *The Gospel of John; a Commentary,* trs. G. R. Beasley-Murray (Philadelphia: Westminster, 1971); esp. passages dealing with chapters 14 and 16.

58. *Theology,* vol. I, p. 206.

59. Sympathetic assessment of Bultmann in Stephen Neill, *The Interpretation of the New Testament, 1861-1961* (London, 1964), pp. 222-235; Walter Schmithals, *An Introduction to the Theology of Rudolf Bultmann*

(Minneapolis: Augsburg, 1968); Heick, *History of Christian Thought*, pp. 284-288; Charles W. Kegley, ed., *The Theology of Rudolf Bultmann* (London and New York, 1966, with autobiographical sketch). Bultmann's existential interpretation of "walking in the s/S/pirit" in *Theology of the New Testament*, vol. I, pp. 205-209 and esp. 330-340; the Spirit as Paraclete in *The Gospel of John, A Commentary* (Philadelphia: Westminster, 1971), pp. 552-554, 558, 561-565, 566-572, 585, 613-631. Helmut Thielicke, *The Evangelical Faith*, trs. by Geoffrey W. Bromiley (Grand Rapids: Eerdmans, 1974), though a rigorous critic, also defends Bultmann, p. 174: "This is pioneer work, and there are bound to be casualties on the way. The Church should rather keep in view Bultmann's ultimate objective, which is to secure a firm basis for her own proclamation. He is concerned with the kerygma. We are justified not by the way we travel, but by the Lord to whom we look." Tillich, *Perspectives*, also defends Bultmann, pp. 227-228, 242: "Bultmann saved the historical question from being banished from theology," but regrets that Bultmann, when he "deliteralizes" biblical terms, is not able to bring this into a real systematic structure, not even with the help of Heidegger's existentialism.

60. *Systematic Theology*, 3 vols. in 1 (Chicago: University of Chicago, 1967), vol. 3, pp. 11ff.

61. *Ibid.*, p. 285.

62. *Ibid.*, p. 294. Wilhelm and Marion Pauck, *Paul Tillich, His Life and Thought*, I (New York: Harper and Row, 1976), pp. 232-45 on Tillich's own wrestling and unhappiness with this part. Cf. a useful digest and modest critique of "Life and the Spirit" in Alexander J. McKelway, *The Systematic Theology of Paul Tillich: A Review and Analysis* (New York: Dell, 1964), pp. 189-220; penetrating reviews of vol. III by John H. Randall Jr., Father George H. Tavard, and Kenneth Hamilton in the *Journal of Religion* 46 (1966), 218-228. As the Origen of our troubled times, Tillich was the brilliant bridgebuilder, the man who always transcended boundaries, who simplified or settled ambiguities and reconciled antinomies. His formula of the Spiritual Presence, that Spirit works upon or touches the human spirit, is succinct but ambiguous; he does not and perhaps cannot explain this action. In a postscript to *Paul Tillich in Catholic Thought*, eds. Thomas A. O'Meara and Celestin D. Weisser (Dubuque, Iowa: Priory, 1964), pp. 302-303, Tillich wrote, "Every knowledge of God, like every prayer, like every act of obedience, like every experience of awe and blessedness, is the work of the divine Spirit, i.e., God himself, present to our spirit. . . . Equally impossible is it to call such a relation to God subjectivistic, for the Spiritual Presence transcends the split between subject and object."

63. Dietrich Bonhoeffer, *The Communion of Saints, A Dogmatic Inquiry into the Sociology of the Church* (New York: Harper & Row, 1963). See J. D. Godsey, *The Theology of Dietrich Bonhoeffer* (Philadelphia: Westminster, 1960); Heick, *op. cit.*, pp. 289-291; and the biography of

Eberhard Bethge, *Dietrich Bonhoeffer: Man of Vision* (New York: Harper & Row, 1970).

64. For Paul Althaus, see Heick, *op. cit.*, pp. 291-296, and *Die christliche Wahrheit, Lehrbuch der Dogmatik,* 6th ed. (Gütersloh, 1962), esp. pp. 494-499, the criticism of the old *ordo salutis,* pp. 499, and 523-528. Wolfgang Trillhaas, *Dogmatik,* 2d ed. (Berlin, 1967), unfolds a well articulated Pneumatology in pp. 405-440, including an approach through the history of the doctrine, and attention to the gifts of the Spirit and enthusiasm. See John Macquarrie, *Principles of Christian Theology,* 2d. ed. (New York: Scribners, 1966), ch. 9 on the Triune God, ch. 14 on the Holy Spirit and Salvation, pp. 328-350, esp. 332-337 on the Spirit's "work."

65. *Der christliche Glaube,* 3d ed. (Hamburg, 1956), p. 396.

Karlfried Froehlich

Charismatic Manifestations and the Lutheran Incarnational Stance

The topic that is before us involves a peculiar dilemma for a Lutheran theologian. Charismatic movements are a reality today, not only on this continent but everywhere in the Christian world. Claiming a supposedly strong biblical basis, these movements have found vital expression not only in the traditional Pentecostal communities but in the main-line churches as well. The Lutheran church bodies are no exception. On the contrary, together with Episcopalians and Roman Catholics, they seem to be in the center of where the action is. On the other hand, official caution and outright criticism have nowhere been more pronounced in theological terms than here.[1] This may be a result of the other side of the dilemma. The Lutheran confessional writings, the basic doctrinal standard for the interpretation of Scripture in all Lutheran churches, do not deal with the phenomenon of charismatic manifestations as a theological issue. They do not even quote any of the crucial New Testament texts except once in a seemingly unrelated side argument.[2] In short, they do not seem to afford much help in dealing with the problem the charismatic movement is posing in the context of a confessional Lutheran stance.

Many Lutherans are inclined to take the absence of a discussion in the Confessions as an excuse for meeting all the manifestations of the charismatic movement in their own ranks with extreme reserve. And there seems indeed to be good, solid, biblical warrant for such an attitude. The presence of extraordinary charismatic phenomena cannot

136

be denied in the New Testament. However, they do not appear to play a central role, their mention being restricted to a limited area of the New Testament witness about the Holy Spirit. A somewhat cursory look at the biblical evidence will help us to assess the situation.

I.

The Synoptic Gospels reserve the Holy Spirit primarily for Jesus. The stories of his conception, his baptism, his work as an exorcist carry the reference to the Holy Spirit as part of the fulfillment pattern of the Old Testament prophecy of the New Age. As Luke 4:18 puts it: In Jesus, Isaiah 61:1 is fulfilled—"the Spirit of the Lord is upon me." It seems to be Luke among the three Gospel writers who, in his interpretation of Jesus' ministry, gives emphasis to the idea that Jesus was "led" by the Spirit,[3] and the same interest continues in the book of Acts with respect to the apostles. The instances are well known: Pentecost, the mission of Philip to the Ethiopian eunuch, of Peter to Cornelius, of Paul and Barnabas, of Paul on his later missionary journeys.[4] But beyond this sustained Lucan interest in the Spirit's "guidance" in the apostolic church, the Synoptic Gospels show very little evidence even of a promise of the Spirit for the time after Easter. The only major exception is the promise of the Spirit's assistance in the situation of persecution (Mark 13:11; Matthew 10:20; Luke 12:12). Luke again is the one who adds the other instance: ". . . how much more will the heavenly Father give the Holy Spirit to those who ask him" (Luke 11:13), apparently interpreting the "good things" of the Matthean parallel (Matthew 7:11) according to his theology.

The picture is admittedly different in the Fourth Gospel. Here, too, Jesus' baptism is interpreted in terms of his having the fullness of the promised Spirit (John 1:32—the baptizer saying that he saw the Spirit descending *and remaining* upon Jesus). However, the fourth evangelist also knows the notion of the Spirit as the gift of the exalted Christ to his disciples, a gift replacing the visible presence of the Lord in the time after his glorification. During Jesus' earthly ministry, "the Spirit had not yet been given, because Jesus was not yet glorified" (John 7:39). The Paraclete sayings in the Farewell Discourses and the Johannine parallel to the Pentecost narrative in John 20:21-23 ("Receive the Holy Spirit . . .") give content to this theological argument.

For our discussion it is important to note that in these latter passages there is no allusion to special charismatic manifestations such as exorcisms, speaking in tongues, miracles, healings, as we find them in the secondary ending of Mark (Mark 16:17-18, though here without reference to the Spirit).[5] Instead, when it points beyond the apostolic generation to the believer of the author's own day, the Johannine material suggests a strong link between Spirit and *baptism* (John 3:5; 1 John 2:20, 27).

This link itself is apparently firmly rooted in early Christian tradition, being prominent in Paul and already in the pre-Pauline tradition. In baptism, every Christian has received the Spirit (1 Corinthians 12:13). Romans 6:3f. links *baptism* with resurrection, Romans 8:9ff. links *Spirit* and resurrection. As Romans 8 makes clear, this link between Spirit and baptism is the basis for Paul's appeals to "walk in the Spirit" (Galatians 3:2f.; 5:16, 25). A text like Ephesians 4:4 documents this same reading of Paul in the deutero-Pauline literature.

But it is precisely Paul who seems to have connected his talk about the Spirit received in baptism with the notion of *pneumatika* or *charismata*,[6] special gifts of which every Christian has received his or her kind or measure (1 Corinthians 7:7), and among which the manifestations treasured by the charismatic movement have their place. Paul's discussion of these gifts in 1 Corinthians 12-14, in fact, furnishes the main biblical basis for the claims of the charismatics.

Lutherans are quick to point out that there are problems with these claims on the basis of the texts. Paul's lists of charisms are at variance with each other. They always stress the one source, God's Spirit, but at the same time envisage variety in their manifestations. Not only are some gifts extremely difficult to identify (e.g., "word of wisdom," "word of knowledge," 1 Corinthians 12:8), but the lists include such ordinary phenomena as service, aid, giving, faith, administration. Romans 12:6-8 mentions prophecy, but contrary to the two lists of 1 Corinthians 12 does not refer to either glossolalia, healing, or miracle working. The mention of the latter seems to respond to a peculiar problem in Corinth. While not discouraging their use, Paul seems to be at pains to correct what he sees as an overemphasis on such manifestations among Corinthian Christians where especially the "speaking in tongues" was prominent. Tongues and their interpretation are last in both lists (12:7ff. and 28ff.) and receive an extremely cautious evaluation as a public phenomenon in the church: "In church I would rather speak five words with my mind, in order to instruct others, than ten thousand words in a tongue" (14:19). The thirteenth chapter explicitly points to the transience of speaking in tongues and prophecy (which ranks above tongues in Paul's functional hierarchy of gifts: 14:1-5): "prophecies—they will pass away; tongues—they will cease" (13:8). The polemical tone of the whole discussion is undeniable. Without stepping outside the reality of the life of the Corinthian congregation where charismatic manifestations held an important place, Paul warns of the dangers of leaving free rein to their public exercise and insists on their integration into an orderly communal life (14:40). All of this seems to add up to a picture fully supporting the caution which many Lutherans have displayed toward charismatic manifestations in their midst.

Yet, there is still the other side of the same biblical evidence. The Corinthian chapters leave no doubt that Paul had no intention to challenge the charismatic manifestations as such. For him, they were quite proper expressions of the gifts of the Spirit along with other more ordinary ones. We hear that tongues were an important part of his own experience ("I thank God that I speak in tongues more than you all," 14:18), and, in a way, he does encourage such manifestations: "Earnestly desire the higher gifts" (12:31; 14:1); "Now I want you all to speak in tongues, but even more to prophesy" (14:5); "earnestly desire to prophesy and do not forbid speaking in tongues" (14:39). It is understandable that in the absence of such personal involvement during subsequent decades the Pauline lists could be defused and reduced to the more ordinary gifts and virtues of the Christian life (1 Peter 4:10) or could be interpreted as special gifts bestowed on Christian ministers at ordination (1 Timothy 4:14; 2 Timothy 1:6). But it is very much a question whether this was the only, or even a legitimate, way to apply the Pauline heritage in the light of the total New Testament witness. Even outside the Corinthian correspondence, the references to extraordinary charismatic manifestations in the early church do suggest a reading in the context of the central eschatological message which goes back to Jesus: as possible signs, anticipations, of the inbreaking of the new aeon. It is important to keep this in mind.

The mention of "miracles among you" in Galatians 3:5 or the double warning against "quenching the Spirit" and "despising the gift of prophecy" in Paul's earliest letter (1 Thessalonians 5:19) point in this direction. All the Synoptic Gospels have the logion of John the Baptist which compares his own water baptism with that of the Messiah in clearly eschatological terms: "He will baptize you with the Holy Spirit (and with fire, Matthew/Luke)" (Mark 1:8; Matthew 3:11; Luke 3:16). While the meaning of the original logion is not altogether clear,[7] it is difficult to interpret it as a simple reference to the regular Christian baptismal rite in the redactional setting of the Gospel writers. Admittedly, the terminology and the idea of a "second baptism" of Christians is not present here or elsewhere in the New Testament and should be abandoned.[8] However, the quoting of the "one baptism" of Ephesians 4:5 and Mark 16:16 does not solve the issue posed by this well-attested logion either.

The author of Acts does link this same logion to charismatic manifestations, special gifts of the Spirit, as its quotation in Acts 1:5 and 11:16 clearly suggests. If we leave aside the source problem,[9] Luke's text in the Pentecost story and that of Cornelius' conversion identifies the phenomenon as "speaking in tongues" (Acts 2:4; 10:46). However, while keeping the traditional connection of the Spirit and baptism and adding the charismatic manifestations, Luke is strangely ambiguous about the sequence. Acts 1:8 and 11:17 may imply that Luke saw the coming of the Spirit at Pentecost with its accompanying manifestations as the very moment of the baptism of the apostles. Acts 11:17 also implies (as does the Cornelius story of 10:44-48) that the event of the Spirit "falling upon them" together with its glossolalic manifestations *preceded* baptism. On the other hand, Acts 8:16 and 19:5-6 presuppose a reverse sequence. The incident in chapter 19 describes the charismatic manifestations which occurred *after* baptism as *elaloun glossais kai eprophēteuon* (19:6). It is clear that Luke, following his own interpretation of the Baptizer's logion, does distinguish the water baptism of Christians, at least in some instances, from a reception of the Holy Spirit which was perceived in accompanying charismatic phenomena.

Of course, the interpretation of one biblical author cannot be the only norm. One is tempted to say: particularly in the case of Luke whose narrative seems to imply that charismatic manifestations such as speaking in tongues were a mark of the apostolic period only and ceased thereafter when the apostolic generation had fulfilled its mission "unto the ends of the earth" (Acts 1:8). To be sure, this view remained a convenient basis for dealing with charismatic materials in the New Testament in later periods of church history, including Lutheran Orthodoxy. For these theologians, the biblical phenomenon of charismatic manifestations belonged in the category of *miracula gratiae specialis* which were given only to specific generations or individuals and do not occur anymore.[10]

However, if these biblical manifestations are meant to be read as possible proleptic signs of the breaking in of the kingdom as we have suggested above, there is no reason to follow this argumentation as long as the kingdom has not fully come. We are still living in hope, expectation, and anticipation. The biblical material does not support the view that charismatic manifestations constitute the center of Christian concerns either then or now. Lutherans will resist being swallowed up in Pentecostalism. But the biblical material does not support their complete disregard either. The real question today is that of finding a legitimate place, of making room, for such manifestations in the congregation of the baptized which practices other charisms from Paul's lists. They must have room among us. The concern for charismatic manifestations in the church is biblically grounded.

II.

If we approach the Lutheran Confessions with this result in mind, we do not find the charismatic concern echoed in any way. One rather senses a non-concern, a pervasive animosity which from the beginning seems to preclude the opening up of any legitimate charismatic horizon. It is not difficult to surmise that the reason has to be sought in the consistent front against the Enthusiasts, the *Schwärmer*. However, it must be emphasized at once that the Reformers' fight on this front was not a fight against a charismatic movement of the kind we are encountering today. The fathers of the Lutheran Reformation were not faced by a wave of glossolalia, spiritual healing, or miracles. While the major issues appeared to emerge around eucharist and baptism, the common denominator which Luther and his friends saw in the various forms of *Schwärmerei* was an intellectual spiritualism, a disdain for the "letter," for the palpable manifestations of the Spirit, and an insistence on the possession of this Spirit as an inward reality apart from all outward "means." For the Lutheran fathers, this was a dangerous "theology of glory" which tried to avoid the Cross, the sharing of God's own suffering in the lowly realities of this world. It was a flight into a self-made dream world of pure inwardness, a spiritual elitism which based itself on self-autonomy and self-justification.

Despite this fundamental difference of the situation, the Lutheran fight against the unmediated presence of the Spirit seemed to eliminate *a priori* any chance of even discussing charismatic manifestations by the unrelenting insistence on the Spirit being linked to the spoken Word, the *verbum externum.* Luther's well-known insertion in the section on confession of the Smalcald Articles (Part III, art. VIII) illustrates the problem very well:

> In these matters, which concern the external, spoken Word, we must hold firmly to the conviction that God gives no one his Spirit or grace except through or with the external Word which comes before. Thus we shall be protected from the enthusiasts—that is, from the Spiritualists who boast that they possess the Spirit without and before the Word and who therefore judge, interpret, and twist the Scriptures or spoken Word according to their pleasure. Münzer did this, and many still do it in our day who wish to distinguish sharply between the letter and the spirit without knowing what they say or teach. The papacy, too, is nothing but enthusiasm, for the pope boasts that "all laws are in the shrine of his heart," and he claims that whatever he decides and commands in his churches is spirit and law, even when it is above and contrary to the Scriptures and spoken Word. All this is the old devil and the old serpent who made enthusiasts of Adam and Eve. He led them from the external Word of God to spiritualizing and to their own imaginations, and he did this through other external words. . . .
>
> Even those who have come to faith before they were baptized and those who came to faith in Baptism came to their faith through the external Word which preceded. Adults who have attained the age of reason must first have heard, "He who believes and is baptized will be saved" (Mark 16:16), even if they did not at once believe and did not receive the Spirit and Baptism until ten years later. Cornelius (Acts

10:1ff.) had long since heard from the Jews about the coming
Messiah through whom he was justified before God, and his
prayers and alms were acceptable to God in this faith (Luke
calls him "devout" and "God-fearing"), but he could not have
believed and been justified if the Word and his hearing of it
had not preceded.[11]

Some specific points are noteworthy here. In the second paragraph,
faith and baptism are clearly connected with the support of the quotation from Mark 16:16. But the question of their sequence is left open
in order to press the point that hearing the "external Word" precedes
both. In this connection the traditional link between Spirit and baptism (in this order!) is alluded to. However, rather than discussing its
meaning, Luther again makes his point about the external Word preceding the reception of both, Spirit and baptism. The Cornelius story of
Acts 10 with all its potential for discussing legitimate charismatic
manifestations (or the problem of a "baptism of the Spirit") is quoted
for this reason exclusively. Luther's sole interest is to show that "God
gives no one his Spirit . . . except through or with the external Word
which comes before." This indeed is the main argument against the
enthusiasts as the first paragraph spells it out. The enthusiasts claim
to have the Spirit directly, they think they can unfailingly distinguish
between letter and spirit, glossing over the letter, but they are relying
on their own fancy and thus are involved in the same fatal attempt at
self-justification which started in Adam and Eve and continues right
into the Roman teachings about the pope. Luther sees the sequential
priority of the *verbum externum* to the coming of the Spirit as the most
effective weapon against the works-righteousness he suspects in the
theology of the enthusiasts as much as in the theology of the Romanists. His emphasis does not preclude the discussion of charismatic
manifestations. He simply does not deal with them here.

The same strong bond between Spirit and external Word dominates
Article 5 of the Augsburg Confession on the "Office of the Ministry."
The target of the implied polemic is again the *Schwärmerei* of the
enthusiasts as the condemnation proves:

To obtain such faith God instituted the office of the ministry, that is, provided the Gospel and the sacraments. Through
these, as through means, he gives the Holy Spirit, who works

faith, when and where he pleases, in those who hear the Gospel. And the Gospel teaches that we have a gracious God, not by our own merits but by the merits of Christ, when we believe this.

Condemned are the Anabaptists and others who teach that the Holy Spirit comes to us through our own preparations, thoughts, and works without the external word of the gospel.[12]

The connection with Article 4 suggests that the hidden agenda concerns the means of grace. It is in this context that the rejection of the enthusiasts is to be understood. Their insistence on the Holy Spirit as the center of the means of grace is not questioned but, in fact, confirmed. It is indeed the Spirit who "works" (German) or "effects" (Latin) the faith, and therefore he is himself *the* means of grace. What is rejected is the alleged immediacy of access, a Spirit without the external Word. Interestingly enough for our discussion, the charge of works-righteousness is spelled out in concrete terms here: the enthusiasts start with "preparations," works over which man has control. They commend the mystical exercise of self-emptying, of practicing yieldedness *(Gelassenheit)*. To be sure, these are not charismatic manifestations. In their contemplative, passive nature they seem to belong rather to the other end of the spectrum. But the authors of the Augsburg Confession detect here more than the claim to immediacy. These phenomena become a rival option to the bond between external Word and Spirit, and thus put the enthusiastic aspirations into the category of mysticism and its pelagian potential for self-justification. The article's insistence on the external Word as the indispensable antecedent to the reception of the Spirit is meant to protect the understanding of justification as coming not by any merits of our own but by the sole merit of Christ. It is true that the beginning of the Article speaks of this antecedent as "the Gospel *and the sacraments.*" While in a wider context we cannot overlook the "and," the emphasis is decidedly *not* on the sacraments, as their subsequent omission makes plain. For an anti-Roman as well as anti-enthusiastic stance, the Spirit which works faith comes through the instrument of the external Word of the gospel.

The place of the Holy Spirit between external Word and faith suggests one more emphasis. The Spirit belongs decidedly into the beginning of the Christian life. He is the central agent in the process of justification, in the appropriation of the gospel as the assurance of the forgiveness of sin. This importance of the Spirit for the *initia vitae Christianae,* his function as the one who "sets right our thinking about God," is a characteristic feature of the Spirit's place in the Confessions. We could point to the Augsburg Confession [13] and the Apology,[14] as well as to Luther's explanation of the Third Article in the Small Catechism:

> I believe that by my own reason or strength I cannot believe in Jesus Christ, my Lord, or come to him. But the Holy Spirit has called me through the Gospel, enlightened me with his gifts, and sanctified and preserved me in true faith, just as he calls, gathers, enlightens, and sanctifies the whole Christian church on earth . . .[15]

The text, of course, leaves no doubt that the role of the Spirit is not restricted to that initial place. It speaks of the Spirit's enlightening, sanctifying, and preserving work; and although these references appear, curiously, in the same past tense as the Spirit's initial "calling" with reference to the individual ("me"), the text repeats them as a reality constantly present in the church. In this movement from individual experience to ecclesial context it follows the logic of the creed itself. Similarly, the Augsburg Confession, Article 5, is followed immediately by the article on the new obedience which speaks of the good fruits and good works of the faith, and then moves into the article on the church. Much has been made of the implied communal context of sanctification against enthusiastic and pietistic individualism. The explanation of the Third Article in the Large Catechism supports this aspect with a much fuller argumentation. What interests us here is another observation.

Rather than staying with the church, the focus in all these texts moves quickly from justification at the beginning of the Christian life to justification at the end, i.e., to the Spirit's role in the eschatological judgment. The quotations from Luke 17:10 and Ambrose in the Augsburg Confession, Article 6, are no less telling in this regard than the continuation in the Small Catechism:

> In this Christian church he daily and abundantly forgives all
> my sins and the sins of all believers and on the last day will
> raise me and all the dead and will grant eternal life . . .

Life in the church, where the Spirit is continually at work, is a daily
repetition of the Spirit's first work and a daily anticipation of his final
work of abundant forgiveness of sins. Thus, the ongoing work of the
Spirit, mediated through the Gospel of forgiveness, has its place not
in a spiritual community of mystical conversion, illumination, or
inspiration, accessible to the one who prepares himself properly, but
in the crucial act of justification there (at the beginning) and then
(at the end). Augsburg Confession, Article 18 on Free Will, seems to
suggest that this emphasis is not only directed against the Pelagianism
of the enthusiasts, but just as much against the Pelagian tendencies of
the Roman sacramental system which made the Spirit's work available
at the bidding of the church, or the humanists' reliance on reason as
the Spirit's major ongoing working ground.

It seems to me that the later Lutheran doctrine of a four-fold office
of the Spirit confirms this line.[16] It displays the same dialectical concentration on the beginning and the end of the *vita christiana*. If one
looks at them closely, the *officium elenchthicum, didascalicum,* and
paideuticum all three focus on the beginnings, the *officium paracliticum*
on the end of the Christian life.

The question then remains: What about the Spirit's role in between?
As we have seen, the Confessions do speak of the "enlightening, sanctifying, preserving" work of the Spirit. Could these terms not provide
the context for a variety of charismatic manifestations? Is there not a
place for "gifts of the Spirit" in the sanctification, illumination, and
preservation of the Christian life?

Indeed, we do encounter in this context the reference to the Spirit
and his gifts, and the basis of this phrase in the Pauline terminology
of Romans 12 and 1 Corinthians 12 is often unmistakable. The Large
Catechism describes the church as "called together by the Holy Spirit
in one faith, mind, and understanding, with a *variety of gifts,* yet is
united in love . . .".[17] The German text of the Augsburg Confession
mentions as actions of the Risen Christ through the Holy Spirit the
"bestowing of life and of a *variety of gifts* and goods," [18] and the last
stanza of *Ein feste Burg* declares: *Er ist bei uns wohl auf dem Plan /*

mit seinem Geist und Gaben.[19] Yet if we want to know more specifically what is meant by these "gifts," we probably have to go to the medieval tradition rather than to that of the charismatics of Corinth.

The patristic and the medieval tradition spoke of the "seven gifts of the Holy Spirit," drawing this concept from Isaiah 11:2: wisdom, understanding, counsel, fortitude, knowledge, piety, fear of God. This was a list of virtues or, according to the high medieval theologians, of even higher graces bestowed on the Christian soul as a help in its ascent to perfection.[20] It described intellectual qualities, not charismatic phenomena. That Luther's explanation in the Small Catechism connects the "gifts" with the Spirit's *illumining*—not his sanctifying or preserving—role finds its explanation in this background. His German translation of the *Veni Creator Spiritus* refers directly to the tradition, allowing it to re-interpret even the reference to the "tongues" in the hymn:

> *Du bist mit Gaben siebenfalt*
> *Der Finger an Gottes rechter Hand.*
> *Des Vaters Wort gibst Du gar bald*
> *Mit Zungen in alle Land.*

> You are with sevenfold gifts
> the finger on God's right hand;
> you deliver the Father's Word speedily
> with tongues into all the lands.

If the gifts of the spirit are interpreted in this way and, even when tongues are mentioned, remain connected with the vehicle of the external Word, we realize how small the room for an appreciation of special charismatic manifestations in the Confessions really is. But does the notion of the indissoluble bond between external Word and Spirit not itself imply a danger equal to that of Rome and the enthusiasts? Martin Bucer remarked critically on the seventh Schwabach Article which parallels Augustana 5 that God's omnipotence seems threatened if the oral Word is declared to be the "only way and path" to acquiring faith.[21] Is this linkage of external Word and Spirit not indeed a straightjacket for the Spirit? Do we have here a kind of Lutheran *ex opere operato?* Is the Spirit tied to the Word in such a way that the progress from external Word to Spirit becomes virtually automatic? Is there no freedom of the Spirit?

These are serious questions in light of our problems. Of course, Augustana 5 already has a qualifying phrase: " . . . the Holy Spirit who works faith *when and where he pleases*" (Latin: *ubi et quando visum est Deo*). Even if the clause could be read as qualifying the giving of the Spirit rather than qualifying the awakening of faith (as the German and Latin texts clearly suggest), it still does so in terms of God's freedom of choice, and thus most likely in terms of a predestinarian presupposition.[22] But predestination is not a sufficient answer to our questions which are concerned with a much more limited issue: the freedom of the Spirit's work as expressed in his manifold gifts, the full range of charismatic manifestations. We have seen that the Confessions refuse to be pressed on this point. But if the danger spoken of above is real, we have to persist, despite confessional reluctance. Where can we make room in our Confessions for the biblically legitimate expression of charismatic manifestations so that the danger of a "bound" Spirit might be avoided?

I would like to take my clue from Regin Prenter's magisterial treatment of Luther in his book, *Spiritus Creator*. Prenter explains that Luther was so vitally interested in the close instrumental bond between Word and Spirit because he saw in the theology of the enthusiasts a dissolution of his own incarnational emphasis.[23] In their insistence on a sharp distinction between the devalued letter (as part of the visible Word) and the invisible Spirit these people despised the simple external Word as the *instrumentum,* the earthly vehicle of the Spirit. The Word became flesh. The incarnation must have consequences for the theology of the Spirit. The *Schwärmer* looks for the Spirit in his own dreams of a spiritual world above and misses the God who has chosen to reveal himself in the humbleness of "external" signs. For us God is found in the cradle of Word and Sacrament. This choice was a choice of God's freedom. In his freedom God made himself flesh in the humbleness of palpable, down-to-earth, external phenomena—bread, wine, water, word. The Spirit, a person of the Trinity, cannot be thought to be found on a different level, in a separate realm above.

The argument, which I find convincing, may open the road for a legitimate location of charismatic manifestations in the framework of the Confessions. As is often stressed in the New Testament discussion, the Spirit and his gifts belong together. Where the Spirit is, there are the gifts, and *vice versa*. If the Spirit is not found in the lofty world of unreal dreams, then the gifts do not transport us into such a realm either. Like the Spirit himself, they must be linked to the cradle of earthly reality which the Son of God entered in his incarnation. Could the charismatic phenomena of our day not be seen as part of this cradle? After all, the Pauline lists of charisms include such mundane things as giving or administration and, if we count Galatians 5:22 among the parallels, such general human graces as love, joy, patience, gentleness. Could the cradle list be expanded, and this on good biblical grounds: bread, wine, water, word, giving, joy, tongues, healings, song . . . ? To be sure, our modern mentality has problems with such a view. In a world that is not even convinced of God's existence we tend to judge any experience of the Spirit by its apologetic usefulness. But the gifts themselves militate against this tendency. Without the divine promise to which they point, tongues are as ambiguous, healings as provisional, giving, joy, or singing as mundane as bread, wine, water, word. The question is: Can the yearning of Christians today for charismatic phenomena not be seen as part of that incarnational emphasis so deeply embedded in the Lutheran tradition, as a longing for the consolation of the Spirit down here on earth, in the concrete experience of our limited human existence? Could it be that Martin Luther himself would side with the charismatic movement in the church today for precisely the same reasons that forced him to reject what he saw as the flight from this earth in the enthusiasts?

I can only raise these questions. The answer depends on both the self-understanding, the motivations, and the effects of the movement itself and on one's reading of these from the outside. I do not speak from the inside. As an "outsider" I am, however, very much aware of the suspicion that, far from enforcing the incarnational emphasis, the movement in Lutheranism and elsewhere in fact follows the lead of the *Schwärmer*, indulging in spiritual elitism and individualistic piety, taking the flight from this world, making the Spirit serve their self-justification. I am convinced it need not be so. In an article on glosso-lalia,[24] Roy Harrisville raised as the basic problem the question whether or not speaking in tongues offers proof of a transcendent reality, whether or not it gives incontestable evidence of the presence of God. He rightly denied this, pointing to the ambiguity of the phenomenon and the Lutheran incarnational stance. But he loses me in his fascinating argument when he seems to assume that this *is* the question which the charismatic is interested in. Is this really so? Is the illicit hunger for unambiguous proofs of the transcendent the only possible motivation for an earnest striving after charismatic gifts? Do charismatics shut their eyes to the ambiguity of glossolalic phenomena, to the provisional nature of healings, to the human limitations of expressing joy in song and dance? Can they not rejoice, can the whole church not rejoice at a wide spectrum of charismatic expression in its midst precisely because all of these manifestations, from the simplest to the most complex, are not taking us out of this world, but help us to live in it more joyously? The incarnational emphasis of our Confessions seems to me not only a possible cover for charismatic manifestations but the proper place for them in a church that is interested in the full range of the gifts of the Spirit.

III.

This result, I believe, is in essential agreement with the treatment of charismatic manifestations in Luther's writings. For Luther, too, the incarnational emphasis provides the framework for their positive consideration. Surprisingly, as far as I can see, the relevant materials have not played a significant part in the recent discussions among Lutherans. In fact, Erling Jorstad states in his 1974 monograph: [25] "All participants in the movement as well as its critics agree that Luther did not make any reference to the heart of Pentecostal-charismatic renewal, the charismatic gifts of 1 Corinthians 12:8-11." This is incorrect. 1 Corinthians 12:1-11 was the Epistle lesson for the 10th Sunday after Trinity, and the Weimar Edition contains transcripts of at least four sermons (1524, 1531, 1535, and 1536 respectively) in which Luther deals with the text.[26] Other relevant material may be found in sermons or statements on other texts such as 1 Corinthians 13; Mark 16:17-18, and in the treatises and letters. What follows is no more than a preliminary check of my thesis against the most obvious materials.

There can hardly be any doubt that Luther upheld and reckoned with the presence of charisms, not only in the form of ordinary offices and services among Christians, but also in the form of extraordinary charismatic manifestations. Their continued occurrence was for him a simple consequence of his concept of faith. Faith makes everything possible. The argument can be easily traced in Luther's sermon on Mark 16:17-18 preached on Ascension Day, 1522.[27] He starts by refuting an interpretation of the "signs" accompanying the preaching of the gospel (casting out of demons, speaking in new tongues, nature miracles, healings) that would either spiritualize them or attribute them as *notae ecclesiae* to the whole church:

> These words do not refer to the congregation but to each one individually. The idea is: If a Christian has the faith, he shall have power to do these signs. . . . For a Christian has equal power with Christ, is one cake with him . . . Where there is a Christian, there is therefore the power to do such signs even now if it is necessary. But nobody should presume to exercise it if it is not necessary or required. For the Apostles did not always exercise it either, only in order to proclaim the Word of God and to confirm it by miracles. . . .
>
> Since now, however, the Gospel has spread and has been made known to all the world, it is no longer necessary to do signs as in the times of the Apostles. However, if need be and if they should threaten and oppress the Gospel, then it will probably be our turn, too, and we will have to do signs before we allow the Gospel to be suppressed and dishonored. But I hope that it will not be necessary and come to that, that I must speak in new tongues. It is indeed not necessary, for you all can hear and understand me well. Should God, however, send me elsewhere where they do not understand my language, he could well bestow on me their tongue or language so that I may be understood. But if some presume without need to perform such signs, I do not know what to say to that. Some drive out the devil. But I know it is dangerous. . . .

Rejecting anything less than a down-to-earth interpretation, Luther naturally assumes the presence of miraculous powers among Christians of his generation. However, he sees such signs only as responding to a "necessity," i.e., in strictly functional terms, and warns of the danger of getting too deeply involved: exorcisms are no child's play.

The sermons on 1 Corinthians 12 stress the ordinary gifts more than the extraordinary ones. Luther understands Paul to have done the same. According to him, every Christian has the Spirit and ought to put this gift to good use. But he insists that "the text speaks of the *manifestation of the Spirit* to confirm and witness to his gifts, not simply of the Spirit." [28] Gifts—this means manifestations, whether ordinary or extraordinary ones. It is probably this incarnational emphasis, developed in the front against the enthusiasts, that makes him interpret some of the extraordinary gifts from Paul's list in ordinary terms.

For instance, while the "gift of faith" (1 Corinthians 12:9) is interpreted as the power to work miracles (moving mountains, crushing serpents, and the like), the "gifts of healing" in the same verse are somewhat deflated:

> Here the Apostle leaves the miraculous deeds. The latter are more than the gift of healing where those (who have it) do no more than know how to heal *people*. It is a gift which only touches the body.[29]

Yet this does not mean that healing could not be seen as a "hot" phenomenon by Luther as other texts show. A letter to Severin Schulze from the year 1545 clearly counsels in a particular case what we would call a faith healing procedure, very much in the style of Blumhardt. The text explicitly refers to the signs of Mark 16:17-18: [30]

> Then, when you depart, lay your hands upon the man again and say: "These signs shall follow them that believe; they shall lay hands on the sick, and they shall recover." Do this three times, once on each of three successive days. Meanwhile let prayers be said from the chancel of the church, publicly, until God hears them.

The prime example for this incarnational tendency to bring charismatic phenomena down to earth is Luther's interpretation of the Pauline references to tongues. As we saw already in the remarks on Mark 16 quoted above, Luther equated "speaking in tongues" with "using a foreign language," probably on the basis of Acts 2. He simply did not recognize a "hot" phenomenon here. The anti-enthusiastic bias behind this fact comes out in his remark on 1 Corinthians 13:1, the "tongues of angels": [31]

> For even the first piece is impossible, where Paul says: "If I were speaking with the tongues of angels." For it is not pos-

sible for a human being to speak with the tongues of angels, particularly since he distinguishes here between human and angelic tongues. Yea, the angels do not have tongues, but they, the angels, speak with human tongues, but human beings can never speak with the angels' tongues.

The "gift of tongues" meant for Luther something like knowing Greek or Hebrew or another foreign language, and the gift of "interpreting tongues" meant translating. "I believe that what is meant (by the term) is translating. It is a gift of God when one language is being translated into another. I can tell you a tale about that!"[32] On this basis, he even defended speaking in tongues against its criticism by Karlstadt:[33]

> The fool doesn't understand Saint Paul's words correctly, when he writes of speaking with tongues. For Saint Paul writes of the office of preaching in the congregation, to which the people are to listen and to learn from it, when he says: "Whoever comes forward and wants to read, teach, or preach and yet speaks with tongues, that is, speaks Latin instead of German, or some unknown language, he is to be silent and preach to himself alone . . . Now this enthusiast spirit would condemn everything that Saint Paul permits and forbids to condemn." . . .

From the texts cited it should be clear that the surprisingly "cold" view of glossolalia, if it is seen in context, is entirely consistent with Luther's incarnational emphasis which dominates his discussion of all charismatic manifestations. But we have also seen that Luther, in this ordinary interpretation, has no problem in placing next to the mention of the gift of tongues such extraordinary gifts as the power to work miracles or to perform exorcisms. For him, there actually were Christians, "who work miracles that do not just affect human beings; there are those who have been able to move mountains and crush serpents. This all the Holy Spirit works."[34] It hardly needs mention how realistically Luther could speak of the existence of the gift of casting out demons:

> We should not now and cannot drive out the devils with specific ceremonies and words, as did the prophets, Christ, and

the Apostles long ago. We must pray in the name of Christ
and earnestly admonish the Church to pray that the dear God
and Father of our Lord Jesus Christ would deliver the possessed person by his mercy. If such prayer now is said with
faith in Christ's promise: "Truly, truly, I say unto you, if you
shall ask the Father for something, etc.," it is powerful and
strong so that the devil must leave the person as I can tell
several examples.[35]

Ordinary and extraordinary charismatic manifestations are placed
by Luther on the same plane:

The Spirit who has given to one (the gift of) preaching and
to you (the gift of) listening, and who has raised dead people
through still another, this same Spirit has given to another the
gift of comforting people. Before God there is no difference.[36]

All the gifts reflect the Spirit's incarnational reality within the poor
and humble fabric of our human life. And since they all are signs of
God's power which is strong in the weak, God, like Paul, makes no difference but declares them all worthy of equal honor:

When I see someone who knows Hebrew and Greek well, and
I do not know it, why should it harm me if I honor him?
When someone is a real prophet, what harm does this do to
me? When I see that someone has the gift to interpret Scriptures well, what harm is there for me in tipping my hat and
thanking God who has given you these gifts? When someone
has the authority to cast out devils but I don't, why should I
cross myself? How can we fall into such shameful blasphemy
that we stand in the way of God's gifts, since we cannot have
the same gifts? I know well how to write and teach, and
others do not—why should they? [37]

In all of this, Luther never attempts to do away with the ambiguity
which accompanies the exercise of all these gifts in the human situation. "Among the Christians there have been many who had fine charismatic gifts *(Gnadengaben)*. Some were able to do miracles, and yet
this served the devil." [38] The gifts themselves are capable of use and
misuse, and the law of the danger of having them is utterly clear: "The

more beautiful the gifts, and the greater the honor they are paid, the more they tend toward sectarianism. He who has them thinks he understands Scripture and does not allow anyone else a valid place next to him." [39] This, and only this, is the enthusiastic threat: division and sectarianism growing out of human pride. But this threat does not warrant staying away from the gifts. It simply warns Christians to be realistic about them. We do live in the ambiguity of this world into which the incarnate Word has come, taking on the humble forms of our existence. For Luther, the down-to-earth character of the Spirit's gifts, their humanness and ambiguity, is not a threat to their transcendence but the necessary precondition for their helpfulness to us for whose sake they all are given.

Notes

1. For the major facts and developments see E. Jorstad, *Bold in the Spirit: Lutheran Charismatic Renewal in America* (Minneapolis: Augsburg, 1974).
2. The one exception is a reference to 1 Corinthians 14:9ff. and 19 in the Latin text of Augsburg Confession, Article 24 (On the Mass). Paul is quoted in support of the introduction of German chorales as commanding that "in church a tongue understood by the people should be used." The German text does not have the reference. See *Die Bekenntnisschriften der evangelisch-lutherischen Kirche* (Göttingen, 1952), p. 91.
3. Cf. C. K. Barrett, *The Holy Spirit and the Gospel Tradition* (London, 1947), chs. 8 and 9.
4. Acts 1:8; 2:4; 8:29, 39; 10:19; 13:2, 4, 16:6f.; 18:5; 20:23; 21:4, 11.
5. John 14:12 may be an exception. But it does not mention the Spirit and presents problems of its own.
6. For important literature on the term see the brief article on *charisma* by H. Conzelmann in *Theological Dictionary of the New Testament*, vol. 9 (Grand Rapids: Eerdmans, 1974), pp. 402-06.
7. See C. K. Barrett, *op. cit.*, p. 125f.; R. Bultmann, *The History of the Synoptic Tradition*, tr. J. Marsh (Oxford, 1968), p. 111.
8. Jorstad, *op. cit.*, p. 102f.
9. It seems that Luke has combined a language miracle with the report of an event involving speaking in tongues, i.e., an ecstatic phenomenon. For the options in interpreting Acts 2 see E. Haenchen, *The Acts of the Apostles: A Commentary*, translation (Philadelphia: Westminster, 1971), pp. 172ff.
10. An influential example was John Chrysostom's Homily 29 on 1 Corinthians (J. P. Migne, *Patrologia Graeca*, 61:239-250), and his first Pente-

cost Homily on Acts 2 (J. P. Migne, *Patrologia Graeca,* 60:41-50). For the reference to Lutheran Orthodoxy see K. Hase, *Hutterus Redivivus oder Dogmatik der Evangelisch-Lutherischen Kirche,* 7th ed. (Lipsiae, 1848), p. 264.

11. Smalcald Articles, Part III, Article VIII.
12. Augsburg Confession, Article V.
13. Augsburg Confession, Article XVIII.
14. Apology, Article IV, 122-135.
15. Small Catechism, Article II, ". . . sondern der Heilige Geist hat mich durchs Evangelium berufen, mit seinen Gaben erleuchtet, im rechten Glauben geheiliget und erhalten" (Latin: vocavit, illuminavit, sanctificavit, conservavit). See *Bekenntnisschriften,* p. 512. Baptism probably is seen as the common occasion for all these acts.
16. See Hase, *op. cit.,* p. 264f.; Luthardt-Jelke, *Kompendium der Dogmatik* 13th ed. (Leipzig, 1933), p. 313.
17. Large Catechism, Part II, 51.
18. Augsburg Confession, Article III, ". . . ihnen auch Leben und allerlei Gaben und Güter austeile"; *Bekenntnisschriften,* p. 54.
19. Catherine Winkworth's English translation only approximates the exact meaning: "The Spirit and the gifts are ours / Through Him Who with us sideth." A similar reference occurs in Luther's creedal hymn ("Wir glauben all' an einen Gott") where it says of the Spirit: "Der aller Bloeden Troester heisst / und mit Gaben zieret schoene."
20. For the development of the concept of the seven gifts see the writings of O. Lottin, especially his *Psychologie et morale au XIIe et XIIIe siècle* (Louvain: Abbaye du Mont César, 1949 and 1954), vols. 3 and 4.
21. Quoted in Leif Grane, *Die Confessio Augustana* (Göttingen, 1970), p. 49f.
22. *Ibid.,* p. 50, cautions against this reading on the basis of Melanchthon's contention that he had completely avoided the issue of predestination in the Augustana. I find the argument not fully convincing.
23. R. Prenter, *Spiritus Creator,* tr. J. M. Jensen (Philadelphia: Muhlenberg, 1953), esp. pp. 271ff.; 302ff.
24. R. Harrisville, in *Dialog* 13/1 (Winter, 1974), pp. 11f.
25. Jorstad, *op. cit.,* p. 15.
26. The texts may be found in the Weimar Edition (WA) of Luther's works: WA 15, 602ff. (1524); 41, 391ff. (1535); 41, 650ff. (1536); 34/2, 98ff. (1531). WA 22, 170ff. contains a summary rendering of the 1535 sermon. My translations are made from the convenient collection of most of these texts by E. Ellwein (ed.), *Luthers Epistel-Auslegung, 2. Die Korintherbriefe* (Göttingen, 1968).
27. WA 10:3, 145f. I am translating from the text as found in E. Muelhaupt (ed.), *Luthers Evangelien-Auslegung, 5. Passions- und Ostergeschichten* (Göttingen, 1950), p. 454f. The same emphasis on charismatic gifts as a consequence of faith dominates Melanchthon's interpretation of the Corinthians passage. R. Stupperich (ed.), *Melanchthons*

Werke in *Auswahl,* vol. 4, *Frühe exegetische Schriften* (Gütersloh, 1963), p. 65ff.

28. Ellwein, *op. cit.,* p. 146.
29. *Loc. cit.*
30. T. G. Tappert (ed.), *Luther: Letters of Spiritual Counsel* (Philadelphia: Westminster, 1955), p. 52 (Library of Christian Classics).
31. Ellwein, *op. cit.,* p. 177.
32. *Ibid.,* p. 146.
33. "Against the Heavenly Prophets," tr. B. Erling in: *Luther's Works,* vol. 40 *(Church and Ministry,* II) (Philadelphia: Muhlenberg Press, edited by Conrad Bergendoff, 1958), pp. 142f.
34. Ellwein, *op. cit.,* p. 147.—The legends of the saints provide examples: ". . . Agnes and Anastasia did miracles and had gifts so that they confessed Christ and preached before the tyrants . . . ," *ibid.,* p. 162.
35. WA Tischreden I, no. 1170, p. 578.
36. Ellwein, *op. cit.,* p. 162.
37. *Ibid.,* p. 149f.
38. *Ibid.,* p. 167.
39. *Ibid.,* p. 153.

Warren A. Quanbeck

Developmental Perspective and the Doctrine of the Spirit

The doctrine of the Holy Spirit has never been worked through as thoroughly as the doctrine of the Trinity or the doctrine of Christ. Because of the centrality of these doctrines and the intensity of the discussion about them, they have received attention in almost all periods of the church's life. In our time the doctrine of the church is the center of comparable attention, both within denominations and in ecumenical discussion. The doctrine of the Spirit, however, has not received such thorough treatment at any time in church history.[1] The reasons for this somewhat surprising neglect are no doubt many, among them the fact that major doctrinal disputes have not focused on the work of the Spirit, the difficulty of treating matters which are so interior and inaccessible, and the tendency for groups making much of the Spirit's work, from Montanism to modern Pentecostalism, to form separate communities and thus remove the discussion from the mainstream of the church's life.

Today, for a variety of reasons, the doctrine of the Spirit is receiving more attention and in the process is being enriched and transformed. Historical studies, both in the Scriptures and in the development of doctrine, have made enormous contributions to this study, as have also the encounters among the various traditions in the ecumenical movement and the new perspectives and insights provided by developments in the human sciences, especially psychology, sociology, and anthropology. Another important factor is the growing awareness among the churches of the minority status of Christians in the world and a resultant concern for the mission of the church and the work of the Spirit.

The doctrine of the Spirit, like everything else in theology, has been greatly affected by the historical and cultural revolution of the nineteenth century. Theology has many functions: doxological, giving proper orientation to worship, witness, and service; identifying, helping Christians understand who they are and what their mission is; evangelistic, finding the language that will communicate the gospel in a specific time and culture. The controversies following the Reformation gave the identifying function great prominence in the churches; indeed at times theology seemed primarily a defense of the ecclesiastical status quo. Today, without neglecting the identifying or catechetical function of theology, it may be necessary to stress once again the doxological and evangelistic functions; the doxological, in order to integrate the life of the Christian community once again in a healthy balance of worship, witness, and service; the evangelistic, to communicate the gospel in a world increasingly secularized and materialistic.

What is the historical and cultural revolution of the nineteenth century? It is a radical change in conceptuality, a shift in cultural perspective from the substantialist outlook of the Hellenistic world and its western heirs to the developmental perspective of the modern world. This shift obviously did not take place overnight. R. G. Collingwood sees its roots in the message of the prophets of Israel and traces its growth through the impact of biblical historical thinking on Graeco-Roman civilization and its successors.[2] It is one of the ironies of history that some of the heirs of the prophetic tradition should oppose, in the name of perennial theology, the working out of the prophetic insight and impulse in human affairs.

Substantialist thinking has a conviction of the unchanging character of reality, seeks to understand the world and human experience in terms of enduring essences, and has considerable confidence in the capacity of metaphysical language to express the inner reality of things. Developmental thinking sees the world and human experience as in constant process, does not attempt to state what something is, but rather to understand what it has been and is becoming, and has little confidence in the capacity of metaphysical language to communicate the essence of things. This shift of perspective is a major watershed in human experience. People who live on the two different slopes may use the same language, but view things from different perspectives, operate with different conceptualities, ask different questions and seek different answers.

The radical character of this shift enables us to understand the unrest in the churches and the distress of theologians. The change of perspective requires a reworking of the entire theological apparatus in the church; it demands much time and places heavy burdens on theologians, specifically in three areas:

1. It requires that the theologian know the apostolic gospel as it is transmitted in the Scriptures and through the tradition of the church. He must comprehend the many-sidedness of the biblical message and its implications for human life. He must be able to interpret the Scriptures so that the Word of God is heard in its dialectical relationship of law and gospel. He must understand the development of doctrine in the church, especially of the great landmarks of the faith, the creeds and confessions.

2. The theologian must understand the social-cultural situation in which he lives so that he recognizes the anxieties and questions of the day and the conceptuality in which they are expressed.

3. He must be able to find language which communicates the strange good news of the gospel message in the vocabulary and conceptuality of the people whom he addresses.

The task of doing theology in our time has become very demanding. Everything that theology has said about God, man, and the world must be restated in the new developmental perspective. The entire life and mission of the church, the doctrines of the Trinity and of the two natures of Christ, which were stated in the language of hellenistic metaphysics, must be expressed anew in the language of developmental thought.

This does not mean that the theologies developed before the nineteenth century are utterly worthless and should be consigned to the shredding machine. They remain channels through which the gospel has been transmitted to us, and some of them are especially valuable witnesses to the way the prophetic and apostolic message has been formulated at critical periods in the life of the church. The nineteenth century has made clear that any document or artifact must be interpreted in the context of its historical situation. This insight was anticipated in various ways and in certain degrees by many theologians in the life of the church and is decisive for the life of scholarship in our time. We understand theologies of the past as we see the way they addressed the problems of their time. Their effectiveness as evangelistic tools is largely for their own time. We do not communicate effectively today by simply repeating their statements, for they are addressed to the questions of their time and not to the somewhat different questions of our day. These theologians are an essential part of our self-identification as Christians and Lutherans. To read them with historical perceptiveness is a necessary part of our growth as theologians. To insist on their use as a perennial theology, as answers to the questions of all times, is to misunderstand their role and to hamper the church in its missionary task today.

Even after a century the implications of this radical shift of perspective have not all been worked out in all disciplines. The changes, however, are dramatic. The natural sciences no longer seek to penetrate beyond appearances to the substantial reality behind or underneath them. New sciences have developed and are developing, and the life sciences have come to a leading role in modern thought, seriously influencing the methods, categories, and perspectives of virtually all intellectual work. Historical and human sciences have emerged with new stature. Earlier regarded by many natural scientists as hobbies of dilettantes with no serious claim to scientific status, they have today immense prestige in the world of thought and great influence in the world of literature and the arts.

The new perspective is especially significant for the doctrine of the Spirit. The older conceptuality was less effective in expressing the work of the Spirit than it was in some other areas of theology. Its static, substantialist character was ill-adapted to give expression to the dynamic, growing, and elusive work of the Spirit. In our day, moreover, questions are being raised which were not on the horizon of theologians in the thirteenth or sixteenth centuries: the role of women in the church and in its ministry, the theological meaning and value of the world religions, the role of the people of God in a secularized society. Attempts to answer these questions today with the resources of scholastic theologies have had almost uniformly unhappy results, an ineffective proclamation of the love of God, and the alienation, not only of agnostics and secularists, but of many earnest friends and members of the church.

Not all Christian theologians have reacted to these changes with enthusiasm. Some indeed still oppose them as hostile to the gospel and destructive of theology. It must be admitted that there is more reason for this attitude than simply fear of change or a fortress mentality. Not all theologians who accepted the new perspective were able to give effective expression to distinctive and essential elements in the Christian tradition. The rejection of supranaturalistic metaphysics caused some of them to deny or understate the element of the transcendent in the Christian faith. The Scriptures were treated in a completely relativistic way and the doctrines of the church handled in the same way. No grounds seemed available for mounting prophetic criticism of the present situation.

The same standpoint, however, that challenged the metaphysics of the Middle Ages made it clear that no single perspective or conceptuality is to be absolutized. The rejection of scholasticism as a theological method for today does not mean the end of theology, but rather the quest for a theology which can enter into dialogue with the scientific and philosophical viewpoints emerging in the modern world. Theologians such as J. C. K. von Hofmann and K. M. A. Kähler combined acceptance of the new scientific perspectives with a confession of the apostolic gospel, thus foreshadowing the new evangelical theologies which appeared after World War I.[3]

The discovery of cultural and historical relativity is, however, also the discovery of pluralism. Medieval thinkers could suppose that what they labeled natural law was *the* human way of thinking. We can now recognize that it is *a* human way of thinking, that of western European Christian humanists. Theirs was a great intellectual and cultural achievement and we are still clipping the coupons from their investments. But there are many other ways of thinking. Each culture has its own perspective on the world and its own way of slicing the pie of human experience. The Middle Ages came close to having a common universe of discourse. They had relatively few different approaches to scientific and theological problems, as is illustrated in the differing approaches of Thomas, Bonaventure, Scotus, Occam, and Bernard. We have no such approach to a common language, and therefore nothing approximating the all-encompassing philosophy and theology of a Thomas.

The nature of our missionary task demands that we recognize historical and cultural relativity and accommodate ourselves to a pluralism of conceptualities. This, of course, does not mean that just anything is acceptable and that there are no longer criteria for theological work. We remain committed to a long and rich theological tradition which has shown that certain ways of speaking about God and man are appropriate and that others are unsatisfactory and misleading. We have agreed that it is improper to deny that Jesus was really a human being, or to deny that God is revealed in him. But the formulas in which Christians have asserted these insights are not casually to be detached from their historical situation or to be applied without proper interpretation to any or all other cultural situations.

The impact of the developmental perspective on the doctrine of the Spirit may be summarized in three areas: 1) the contribution of the human sciences, the study of language, and comparative religion; 2) the contribution of biblical studies; 3) the contribution of studies in the development of doctrine. Of special significance for Lutherans is the contribution of the renaissance in Luther studies.

To these should be added two other movements: 1) the ecumenical movement, which has given new dimensions to the theological work of almost all the churches; 2) the charismatic movement, which has aroused new interest, not only in the doctrine of the Spirit but in the experience of renewal, of community, of the gifts of the Spirit in the life of the church.

When the Christian community embarked upon the mission to the Gentiles it undertook at the same time the task of the theological penetration into hellenistic thought. It could no longer operate in the prophetic, eschatological atmosphere of the covenant people but had to come to terms with metaphysical thought. The questions raised from this new perspective were different questions than had previously engaged the minds of Christian missionaries, and had to be answered in the same coinage in which they were asked. An essentialist metaphysic is not, however, an especially congenial instrument for the expression of biblical thought. It is too static, abstract, and impersonal in its approach to the meaning of human life to be able to render the eschatological dynamism of the Scriptures. Biblical ideas such as the creaturehood of humans, their created goodness and their existential disobedience as sinners, the life of the Christian as a tension between the now and the not yet, are not readily expressed in the vocabulary of hellenistic psychology. Neoplatonic or scholastic theology set up useful dialogue with the science and philosophy of their time, and transformed hellenistic civilization into a kind of Christian civilization, but at the expense of understatement or distortion of key biblical themes. Bernard's attack on the theology of Abelard or Luther's strictures on Occamistic scholasticism are comparable attempts to correct theologies which were at once constructive in their impact upon culture and yet dangerous in their distortion of the gospel.

Modern psychology shows the inadequacy of the older faculty psychology in its abstract and impersonal treatment of the human being. It offers an alternative conceptuality much more congenial to the prophetic and apostolic anthropology, stressing the dynamic-process character of human personality and the unity and dignity of the person. For some students it has been a pathway to the recovery of a biblical estimate of human life. It prefers images drawn from human relationships to those derived from physical or mechanical models. Its usefulness to the theology of the Spirit can be seen in the following examples:

The relationship of God to his world and his creatures cannot be adequately set forth in mechanical models or monergistic language. God is not simply a power center bringing force to bear upon objects outside himself. He is rather person, supremely person, relating himself to his creation in the mystery of speech, the word. His relation to his creatures is not adequately seen in illustrations drawn from school, prison, or boot camp, but is suggested rather in images drawn from the life of the family, the father and his children, friendships, or the complex and mysterious relationships of husband and wife. The traditional handling of the problem of divine sovereignty and human freedom appears by this standard to be too static and undialectical. The problem has been most commonly resolved by the denial of human freedom, which is to say that it is not so much resolved as that one of the elements in the problem is suppressed or denied. But if images drawn from personal relationships are the most effective models for understanding the relations btween God and man, both factors can remain, but with emphasis on God's initiative in creation and redemption and a corresponding accent on the reality and limitation of human freedom. It is interesting that the authors of the Formula of Concord already express an uneasiness about stick and stone imagery in this area.[4]

Psychology and sociology also offer useful insights into the dynamics or human behavior. Careful observation and skilled analysis of the individual and corporate behavior of humans can offer the theologian the contemporary equivalent of medieval natural law: an understanding of the way God the Creator does his work. The Spirit need not enter the cosmos as stranger or interloper; he is Lord of the cosmos and can do his work through instruments which he has made. The human sciences seem to suggest that God does his work not only by encounters with individuals, but through the relationships given in creation, relationships with other persons, with social structures and institutions, and with the world of nature. He works, moreover, in a rich variety of ways. He operates no assembly line, but rejoicing in a diversity, permits each age, culture, and individual to work out that version of worship, obedience, and service that best utilizes the gifts that have been received and the specific concreteness of the social-historical situation.

The tenacious empiricism of modern science is another contribution to contemporary theology. The insistence on accurate observation, persistent analysis, relentless searching for resemblances and differences, creates an attitude which is not content with metaphysical abstractions. An older theology was quick to invoke the mystery and transcendence of the Spirit's work, but today's scientists are scornful of what appears to them as laziness or impatience. Psychology and sociology are comparatively young sciences, after all, and need much interaction from different schools of thought before achieving generally accepted results. In the meantime theology may well explore the congruence of the Spirit's work in the processes of creation and redemption.

The developmental perspective has helped to recover and appreciate the doctrine of creation both in the Scriptures and in the theology of Luther. The exposition of Genesis reminds us that creation cannot be treated as an act completed in the remote past; it must be seen as something continually under way, and manifest in the growth of plants, the birth of babies, the development of social and political agencies and structures, and in the works of artists and poets. Traditional scholastic theology has given many the impression that God is completely outside his creation, and can do his work only externally. This theology has nevertheless preserved the classical assertion that the works of God *ad extra* are not to be divided. Creation, redemption, and sanctification are to be seen as the work of the undivided Trinity. Popular theology has recalled that the Logos is the agency of creation, but the role of the Spirit in creation and redemption has not been much emphasized.

The presence of God within his creation is an important insight in the Scriptures and in Luther's theology. He is not to be identified with the creation, as in pantheism. He is the sovereign creator and transcends his creation. But he is present within his creation as the source of its being and the creative power within it. Animism, the vegetation religions, and religious romanticism misunderstand and distort this relationship, but the misuse of a good thing should not cause us to renounce it. We must find fresh ways of stating the presence and power of the Spirit in the world of nature, in human society, and in the dynamics of individual behavior. This can enable us to state more positively the relationship of the Creator Spirit to the fact of change in human society and to the impact of that change on institutions and on individuals. We should not speak so often of the breakdown of the family or of political institutions. Our choice of words indicates that we are still thinking in substantialist terms of institutions which ought to be unchanging. A developmental perspective suggests that we inquire what these structures are becoming as new forces bear upon them.

If we believe that God is one, that he alone is Creator, and that his intention in creation is not at odds with his purpose in redemption, we can face a world of change with confidence and hope. The God who has in Jesus Christ shown himself to be gracious is not otherwise disposed to us in his creation. Evil is a formidable reality, but it cannot finally frustrate the God who has acted in the Cross and resurrection. Churchmen can stop sounding like custodians of dinosaurs or other vanished species and think constructively about what God's people should be doing to relate to God's action in the world today. God's work in our world means in one dimension a growth in freedom, of racial, economic and social liberation. This can be the raw material for Christian obedience as well as a threat to peace of mind. It can be the Spirit driving his creatures toward increased freedom and responsibility and toward growth in maturity.

Recognizing the work of the Spirit in creation can open the theologian to the positive evaluation of the contributions of the human sciences. We do not have to approve everything done by psychologists, sociologists, and anthropologists to recognize that what is emerging from their work is a scientific reading of what the theologian perceives as God at work in his world. Sound sociological work enables us to grasp the dynamics of human behavior in its social groupings, to perceive the grain that the Creator has built into the social fabric. Inasmuch as the greater part of human conduct is conditioned by these social structures it makes sense for the theologian to understand them, and to operate in accordance with them rather than exhausting energies in attempt to restore some supposed golden age. In the same way, sound psychological work discloses to us the dynamics of human personality. Rather than opposing this work and attempting to rehabilitate an older psychology, we can acknowledge its contribution and use its insights to discern the psychological structures through which the Creator Spirit works. He does not come upon us as a stranger, but works through the grain of his creation.

In this work we should, of course, shun the twin pitfalls of naturalism and dualism. God transcends his creation, and has in Christ disclosed his purpose for reconciliation with his creatures. Therefore we should not talk as though God were simply a resource for human success in one dimension or another. He is sovereign; our happiness is in his will. But neither should we pursue our investigation of God's work in human personality only spasmodically, breaking off now and again with references to the mystery of his ways. If God works through his creation, psychological study may yet uncover far more about his ways of working than we now know.

Another aspect of the Spirit's work in creation which calls for concentrated study in our time is his role in relation to the world religions. If all that is, with the exception of sin and evil, is the work of God, then the work of creation also includes the lives, actions, aspirations, and insights of those beyond the Christian fellowship. This is not to suggest that the world religions are redemptive and alternatives to Christ as the way to the Father. Nor is it to suggest that they have the same relationship to the redemptive work of Christ as does the community of the old covenant. But neither can they be treated as though they have no religious significance or as though they were the manufacture of the prince of darkness. Luther and his generation did not give attention to this topic for the simple reason that it was not on their horizon. They were bounded by the *corpus christianum* with an occasional side glance at Jews and Turks. World missions lay in the future for Lutheran churches. The Reformers' attention was so fully engaged in the battle for survival that there was no inclination to explore the significance of world religions for Christians. We, however, are faced with this problem and must explore it in the light of the relationship between creation and redemption.

Secularism and atheism confront the Christian theologian today as problems of comparable dimensions. Secularism seems in one aspect to be a product of the desacralizing activity of the Reformation; in another dimension it is an emphatic denial of the Reformers' message concerning the sovereignty of God. Atheism also has a complex relationship to the Christian tradition. In one sense atheism is largely possible because of the prophetic-Christian insistence on the unity of God. Older alternatives to the gospel ranged from animism to gnosticism, but few of the opponents of the gospel had imagination enough to contemplate the possibility of atheism. In another dimension, many atheists owe their convictions to the misuse of Christian theology and pastoral office by incompetent and tyrannous churchmen. Both subtle and overt forms of coercion have driven their victims to assert their human integrity and dignity by attacks upon oppressive church institutions and the God they have regarded as responsible for them. These assertions sometimes take extravagant forms, as in the assertion of the autonomy of the human spirit made by contemporary secular humanism. Inasmuch as the data provided by the human sciences do not furnish much support for this assertion, it may be a measure of the fury generated by ecclesiastical oppression that it is able to energize so radical an assertion.

The developmental perspective opens the way to many insights when applied to the study of the Scriptures. First of all it shows us the development of the understanding of Spirit within the Bible itself.

In ancient Israel, as in other Semitic cultures, *ruach* means breath, wind, the breath of life, vitality, the power of life. In primitive religion the term is applied to every manifestation of power or vitality, whether good or evil. Within the religion of the covenant this leads to difficulties, for the God of the covenant is seen as the source of all power, even those manifestations which are evil. The lying or deceiving seer appears at this stage to be as much a manifestation of God's power as the true prophet. God sends the lying spirit to test his people or as a judgment upon them (1 Kings 22:22-23).

A later stage of development introduces ethical criteria into the understanding of Spirit. The God of the covenant does not lie or deceive; he is not the author of evil, except in the sense that he judges a disobedient people. God is good and gracious; his Spirit is always in the service of his covenanted love, never opposed to it. The Spirit sent from God can be distinguished from evil spirits by its relation to God's grace and love.

About the time of the exile the word Spirit as used of God is further refined. Spirit is the mode of God's gracious and holy presence among his people. It is not merely a messenger sent from God; it is the self-manifestation of God. The religion of the covenant had its beginnings in the general world of Semitic religion. The prophetic movement sets up a process of criticism and correction which distinguishes Israel from its neighbors and creates an environment in which the prophet *par excellence* can do his work of judgment, revelation, and self-giving.

Some older theologies used the Scriptures as though every passage were on the same level. The historically informed use of Scripture recognizes that there are different stages or levels of God's dealing with his people. The word spirit begins in contexts of animalistic or vegetation religion, but is gradually detached, given new contexts and equipped to serve as an expression of the gracious presence and purpose of the One God.

Second, the developmental perspective enables students of the Bible to recognize the importance of eschatological dynamism. The theological vocabulary of Neo-Platonism or scholasticism did not have adequate categories to express this surging eschatological thrust, and for a millennium the church had to operate with static and legal categories rather than dynamic, historical, and purposive terms. The Reformation recaptured the movement and color of biblical terminology, and historical studies have made our day even more keenly aware of it. The Spirit is seen as eschatological sign: the earnest money, giving assurance that God will carry through his redemptive work, the seal of God's signet, authenticating the message and action as God's, the first fruits, giving assurance that the harvest is at hand. The church as the community of the Spirit also has this eschatological character. In the church God gives a demonstration of what he intends to do with his entire creation, renewing it by the Spirit of Christ. The unity of the people of God in the love of Christ is an especially important aspect of this eschatological sign, according to the Fourth Gospel. It is the love within the Christian community that can convince the world that Jesus has really been sent by the Father. The sacraments share this eschatological character. Baptism is union with the crucified and risen Messiah, the bestowal of the Spirit of the age to come, renewal and cleansing. The Supper projects God's eschatological act in the Cross and resurrection, offers communion with the Risen One, anticipates the messianic banquet.

The developmental perspective in biblical studies has shown how important is the role of the Spirit in the work of redemption. Jesus is the Spirit-filled man, the bringer of the new age. He is a prophet, indeed *the* prophet. The Spirit of God is upon him to proclaim good news to the poor, to accomplish messianic signs of healing, exorcism, cleansing, and life giving. In him God's love is seen not only as generous, but as inexorable. He wants not only to forgive sinners, but to transform them. The parable of the unforgiving servant shows God's impatience with those who consume God's grace but do not become gracious.

The life and ministry of Jesus is attended and empowered by the Spirit from beginning to completion. His conception is the Spirit's work, asserting God's will to newness. His ministry is attended by the signs of the Spirit's power in him. His resurrection is an act of the Spirit. The rediscovery of the role of the Spirit in redemption gives us a new appeciation of Luther's teaching that Jesus is both *sacramentum* and *exemplum*. He is God's deed for us, the accomplishment of our redemption and reconciliation. He is also God's paradigm of human life, for he shows that true humility is not merely consumption but self-giving.

The biblical stress on the role of the Spirit in the ministry of Jesus has interesting repercussions on Christological formulations. The dogmatic language about the impersonal humanity of Jesus was for the seventeenth century an adequate assertion of the universal humanity of Jesus Christ. To us it seems psychologically unreal and dogmatically semi-docetic. The wealth of observation and insight given us by the human sciences makes us impatient with such dogmatic abstractions. We prefer to speak of the specific individual Jesus of Nazareth, whose knowledge was that of his time, whose speech most likely betrayed his Galilean upbringing, whose thinking shows the impact upon him of the Scriptures, the synagogue, the rabbis, and the apocalyptic writings. Precisely this historical person is for us the authoritative interpreter of God's will, the revealer of God himself, the way, the truth, the life. The New Testament teaching on the Spirit pushes us in quest of a more properly pneumatic or trinitarian Christology.

Notes

1. For further information see essays by Rusch and Holm in this volume.
2. See the discussion in R. G. Collingwood, *Essay in Philosophical Method* (London, 1933), and *An Essay on Metaphysics* (London, 1940).
3. For a survey of these theologies see F. W. Kantzenbach, "German Lutheran Theology of the 19th and 20th Centuries," *The Encyclopedia of The Lutheran Church* (Minneapolis: Augsburg, 1965), vol. II, pp. 914-916.
4. See, for example, *Formula of Concord*, Solid Declaration II, in Book of Concord, Theodore G. Tappert, ed. (Philadelphia: Fortress, 1959).

Olaf Hansen

Spirit Christology:
A Way Out of Our Dilemma?

I.

Christology is in crisis. This is not a startling statement since the nineteenth and twentieth centuries have been ones of constant Christological turmoil. Among those set forth is Spirit-Christology which claims to be a convincing and illuminating solution to the Christological problem. Before we examine these claims it is well to take note of certain characteristics of Christological inquiry in the last several decades which are worthy of notice.

The first is the tension between a functional and an ontological approach to Christology. It is Oscar Cullmann[1] among others who reminds us that the New Testament hardly ever speaks of the person of Christ without at the same time speaking of his work. John Knox[2] distinguishes between "event" Christologies and "person" Christologies. His contention is that "the uniqueness of Jesus was the absolute uniqueness of what God did in him."[3] The divinity of Christ is to be understood as the purposeful activity consummated in and through his humanity. The significance of Jesus Christ is to be found in that which God was doing rather than in what he was.

There is little doubt that the functional approach does reflect the thrust of the Scriptures, and that ontological patterns can and do clash with biblical motifs. But, while it is wrong to seek justification for the metaphysical considerations of the fourth and fifth centuries in the New Testament, this is not to say that the New Testament is disinterested in ontological concerns. The Scriptures do not treat ontology as an end in itself, but invariably relate it to function. Thus it is no solution to reject all ontologies simply because many have been found inadequate and even alien to biblical motifs. Bringing ontology into closer conformity with the biblical witness will result in, among other things, more personalistic and dynamic categories than what the metaphysics of the later Greek Fathers would allow.

Reginald Fuller [4] reminds us that while functional terminology and intent characterize the earlier two strata of Christological language, the gentile mission advanced beyond that to make ontic statements about the Redeemer. In that context, Jesus did not merely function as *kyrios*, but was given the name of God himself. Of his incarnation it is asserted that the Logos "became" flesh.

The beleaguered status of the Chalcedonian Formula is another characteristic of the contemporary Christological turmoil. H. R. Mackintosh [5] reflects the impatience of many when he criticizes the Formula on two counts. He argues that the doctrine of the two natures in one person imports into the life of Christ an incredible and thoroughgoing dualism. It gives us two abstractions instead of one reality, two impotent halves in place of one living whole. In his words, "it hypostasies falsely two aspects of a single concrete life." Moreover, the Formula assumes that "in both God and man there exists a complex whole of attributes and qualities which can be designated and spoken about as 'nature' enjoying some kind of real being apart from a unifying or focal ego." To abstract from a person a residuum designated as "nature" is to posit a psychological puzzle and a meaningless abstraction, Mackintosh contends.

The dilemma, constituted by Chalcedon's distinction between the "who" as the personal object implied in the name and the "what" as the qualities or specific personality traits, is that we are caught between dualism and docetism. Innumerable attempts have been made, on the one hand, to avoid positing two centers of consciousness and subjects of activity without an adequate substitute for the hypostatic union and, on the other hand, to avoid losing the self-consciousness and finite subjectivity of Jesus in the Logos. It is clear that if we take the idea of the two natures as one which asserts the realities of humanity and divinity, and then try to conceive of the consequences of those two realities being united, neither fused nor lost, in a person who does not result from the union but is prior to it and enters into new conditions because of it, we are confronted with difficulties that have escaped so far a satisfactory solution.

While it has not given us a solution to the mystery of the person of our Lord, the Formula has nevertheless safeguarded three vital dogmas: the unity of God, the divinity of Christ, and the unity of Christ's person. It has decisively prevented the conversion of a doctrine of Incarnation into some form of divine immanence. M. F. Wiles [6] reminds us that it is not possible to restate Chalcedon in modern terms without being prepared to revise the formulation of Nicaea. Nicaea gave us a fixed starting point in which the problem of Christ's person could be posed in only one way, namely, how the Second Person of the Godhead, distinct yet *homoousios* with the Father, had become man. Thus the Antiochene approach of much of contemporary thought takes issue not merely with Chalcedon but also with Nicaea.

This leads us to the third characteristic of contemporary discussions, namely, the insistence that the starting point must be the historical individual person of Jesus. It is Pannenberg who has popularized, though not originated, the terminology of Christology "from above" and "from below." In contrast to both Bultmann and Barth, Pannenberg urges that the historical events of the earthly Jesus be the point of departure for an understanding of Christ. His contention is that Christologies "from above" minimize, if not reduce to insignificance, the historical particularity of Jesus, and ignore the patent fact that we cannot stand, as it were, in the position of God himself and determine how the divine Logos would be thought apart from the Incarnation, simply because we are bound to a historically determined human situation.[7]

It should be noted that this Antiochene approach is as strongly soteriological as the Christology "from above," but it employs a different soteriological principle, namely, that of Gregory of Nazianzus, "what Christ has not assumed he has not healed." [8] The humanity is a necessary element in his saving work as much as his divinity so strongly emphasized in Athanasius' victory over Arius.

But a Christology "from below" is not without its difficulties. Just as a Christology "from above" too easily assumes that it understands what "divinity" is, it suffers from the presumption that it knows what "humanity" is. But the assertion that Jesus was a "man" is not unambiguous. Is it perfect man, or inclusive man, or essential man, or integrated man? There is no generally accepted ideal for humanity which Jesus can be regarded as having perfectly embodied and thereby savingly revealed. The usual nineteenth century idealist portrayal does not meet with much response in our day. As S. W. Sykes [9] suggests, if Jesus is to be understood as the image of man, he ought not to be misunderstood as an idol. The idolized version of Christ is that description of him which is supposed to encapsulate the timeless truth about him, usually by taking some aspect of his personality or teaching and investing it with authority. Thus, it is common to extol the moral quality of Jesus, especially his love, as reflective of his full humanity.

The question is whether such a human Jesus can account for the moral qualities so praised. To emphasize that Jesus was a human being participating in the limitations and ambiguities of life as other men simply underscores a dilemma. It is that any account which does not distinguish him from the rest of humanity is not acceptable as a credible Christology, while at the same time any account which does so distinguish him runs the risk of undercutting his "mere" humanity. Nor is there any guarantee that a Christology "from below" will give the concrete historical figure of Jesus its full significance. It is Peter Hodgson [10] who observes that while Pannenberg insists that Christology must begin with the Man Jesus, the first question he raises about him is his unity with God. This he finds not in the life and ministry of Jesus, but in the Easter traditions. Nor is the divinity problematic for Pannenberg since, in obvious dependence upon Hegel, he posits a divine-human relationship in which the historical life of Jesus is finally without decisive significance.

Peter Hodgson well summarizes the present situation and intention of Christological discussions in the following statement:

> What is needed is a way of avoiding the supernaturalism and docetism of the Logos-flesh Christology, of overcoming the subjectivistic bias of a self-transcending anthropology, and of moving beyond the impasse of the doctrine of the two Natures entirely, while at the same time holding radically to the historical man Jesus as the criterion of Christology.[11]

Spirit-Christology believes that it meets those stipulations.

II.

Generally speaking, there is a twofold relationship between the Spirit and Christ that is set forth in the New Testament, namely, as the bearer of the Spirit in his life on earth, and as the sender of the Spirit in his state as risen and exalted Lord. The striking thing, however, is that while the Spirit figures prominently in the life of the earthly church, he scarcely appears as a theme in the Synoptic Gospels. This underscores the credibility of the Synoptic Gospels since it makes clear that the later experiences of the Spirit on the part of the church were not projected back into the life of Jesus. It also reflects the fact that the Gospels represent a period of transition between the old covenant when the Spirit was sporadically given and the New Age which began with Pentecost in which the prophetic hope of a permanent presence of the Spirit was fulfilled.

J. Jeremias observes that though Jesus was regarded as a prophet by many of his contemporaries this did not mean that he was simply another in the line of the Old Testament prophets. That prophetic sequence had been broken off, and at the time of Jesus the dominant view was that the Spirit had been "quenched." [12] Thus the several mentions of the Spirit in the first two chapters of Luke reflect that Old Testament view of the sporadic gift of the Spirit upon John the Baptist, 1:15, 17, 80; Elizabeth, 1:41; Zachariah, 1:67; Simeon, 2:25, 27. John the Baptist stood, as it were, on the border line between the old and new. Apart from the reference to "power" (Luke 1:17) and "Spirit" (Luke 1:15, 17) in connection with the birth of John, nowhere else in the Synoptic Gospels is it said that anyone but Jesus received the Holy Spirit. There is no occasion to find in the mission charge (Mark 3:15; 6:7) any indication that the Spirit had been given or was then given to the disciples. They were heralds rather than prophets.

With respect to the virginal conception, Luke 1:35, the angel is clearly referring to the Holy Spirit to explain two points: (1) how Mary, though a virgin, could conceive; (2) that the child would be called the Son of God. The complicated discussion on the birth narratives need not involve us here, except the observation that Matthew and Luke are interested in the virginal conception as a phenomenon with theological import. It is clear that Matthew believed in the virginity of Mary before the birth of Jesus (1:25) and regarded the activity of the Holy Spirit as the explanation of Mary's virginal conception (1:18, 20). The clear allusion to Isaiah 7:14 would have little point if Luke did not take *parthenos* to mean "virgin" and were not intending to emphasize the virginal conception.

The language of the Lukan text is a frustrating one for anyone who looks for precision with respect to the virginal conception. "The Holy Spirit will come upon you, and the power of the Most High will overshadow you." *Epeleusetai epi se* is used elsewhere of the descent of the Spirit upon persons. In the description of the promise of the Spirit at Pentecost given by our Lord at his ascension, this term is used as it is in Isaiah (32:15)as he prophesies destruction "until the Spirit is poured *(epelthei)* upon us from on high." Gabriel's words seem to imply that because Jesus is conceived by the power of the Holy Spirit he will himself be holy.

The connection between "power" and the creative function of the Holy Spirit is of considerable importance. The Old Testament and rabbinical writers refer God's creative activity to his "power." This is echoed in Hebrews 1:3 in God's almighty power over creation. The parallelism of Gabriel's words, "The Holy Spirit will come upon you, and the power of the Most High will overshadow you," reflects the close connection between power and the Holy Spirit.

Any attempt to articulate an understanding of Jesus Christ in terms of the Spirit pays a great deal of attention to his baptism. Was the descent of the Spirit the moment of Jesus' adoption as the Son of God and appointment as Messiah or merely the climax and confirmation of a growing conviction that he was Son and Messiah? There is no support in the passages for an adoptionist Christology. Luke, for instance, does not intend in the baptism event to deny what he has said earlier. Jesus is Messiah and Son of God from his birth (1:35, 43, 76; 2:11, 26, 49). Baptism is another stage of his unveiling or revelation, just as the resurrection and ascension (Acts 2:36; 13:33) likewise was another stage in the revelation of Jesus as Messiah and Son of God. For Luke, therefore, the association of the descent of the Spirit with the baptism of Jesus has a revelatory rather than an adoptionist significance. At the baptism the Spirit descends, according to the Lukan account, in "bodily form," which is to suggest that it was in a manner different from the often temporary inspiration of an ordinary prophet.

Luke 3:23 as well as John 1:32-34 suggest that the baptism marked a new beginning in the life of our Lord. At the inception of his messianic life, he must receive a new outpouring of the Spirit. By the visible descent of the Spirit upon him at his baptism, Jesus is identified as the one who will dispense the Spirit and inaugurate the distinctively Christian baptism. Two items may be cited as support for this contention. The primitive *kerygma* reflected in Acts 10:38 held that the Spirit's descent was not the act by which Jesus became Son of God, but it was an anointment of Jesus "with the Holy Spirit and with power." Joachim Jeremias, arguing that it is only Isaiah 42:1, rather than a composite of Isaiah 42:1 and Psalm 2:7, that is cited, refers to the custom in the Judaism of that period that large portions of Scripture were known by heart so that it was customary to quote only the beginning of a passage. He thinks that Mark 1:11 (Luke 3:22) may be such a case of an abbreviated quotation since the really decisive clause, "I have put my Spirit upon him," does not appear in the citation. Thus the emphasis, he concludes, is upon the communication of the Spirit, and the proclamation had nothing to do with the enthronement of a king or adoption.[13]

Each evangelist treats the baptism differently. Two changes made by Luke indicate that he wished to make it clear that Jesus receives the Spirit as an abiding possession in his own right. Mark and Matthew have Jesus see the Holy Spirit coming down on him. Luke makes this a statement of objective fact. Again, while Mark connects the descent of the Spirit with Jesus' climbing up out of the water, and Matthew with the completion of baptism, Luke wants nothing to clutter the account of Jesus receiving the Spirit. It is while Jesus is at prayer, after his baptism, that the heavens open and the Spirit descends, indicating that the descent of the Spirit was because of who he was, rather than because of a particular rite performed.

What Jesus experienced at the baptism was that from that time he knew that he was in the grasp of the Spirit. God was taking him into his service, equipping him and authorizing him to be his messenger and the inaugurator of the time of salvation. At his baptism Jesus experienced his call. Mark 11:27-33 is evidence that Jesus attached supreme importance to the moment of his baptism. His counter-question whether the baptism of John was or was not from God is hardly an evasion. If meant seriously the counter-question meant that his authority rested on John's baptism or, in other words, what happened at John's baptism constituted his authority.

While Jesus is not described in any impressive terms as the bearer of the Spirit, nevertheless the attention given to the exorcisms indicates that Jesus was regarded as a man of the Spirit. The Spirit, as a matter of fact, is mentioned only once in connection with the demons, namely, in Matthew 12:28 (Luke 11:20). Whether it is the "Spirit of God" as in Matthew or the "finger of God" in Luke, the fact is that it speaks of a divine power residing in Jesus. James Dunn observes that the ministry of exorcism by the power of the Spirit proves that the Kingdom has come:

> . . . the Kingdom is present in Jesus *only* because He has the Spirit. It is not so much a case of where *Jesus* is there is the Kingdom, as where the *Spirit* is there is the Kingdom. So in Matthew 12:28 the fact which demonstrates the presence of the Kingdom there and then is not the presence of Jesus, and not even the power of Jesus (the power to cast out demons was nothing distinctive in itself), but rather the fact that it is *by the Spirit of God* that exorcism is accomplished (note how emphatic is the "en pneumati Theou"). It is because the *Spirit* is at work that they can be sure that the Kingdom has come.[14]

The sin against the Holy Spirit (Mark 3:28-30) is only comprehensible against the background that the Spirit had been quenched and that he was at work once again in the ministry of Jesus. With the new activity of the Spirit the time of salvation has begun, and the eschatological return of the Spirit means that God will remain with his community to complete his saving work. Jesus claims to be the eschatological messenger of God, the promised prophet like Moses, who brings the final revelation and therefore demands absolute obedience. The difference between the blasphemies that can be forgiven as in verse 28 and the blasphemy against the Holy Spirit which cannot be forgiven is that the former were sins against the God who is still hidden. The active presence and power of the Spirit in Jesus makes sin against him a sin against the revealing God and therefore incapable of forgiveness.

In the Pauline literature, reflecting as it does the post-Pentecost experience of the risen and exalted Christ, the emphasis is primarily upon Jesus as the sender of the Spirit. The Spirit is the living contact between the victorious Jesus and all who are united with him. It is clear that Spirit and Christ are inseparable. The manner in which they are related, however, is what concerns us. The tendency to reduce the Pauline concept of Christ as Lord to an ephemeral and universal Spirit is to be rejected because Paul maintains that the specific identity of the ascended Lord Jesus is none other than Jesus of Nazareth. For Paul, Spirit is not a metaphorical expression that points to the ongoing influence of a Jesus who is dead and gone. On the contrary, the life-giving experience of the Spirit is what bound the historical Jesus and the risen Lord together, establishing a real continuity between them. It is important to realize that when Paul speaks of the Spirit, he states his conviction that to possess the Spirit is nothing less than to possess Christ himself. In Ingo Hermann's fine phrase, the Spirit is the "christological category of realization." [15]

There are several passages that need to be examined as to the manner in which Paul conceives the relationship of Jesus and the Spirit, notably 2 Corinthians 3:17; Romans 1:3-4; and 1 Corinthians 15:45. "The Lord is the Spirit" is the statement in 2 Corinthians 3:17. The context is the discussion by Paul of the change in the history of salvation effected by Jesus Christ. He is arguing for the superiority of the new covenant over the old by affirming that the new is the time of the Spirit. The Spirit plays much the same role in the new covenant as the law did in the old, only the Spirit gives life. Though the Spirit is the prevailing power of this new era, the new covenant is instituted and established through the work of Christ.

In the equation of Lord and Spirit, Paul is making a functional, rather than an ontological, identification. We can hardly assume that the Spirit as a person in the Trinity distinct from the Son is now literally identified with the Lord as Christ. Christ is Lord because he has established the new covenant, but the experience of the life and freedom of the new era is effected through the Spirit. Ingo Hermann [16] argues that the identification of Christ and Spirit is an identification not in divine substance but in Christian experience. We experience the exalted Christ as Spirit, so that Spirit is a functional concept and describes the means by which Christ is at work in the Christian community.

This is reinforced by Paul's statement in 1 Corinthians 15:45, "The last Adam became a life-giving Spirit." Paul is drawing a line between Adam and Christ. Adam is the prototype of man's death-destined life as mortal, weak, and physical. The second Adam is the prototype of a new kind of life effected and affected by the resurrection. He becomes a life-giving Spirit at the resurrection. The power that Paul attributed to the risen Lord is the power everywhere ascribed to the Spirit. In the Old Testament, the Spirit is he who broods over creation and brings forth life from chaos. God withdraws his Spirit, and living flesh fades as grass (Psalm 104:29). He sends out his Spirit, and the dry bones come alive (Ezekiel 37). Now at the resurrection Christ assumed these life-giving activities of the Spirit.

The phrase *pneuma zoopoioun* (life-giving spirit) as Paul uses it here refers to Jesus in a representative capacity, particularly to his resurrection and his resurrection-body. The experience of Jesus as a *pneuma zoopoioun* implies a *soma pneumatikon* because that is the inevitable end result of a process already under way, namely, that of being transformed into the image of Christ by his Spirit. Jesus became the last Adam at his resurrection. Thus for Paul the resurrection marks the beginning of the humanity of the last Adam. Christ's role as "second man" does not begin either in some pre-existent state, or at the Incarnation. Both the recapitulation theory of Irenaeus and the incarnation-based soteriology of F. D. Maurice misinterpret Paul here.[17] In the Incarnation Jesus took on the flesh of the first Adam, sinful flesh, fallen humanity, and by his death destroyed it. The new humanity stems from the resurrection.

What is of interest to us in Romans 1:3-4 are the phrases *kata sarka* (according to the flesh) and *kata pneuma* (according to the Spirit). It is entirely probable that the *kata sarka/kata pneuma* antithesis not only describes two distinct and successive phases in the life of Jesus separated by the resurrection, but refers also to the pre-resurrection life of Jesus as lived according to the flesh and according to the Spirit. *Kata sarka,* if it is to follow the prevalent Pauline usage, is pejorative because as Paul argues elsewhere in Romans the physical relationship is precisely Israel's stumbling block. Moreover, it usually stands in open antithesis with *kata pneuma.* Thus insofar as Jesus lived on the level of the flesh, he was bound and determined by the weakness and inadequacy of the human condition and was merely the Son of

David and no more. But he also lived *kata pneuma,* for it is clear that Jesus' experience with the Spirit did not begin with the resurrection. Sonship for Paul is clearly a function of the Spirit. If the "Abba" cry of the Christian was constituted by the Spirit, so it certainly was recognized as a reproduction of Jesus' own experience of being the Son of God. Insofar as Jesus lived on the level of the Spirit and was controlled by the Spirit, he manifested that he was indeed the Son of God and thereby proved his right to be installed—"designated"—he did not become the Son of God by resurrection—Son of God in power as from the resurrection of the dead.

James Dunn argues that Paul has in mind Jesus as the prototype for the Christian who is caught in the tension and conflict of the flesh and the Spirit, since he was also caught in the same overlap of the ages.[18] According to Romans 8 the Christian's sonship falls into two stages—adoption which comes with the Spirit of adoption in verse 15, and the full adoption in glory which awaits the resurrection of the body, verse 23. Sonship in both instances is a function of the Spirit. The parallels between Romans 1 and 8 are too close to admit any doubt that the sonship of Jesus in the first stage is likewise a function of the Spirit.

On the other hand, Paul's intention in this passage is to express continuity as well as change by attempting to formulate the relation between the historical Jesus and the exalted Jesus, the Jesus which Christians once knew and the Jesus they now knew and worshiped. It is Jesus' relation to the Spirit that provides the clue. It was because the historical Jesus was recognized as the unique man of the Spirit that the exalted Jesus could be acclaimed as the Lord of the Spirit. Jesus' exalted life in terms of the Spirit *(kata pneuma, en pneumati, pneumati)* was recognized to be continuous with the earthly life in terms of the Spirit, the latter being, as we have seen elsewhere, the necessary presupposition for the former. The transformation from the Spirit inspiring Jesus to the Spirit of Jesus took place at the resurrection. It was precisely in and by the resurrection that Jesus fully "took over" the Spirit, ceased to be a man dependent upon the Spirit and became Lord of the Spirit.

Paul thus understands the formula of Romans 1:3f. in terms of a two-stage Christology. At both stages Jesus is the Son of God, and at both stages his sonship is determined by the Spirit and Jesus' response.

In Paul's view the sonship of the earthly Jesus was constituted by the Holy Spirit. He was Son of God because of the Holy Spirit in him and because he lived in obedience to that Spirit. Jesus' possession and experience of the Spirit is what Paul called Jesus' sonship and what later dogma called his divinity. The deity of the earthly Jesus is a function of the Spirit.

> The uniqueness of Jesus was not that he was the first to possess the Spirit in a distinctive (Christian) way, but that he was uniquely "full of the Spirit," and that he impressed his character and personality on the Spirit, so that thereafter the mark of the Spirit was his inspiration of an acknowledgement of the Lordship of Jesus and his reproduction of the character of Jesus in Christians (1 Corinthians 12:3; 2 Corinthians 3:18). In short, to express the point in an epigram, if the Spirit gave Jesus his power, Jesus gave the Spirit his personality." [19]

In conclusion, biblical evidence certainly points in the direction of a Spirit-Christology. At the decisive moments in both his earthly and exalted ministry, Jesus is intimately related to the Spirit. The resurrection appears to be the point at which a transformation from Jesus as a man of the Spirit to the Lord of the Spirit took place. While he was already the Son of God *kata pneuma*, he became the Son of God in power by means of the Spirit of holiness.

One must readily admit that here is a much more congenial portrait of our Lord than the wooden, abstract categories of the Chalcedonian Creed. The living, human experience of the Spirit possessing and empowering Jesus strikes a responsive chord in us because it is analogous to our own experience. As a matter of fact, this is probably the strong appeal in this approach. It proceeds from one's experience of the Spirit, by way of analogy, to the experience of Jesus, the difference being a matter of degree. Nowhere is this more clearly alluded to than in the use of the "Abba" formula in the address to God. Romans 8:15 and Galatians 4:6 make it abundantly clear that the cry "Abba" uttered by the Christian is beyond all human capability and is only possible with the new relationship with God, established by the Son but effected by God himself through the Spirit. It actualizes the divine sonship wherever it is spoken. Whenever you cry "Abba," Paul says to the Christians, God assures you that you are certainly his children. The significance of this is that the use of the term "Abba" is uniquely a term used by Jesus because as Jeremias observes, "there is no analogy at all in the whole literature of Jewish prayer for God being addressed as Abba." [20] It was by the Spirit that Jesus sustained his relationship to the Father. The Spirit thus becomes the common ground between the believer and the exalted Lord Jesus.

III.

A Spirit-Christology essentially holds that Jesus was a man so totally possessed by the Spirit that the outcome of his life and ministry was a revelation of God as full and complete as can be expressed in a finite human life. Because of the disastrous history of such a notion, it eschews the temptingly easy and reductionist way of Adoptionism, namely, to think of Christ as simply the man upon whom the Spirit came in order to raise him to a unique place and function. It is convinced that the Gospels tell the story of a human life, a life full of meaning and significance, but that humanity is not the last word about it. To say no more than that he is the highest achievement of the race, the revelation of the Spirit in the form of human personality, is to fail to recognize his uniqueness. Spurred by the inadequacy of the traditional Logos-Christology, it essays a re-interpretation of our Lord's Person that will be expressive of the church's conviction that indeed in him we meet with nothing other than God himself. It brings to the Christological enquiry some valuable and hopeful insights and approaches. It is appropriate to state its strengths.

There is a strong emphasis upon the historic, personal life of Jesus in the Gospels. As a Christology "from below," it starts with the Gospel accounts in which there is no hesitation as to the reality of Christ's humanity as the vehicle of the Spirit. One controlling factor, however, is that the human life of Jesus is seen not as the supreme anomaly, but the classic instance of the manner in which God works in and through human life. Creation is held to be instinct with the presence and activity of God as Spirit. At many points and many places, God has entered and continues to enter into the human situation. The created order is regarded as always open to the divine activity and initiative.

Various metaphysical systems are used to articulate this conviction in a coherent fashion, the most contemporary and in many ways persuasive being that of process philosophy. They are strong in their insistence that the activity of God is not a *deus ex machina* intruding from the outside into the created world. They affirm that God the Spirit is moving in every created entity from the celestial bodies to the mind of the human, urging each entity to become that which it was intended to be. At each of the successive levels, from the inorganic to the living and conscious levels, the Holy Spirit is at work establishing whatever perfection is proper to that level.

In Jesus the work of the Spirit is known on the level of conscious, personalizing action. The significance of Jesus is that he is very much a part of the process and that therefore he is, in Norman Pittenger's words, the "focusing and concentrating of what God is always doing in the creative advance." [21] Allowing for a difference of degree of intensity and quality, the work of the Spirit in the natural and historical order is of one piece with that in Jesus Christ. The particular incarnation of God in Christ through the Spirit is analogous to the manner of all God's work in his world. To regard the person of Christ in any other manner would mean to turn him into a meaningless prodigy which contradicts rather than illuminates the way of God in his creation.

A further implication of this approach of Spirit-Christology to the mystery of our Lord's person is the recognition of *kenosis* as a mode of activity of God. It is H. Wheeler Robinson who speaks of the divine *kenosis* of the Spirit.[22] By *kenosis* he means that there is the acceptance of the "lower" as the medium of the "higher." Robinson suggests that spirit, as a higher level of reality, constantly takes the lower into itself and thereby gives it a new meaning and reality. *Kenosis* is in effect the sacramentalization of the created order by which the Spirit embodies himself in the lower, usually the material and physical, in order to express and realize himself. This is another way of stating that the human is not inimical to the expression and even the realization of the divine.

The concept of *kenosis* reflects God's freedom over his creation in entering it. In the possession of a man with fully human consciousness, his freedom reaches its highest expression. Spirit is God's unique manner in which God, in inspiring man and becoming involved with him, does not cease to be God. Traditional theology has often hedged on this because of its belief that the finite was not capable of bearing the infinite, since the infinite would inevitably overpower the finite. The indwelling of the Spirit in Jesus the Christ indicates that this is not so.

Spirit-Christology involves an implicit criticism of the Chalcedonian Formula. It recognizes that the two-nature formula of Chalcedon is a distortion of the actual relation between God and man. Not only are the two natures, divine and human, not as incompatible as Chalcedon would infer, but also the methodology of the Chalcedonian Formula is seriously brought into question. Spirit-Christology involves a new method of formulating the understanding of the person of Christ. The starting point cannot be a preconceived ontology within which the *kenosis* is to be fitted. Traditionally the question has been: how is it possible for a person to incorporate within himself both divine and human natures, the problem acute because it was understood that the divine and the human mixed as uneasily as oil and water. Spirit-Christology suggests: what does the reality of Jesus as the Spirit-possessed man tell us about the nature of God and man?

Christological formulations have tried to guard against the denial of true divinity and also true humanity of our Lord. But there is also the unity of his person to be considered. The distinction between soul and body of a spiritual and of a physical component to man's being is invalid because it distorts more than it clarifies. As a living being is not life plus matter but living matter, so our understanding of our Lord must likewise reflect this unified understanding of his total reality. Man is not matter plus spirit but animated matter, capable of those activities which we call spiritual. So our Lord is neither God plus man nor man plus God, an impression which Chalcedon all too readily gives. The very thing that Chalcedon sought to safeguard is destroyed if we interpret it as meaning that the divinity of Christ is a separate thing from his humanity, a one plus one making two.

The comment of Robert North is helpful here:

> The unwillingness of our contemporaries to admit that the transcendent divine and the created human are united in one man results in their seeing the man Jesus as a *mere* man, and to this snare orthodox Catholics also fall prey if they interpret

sacrosanct formulas to mean that the divinity of Jesus is something apart from his manhood.[23]

The import of this statement is that the divinity of Jesus is perceptible
precisely in his humanity and that the human form of Jesus is the revelation of God. Spirit-Christology would concur in Edward Schille-
beeckx's suggestion that we speak of "hypostatic *unity* rather than
union" as more representative of the person of our Lord.[24] He argues
that God is more with every single man than that man is one with
himself. Any man's "being-of-God" is constitutive of his "being-him-
self," his human subjectivity. So the "being-of-God" on a higher plane
in Jesus *is* his human subjectivity. Jesus thus does, though uniquely,
what every creature and especially every man does, namely, "re-pre-
sent" God by what he himself is.

Does the correlation of spirit/Spirit offer any insight to the understanding of the person of Christ? Obviously, this is a difficult project
because of the ambiguities regarding the presence of spirit in man.
Karl Barth, for instance, vigorously insists that man never is spirit but
"has" spirit only as he has the Spirit.[25] Soteriological considerations
affect Barth's position since he wants to deny that man in any way
has that with which he may understand or approach God. However,
it would appear that "spirit" may be designated of man, but not as a
synonym for soul, or some psychological functioning on the part of
man. As George Hendry,[26] reflecting Bultmann, observes, "the spirit of
man, as the spirit of the creature whom God created for himself, has
the true goal of its aspiration in God; yet as spirit is free, its direction
to God appears in a phenomenological view, as only one possibility."
Spirit is the "medium," or the organ of man's encounter with the
Spirit of God. Proverbs 20:27, "the spirit of man is the candle of the
Lord," indicates that the human spirit needs and awaits the touch of
the Holy Spirit to kindle it to life and so to the realization of itself.

In this connection it is instructive to remind ourselves of Apolli-
narius' ambivalent understanding of Paul. Because his attitude toward
sin was thoroughly Pauline, he rejected the prevailing Greek belief
that the mind of man and the mind of God are alike. On the other
hand, he rejected the Pauline belief that spirit exists in man only when
he is in relation with the Spirit because his conception of mind was
wholly Greek. Thus, he failed to appreciate that Paul regarded spirit

as the gift of God which, if potentially present in man, is only called into true existence by the action of the Spirit. Spirit-Christology furnishes an answer to this fear of Apollinarianism with its substitution of the Logos for the spirit of man. It affirms that the spirit of man is not a fragment of Spirit, but the image of the divine Spirit.

W. R. Matthews [27] suggests that the phenomenon of inspiration is probably the best way in which to affirm the union of divine and human subjects. An inspired experience, be it that of the artist, or musicians, or philosopher, may be described, as the term indicates, as the "flowing in" of an influence which seizes and masters the person and enlarges the self so as to make it capable of great things. A completely inspired person is one for whom the power of the indwelling Spirit was always and certainly available. Thus of Jesus, he writes:

> The Spirit dwelt in him "as in no other." "As in no other"— that is true in so far as "measure" is concerned, but it is not true with regard to the manner of the indwelling. Just as in the lower and more limited examples of inspiration the Spirit does not supersede or abolish the human being but raises his capacities to a higher potency, using mind, imagination and will for the divine purpose, so here the fact that Jesus was supremely and immeasurably inspired does not make him inhuman; on the contrary it makes him fully man, the representative man, the human person after God's image. He is at one and the same time truly man and truly divine.[28]

Another value of Spirit-Christology is its categories of action rather than of being. Instead of categories drawn from Greek philosophical speculation, it suggests biblical or Hebraic alternatives such as "purpose" and "action" instead. Just as the Bible does not define the nature of God, but speaks of his mighty acts in human history, so the possibility suggests itself that Spirit may be the concept by which we may understand the nature of the divinity of Christ. John Hick [29] points out that Gregory of Nyssa in the fourth century provided the motto for all attempts to base Christology upon the category of action or event when he wrote that "the word 'Godhead' signifies an operation and not a nature *(physis)*," and attempted a doctrine of the Trinity from this point of view. It is a useful insight, and while Hick employs the concept of *agape* as the vehicle for his own reading of the nature of Christ's person, the concept of Spirit would likewise serve the same purpose, perhaps even better in the light of his statement:

> . . . God in Christ has not merely acted *upon* or *into* human history, like a meteor falling from above, but has acted *within* and *through* man's history by becoming an actual part of the ongoing stream of human life and by influencing the course of our history from the inside.[30]

It was Schleiermacher who pointed out that the terms "natures" in the Chalcedonian formula were not commensurate.[31] Manhood and Godhead are not comparable natures to be set side by side, no matter how rightly related. Would it not be more compatible, as Hick seems to suggest, to speak of human and divine functioning or activity? It is clear that the Spirit was the medium of God's redeeming action toward mankind. In Jesus Christ, as the Spirit-empowered person, God was fulfilling the promise of the redemption of human life. As the Holy Spirit is God-in-action, creating and fulfilling the human possibility, so Jesus Christ was the bearer of the Spirit.

The object of the Incarnation is to bring men into a personal relationship with God, into fellowship with him. God condescends to our humanity in order to meet with us humanly and deal with us in human terms. It is precisely this which Christ as the bearer of the Spirit connotes. The activity of Jesus is not merely a representation of God's love for man. It is rather that love in action, by reason of Spirit, so filling Jesus with a fullness of his love that we must conclude that in Jesus we meet with no other than God himself. It is the claim of Spirit-Christology that because Jesus is the source of the transforming power that issues in new life, Christians confess him as divine.

A Spirit-Christology may also have some insight into the perennial problem in Christology of the universality of the manhood of Jesus. As George Hendry has made clear,[32] the key to the success of patristic theology in combining soteriology with Christology lay in the doctrine of the consubstantiality of Christ with mankind. The humanity assumed by Christ as the Incarnation is universal humanity thus establishing an ontological relationship with mankind. This understanding of Christ in ontological relation with humanity as a whole rests upon a tenet of the Platonic philosophy that has been generally rejected by modern thought, viz., that the ideas of things have a real existence that is prior to, and superior to, the existence of the things themselves. Thus humanity is as real, if not more real, than an individual man.

In 1 Corinthians 15:45, "The first man Adam became a living being; the last Adam became a life-giving Spirit," it is affirmed that the new humanity stems from the resurrection of Jesus and that it is a spiritual humanity, a humanity of the Spirit. Man comes to participate in the new humanity not by sharing in the sinful flesh which Jesus came to condemn and destroy, but by sharing in the Spirit which raised Jesus from the dead and which constitutes his new humanity. When a man is united with his Lord he becomes one Spirit (1 Corinthians 6:17).

IV.

We turn in this section to a critical evaluation of Spirit-Christology and would like to raise three outstanding and continuing problems which such an approach fails to solve, even though with the best of intentions it grapples with them. In a stimulating review of Donald Baillie's "God Was in Christ," John Hick notes that there are two different senses in which we can speak of the mystery of the incarnation.[33] There is the active sense, the verbal form in which reference is to the act by which God took to himself human nature in the womb of Mary. *Incarnatio*—the verbal form—addresses itself to the question, what does it mean for God to become man? Traditionally the answer to this question has been in the form of such views as the kenotic theory, Adoptionism, Virgin Birth, etc. However, viewed in a passive sense—*incarnatum*—the concern is with the historical phenomenon of the Incarnate Son and the union of the divine and human natures in the one person. The analysis and description of this phenomenon is the concern and has been expressed in such views as docetism, Apollinarianism, Nestorianism, etc.

This distinction is not only handy and useful, but also important. It is clear that a Spirit-Christology purports to provide an answer to both inquiries. Analogous to the manner in which the Spirit works in man, Jesus the Christ was a man of the Spirit. Knowing himself wholly dependent upon God, totally committed to the realization of his purpose, yet sensitive to the presence or the absence (i.e., the cry of dereliction on the cross) of his Father, Jesus exemplifies for us the perfect man. As almost every exponent of Spirit-Christology is careful to note, such possession does not mean the annihilation of human personality, but rather its heightening.

> God's creative Spirit does not diminish the completeness of a human personality by taking total possession of it. On the contrary, it perfects its own creation, for it establishes a union with God which in no way abrogates the freedom of the human person. This is not an impersonal and quasi-mechanical process, but a relationship between persons. It consists, in its perfection, of the total response of the human spirit to the fully pervasive influence of the divine Spirit, so that the human attains its highest fulfillment in becoming the free and responsive agent of the divine. If the service of God is perfect freedom it cannot be the case that, if God takes the complete possession of a man, his human personality become annihilated in deity.[34]

There was one person, but one person whose personhood was totally captivated by the Spirit. There was one will, that of the man Jesus of Nazareth, but the Spirit so ruled his spirit that it was the Spirit who was the ruling motive of his life. Unlike modern man, who stands in fear of his own freedom and power, Jesus exercised his freedom in responsibility for his fellows. In the fullness of his humanity he reflected the glory of God. This personal existence was not a given, but was a personhood to be won through the struggle, temptation, and doubt that is the lot of all men. The story of the temptations immediately following upon the baptism indicate that wrestling and conflict were very much a part of his existence, and the manner in which the relationship to the Spirit was clarified and consummated. As an obedient Son he learned obedience.

Most who support a Spirit-Christology give attention to the matter of the sinlessness of Jesus. Rejecting any view that it was the innocence of Adam before the Fall that our Lord possessed, the emphasis is upon a real humanity, interpreted as a fallen humanity. Temptation to doubt and disobedience were as real in him as in any man. Yet he was without sin, sin understood in its theological dimension, rather than moral. His character was perfect because he was so completely dedicated to the will of God that no temptation to sin could overcome him. Thus Jesus is the man of God not in spite of the human form and weakness, but in it and because of it. His humanity was not an obstacle, but the medium of God's presence and activity. What brought wholeness to his life is not the human by itself, but the Spirit whose function it is to bring life and light.

But having said all this, the question is whether a Spirit-Christology can deal with the latter concern of a doctrine of incarnation, namely, *incarnatio.* Can it affirm as clearly as the Logos doctrine and the two-nature Christology that Jesus Christ is truly divine? The Logos doctrine provides an explanation of the uniqueness of Jesus since it regards him as the one in whom the Logos dwells. It is not enough to argue that this genuine man, this unique man, revealed God. Both religious experience and the convictions of the church demand to know the truth of this man's relation to God. Is the replacement of the two-nature doctrine with a man in such close contact with God the Spirit as to produce a unitary consciousness sufficient to bear the weight of the confession of Thomas, "My Lord and my God!" (John 20:28)?

In other words, how does Spirit-Christology account for the divine consciousness in Jesus and for the unique presence of the Spirit in him? It is affirmed by almost all that the difference between Jesus and the prophets was that his inspiration was continuous and the prime factor in his everyday life and activity. This would seem to imply that the difference between Jesus and the prophets is fundamentally a difference of degree rather than of kind. So Norman Hook argues:

> Though the difference of inspiration between him and other men was a matter of degree, the degree is heightened to such an extent that it amounts to a difference of itself.[35]

In a phrase reminiscent of Ritschl, Norman Hook holds that the unique factor of insipiration in Jesus yields the "values of incarnation." Yet W. R. Matthews states:

> In view of what has been said already of the need for a metaphysical basis for the doctrine it is perhaps hardly necessary to state that I am not maintaining that the whole meaning of the Incarnation is to be exhausted under the category of inspiration. We are dealing now, not with the ultimate and eternal ground significance of the doctrine, but with the person of Christ as a phenomenon in the order of history, and

there I maintain that the fact of inspiration is the safest guide we have.[36]

It is clear from this statement that Matthews is acknowledging that Spirit-Christology interpreted under the concept of inspiration is useful for understanding *incarnatum* but not *incarnatio*.

Exponents of Spirit-Christology hold that the human life of Jesus as a man of the Spirit is not an exception to the rule, but the supreme exemplification of the rule. None is more vigorous in affirming this than Norman Pittenger:

> A modern christology would also have to say that whatever is divine in that event is no alien intrusion either; it is a focusing and concentrating of what God is always doing in the creative advance. So it is also with the Holy Spirit. There is no absolute chasm between this activity of the Spirit in the natural order and that in the historical order, nor between the historical order and the human experience we all know, nor between that experience and the specific event of Jesus Christ. All is of one piece, although all is not of the same degree of intensity nor marked by the same qualitative impact.[37]

The persisting question with this type of analysis, characteristic of all Spirit-Christologies, is whether the uniqueness of Christ was a uniqueness of kind or of degree. The Spirit, signifying God himself at work in relation to his creation, is at all times seeking to influence and to become united with each human being, so that whenever we can rightly speak of God acting through men or of men responding affirmatively (or even negatively) to God, we have an instance of the Spirit "filling" or "inspiring" a human being in some degree. What the purpose of God is is clearly demonstrated in Jesus Christ, namely, that the Spirit is to control and dominate all men to the same degree that he had already in Jesus Christ. But the inevitable questions, which have pursued all degree Christologies, arise. The first, so apparent in the Adoptionist controversies, is: how did it come about that there has been in all of history only one person who has been so completely inspired by the Spirit and who has been so perfectly responsive to the Spirit? If incarnation is a matter of relative degree, how did it come about that only once did this incessant and universal activity of the

Spirit accomplish its full purpose? There is little hesitation to affirm
that the Spirit's activity is capable of producing such a phenomenon
at any time. Nor is it denied that the Spirit is seeking at all times to
become dominant or to inspire totally human beings in the same manner as in Jesus. But if the Spirit attempted this in the case of the
prophets, or even John the Baptist, why did he succeed only in Jesus?
Or, will he succeed at some future time in another time and place, in
as significant and decisive a manner as in Jesus? If so, then how can
one affirm the uniqueness of Jesus, except in the non-significant manner of the particularity of a historical fact? It cannot be argued that
God caused this perfect human being Jesus to exist in order to make
him the bearer of the Spirit, for this would deny the very premise of
Spirit-Christology, namely, that the Spirit is at work in every man and
that in Jesus we see this to a supreme degree. It is the weakness of
Adoptionism that it leaves to chance that a suitable human instrument
appeared for the indwelling of the Spirit. Moreover, this argument is
weakened further by the realization that it denies that very aspect of
the Spirit that it consciously affirms, namely, the freedom of God in
his operation. God could not create that instrument as and when he
wanted to, but had to wait upon the appearance of Jesus. The designation of God as Spirit to denote his sovereign freedom is thus denied.

Can a Spirit-Christology affirm a substantival deity, in distinction
from the adjectival deity of Christ? It is the virtue of G. W. H. Lampe's
discussion of the issue that he wrestles with this pertinent question.
There are several facets to his argument:

> Spirit christology cannot affirm that Jesus *is* "substantivally"
> God. Since, however, it seems that this affirmation is in the
> last resort incompatible with the belief that Jesus truly and
> fully shares in our humanity, this need not be a fatal objection.
> It does not follow that Jesus is only "adjectivally" God, that is
> to say, God-*like* or "divine" in the sense of being a man who
> possessed to an excellent degree the qualities that we attrib-
> ute to God. An interpretation of the union of Jesus with God
> in terms of his total possession by God's Spirit makes it pos-
> sible, rather, to acknowledge him to be God "adverbially."
> By the mutual interaction of the Spirit's influence and the free
> response of the human spirit such a unity of will and opera-

tion was established that in all his actions the human Jesus
acted divinely. In his teaching, healing, judging, forgiving,
rebuking, God teaches, heals, judges, forgives, and rebukes,
without infringing the freedom and responsibility of the human subject.[38]

It is Lampe's conviction, a conviction that undergirds most Spirit-
Christologies, that it is enough to affirm that Jesus by God's Spirit was
the human agent of God's redemptive activity. There is a functional
uniqueness of Jesus involving, it is contended, an ontological uniqueness. It is well to point out, however, that this would be the result,
rather than the basis, of the unique relationship of Jesus with God.

The crucial question is therefore: is it enough? Even if Jesus were
totally and invariably inspired by the Holy Spirit? An adverbial
uniqueness has the advantage in that it avoids the ontological question
altogether and regards Jesus in almost strictly functional terms. It
enables us, as Lampe and others have pointed out almost with relief,
to dispense with the metaphysical structure of Chalcedonian Christology. But the New Testament itself, with Paul and John delineating
the significance of Jesus in more than functional terms and employing
such ontological concepts as Logos, pre-existence, deity, and resurrection with its attendant understanding of the exalted Lord, does not
allow us. Unless one is prepared to regard this concern in the New
Testament as a false direction for Christology and needless involvement in metaphysical difficulties, then one must be prepared to grapple
with the ontological question of the reality of Jesus as Son of God.

In settling for an "adverbial divinity," Lampe is prepared to accept
its inadequacy largely because otherwise one is forced to relinquish
the full and true humanity of our Lord and his whole relation to the
human race. It is of importance to him that Jesus must be understood
as the New Adam, the archetype and originator of the Spirit-possessed
community, enabling and holding out the promise that the church
may be progressively conformed to the image of God revealed in him
and brought into a union with God which is like, but not equal to, his
own. Lampe also argues:

> The finality and authority of Christ does not arise from his
> absolute uniqueness and discontinuity from the rest of man-
> kind but from the Christians' experience that it is through

Christ, by reference to his disclosure of divine judgment and mercy and love as their norm and criterion, that they are able to recognize and evaluate the continuing communication to them of God's self-disclosure through the Spirit—the Spirit that fully possessed Christ and can be called the Spirit of Christ.[39]

Since revelation through him is historically and humanly limited, Lampe argues that there can be no absolute finality and infallible authority to the words and deeds of Jesus. It may well be necessary at times to "appeal from the words of Jesus to the Spirit in Jesus." The fact that Jesus is the archetype of the indwelling of the Spirit in believers and that the more zealous the saint is the more he patterns himself after Jesus does not convince one that this may be asserted simply on the basis of Jesus' identity with the will of God. Lampe would have us believe that Jesus was not noteworthy in all attributes and that therefore there might well be one more nearly perfect than he or one more properly regarded as a paradigm of divine activity than he. Thus one at the most would be able to claim only a "provisional" divinity for Jesus, subject to the possibility of a further stage of excellence. Schleiermacher saw clearly that this is incompatible with the Christian faith because it would in fact express itself as the wish that the human race will one day pass beyond Christ.

Another difficulty is that Spirit-Christology has far-reaching implications for trinitarian theology. Some historical perspectives may help us in this connection. One of the most interesting questions is why the church has worked to retain a doctrine of the Holy Spirit at all. The Holy Spirit does not easily or naturally fit into any of the theological systems of the Christian writers of the first three centuries. The Cappadocian Fathers were the first to find a way of fully integrating the Spirit within their theological thought.[40] In many ways it would have been much easier for the church simply to drop the doctrine of the Holy Spirit, simply to preach a binitarian God, unhampered and uncompromised by the necessity of including this awkward phenomenon, the Holy Spirit.

In the New Testament the binitarian formulas superseded the trinitarian ones. Colossians 1:15-20 and John 1:1-17, by employing the Logos doctrine, have no place for the Spirit, for the Logos is everything that the Spirit is. In the earlier formulas like Romans 1:3-5; Acts 2:31-33, 10:36-41; it is different. The Synoptics depict Jesus as a man of the Spirit, but when he is understood as the incarnation of the Logos, such references to the Spirit no longer apply, because the Logos is what the Spirit is—God in action, expressing himself.

Spirit-Christology held forth until it was replaced by a Logos-Christology and the consequent formulation of the doctrine of the Trinity. It is evident that the early church actually identified the Spirit with the pre-existent Christ. In the Shepherd of Hermas, Hermas appears to say that the man Jesus was rewarded for his faithful work by being raised to the position of the pre-existent Son, who is the Holy Spirit. Justin Martyr in his "Apology" also reflects the transitional, and therefore confused, state of things when he both identifies and also clearly distinguishes between the Spirit and the Logos. In the former instance, he states:

> The Spirit and the Power from God cannot rightly be thought of as anything else than the Word, who is also the First-born of God. . . . So this (Spirit), coming upon the Virgin and overshadowing her, made her pregnant—not by intercourse, but by (divine) power.[41]

Justin seems to accept a place for the Spirit, but he tends to confuse the use of "Spirit" to express the pre-existent nature of Christ with its use as the name of the Third Person in the Godhead.

Reflecting the prevailing notion that spirit is an essential element in deity, that it is the nature or "vehicle" of deity, the early church Fathers referred to the divine Son as being Spirit. G. L. Prestige cites instances in which the effect of the use of the term "spirit" is the same as that produced by the Nicene use of the word *homoousios* and also in which the term designates not the divine nature, but the personally divine character of the divine Son.[42] It would be a mistake, therefore, to put too precise a construction of these vaguely formulated ideas as Wolfson does in asserting that the early church actually identified the Spirit with the pre-existent Christ.[43]

It is clear from the New Testament that the experience of the early church was an experience of God that revealed a threefold pattern. However, the experience of God as Father and as Son and as Holy Spirit were not three sorts of experiences. It was not an experience of

God and then of the Son, but of God in the Son. There is always the danger of understanding Christian experience tritheistically and of saying, for instance, that the Spirit was the Pentecostal experience, the Spirit as distinct from that of the Father or the Son. With Pentecost God was present for the early church in an altogether new way, but it was God that was present.

While there were three *loci*, there were not three experiences. The function of the triadic language was to affirm that there is no Christian experience which does not encounter this Jesus and there is no Christian experience in which God as Spirit does not enter us, enabling us to make response to Jesus. But neither this polar character of the knowledge of God in Jesus Christ nor the experienced Jesus-Spirit duality—the Spirit was after all the Spirit of Jesus Christ—made it appropriate to regard Father, Son, and Spirit as three individuals, three entities, or even three equal and strictly analogous hypostases. The object of trinitarian discussion and formulation was therefore to express the unity of God in the light of the several ways in which God was experienced. Any use of the Trinity which leads away from monotheism is contrary to its original purpose.

On the other hand, while we need to reject the sort of monarchianism which bases the doctrine of the Trinity in three different experiences and refers these back to the Father, Son, and the Holy Spirit as different functions of God, we need also to affirm that the content of the knowledge of God is inseparable from the distinct form of God's self-giving in Christ the Son, and that the illumination as to the significance of Christ is given through the Holy Spirit. The doctrine of the Trinity is important because it makes impossible a Christology that is not wholly theocentric and pneumatological, and a pneumatology which is not genuinely Christocentric and theocentric. To say that the Holy Spirit is the Spirit of Jesus Christ, that the Spirit reveals Christ and that in the Spirit only Christ is revealed, is to assert that the Spirit partakes of the very Godhead itself. This prevents us from speaking of the Spirit as if he were only some vague energy or power, an impersonal divine *afflatus*. On the other hand, it is to affirm that the presence of the Holy Spirit is not an alternative to, but a mode of the presence of the living Christ.

The eschatological nature of the Spirit's work makes it clear that the Spirit works only with respect to and because of the work of the incarnate Christ. In "extending" the work of Christ, the Spirit does not supersede it, nor render it into something that is inconsequential. On the contrary, the Spirit attests the Lordship of Christ. He represents Christ as risen, ascended, and exalted. While Jesus was indwelt by the Spirit during his earthly life, after the resurrection the relationship is such that as Romans 1:4 suggests the Spirit is indispensable to Christ's effective lordship, to his being the Son of God in power. The Spirit is now the personal power of Jesus Christ extended throughout the world. The Spirit was given within the framework of Christ's death and resurrection, as the climax and consummation of Christ's career, and given in order that it may be established in the world.

> The Holy Spirit is God Himself present in us, but present in such a way that his presence takes Jesus Christ out of the remoteness of history and heavenly exaltation and places him in the midst of our concrete life as a living and redeeming reality . . .[44]

Supporters of Spirit-Christology usually argue that the strict trinitarianism of orthodox Christian doctrine has probably led to too sharp a distinction between the Word or Logos and the Holy Spirit. Cyril Richardson, for instance, is of the opinion that the symbols Son and Spirit are really identical and are two ways of speaking of God's relations with us, significant in their own right as illuminating the encounter with God, but not to be distinguished as persons in the Godhead. The Scriptures give us innumerable ways in which God comes to us, and it is therefore "arbitrary" to limit these to three only. The essential problem as Richardson sees it is to express the two modes of God's being, God as he is in himself, and as he is related to the world.[45] It is along this line that it is held that God as Spirit is immanent in the world, and is also transcendent Spirit whom Christ taught us to call Father. Jesus as being totally and uniquely filled with the Spirit and borne along by the Spirit became increasingly aware of his own unique relationship to God as Son and servant, and is thus recognized as the prototype of the Spirit-filled man.

It is this kind of approach that fails to do justice to the eschatological character of the Holy Spirit, and also to the decisiveness and the finality of the Incarnation. There is nothing of the "novelty" of the eschatological era that is represented by the outpouring of the Spirit at Pentecost represented in this view. To argue that the Spirit governs the whole creative process, and animates the creaturely existence of man, so that it is humanity on the level of Spirit that is capable of full and adequate response, thus realizing the potentiality for sonship, is to ignore the triumphant note of the New Testament that the Spirit is a novel gift to the church, consequent upon and complementary to the work of the incarnate Christ. The cry, "Abba! Father!" is not a universal cry, but that created in us by the Spirit of Jesus Christ. To assign to the Spirit that which has been traditionally assigned to the Son or the Word, namely, the activity of God in which man's creaturely existence is grounded, is to confuse the whole nature of the movement as set forth in the Trinity. Richardson reflects this fallacious manner of approach as follows:

> We conclude, therefore, that in the New Testament the Spirit is God's dynamic activity expressing itself in a great variety of ways, objective as well as subjective. Sometimes it is thought of as identical with God's inner being, sometimes it is distinguished from the Father as a heavenly power whereby he operates and comes into relation with his world. Behind such a distinction lies the need to contrast God's beyondness with his relatedness; and as expressive of this second aspect of the paradox of God's being, the Spirit is logically identical with the Logos. In the New Testament, however, the Spirit is not identified with the Christ. . . . But where Christ is seen to be the incarnate Word himself, then the distinction becomes harder to draw; for the Word fulfills precisely the place of the Spirit, as God in his active relation to the world.[46]

In conclusion the poignant implications of our discussion have been well expressed by Lampe:

> A major question arising from this would be what Christians mean when they claim to "encounter Jesus Christ," and to worship Jesus Christ here and now as contemporary. Would they be satisfied to give an account of their experience in different terms from these: that they encounter here and now, or are encountered by, God, the Spirit who was in Jesus,

meeting them with the identical judgment, mercy, forgiveness and love which were at work in Jesus, inspiring them and recreating them according to the pattern of Jesus; and that they worship God, the Spirit who was in Jesus and who now re-presents to them, and makes real and contemporary, Jesus' Lordship? Or would they, rather, assert that in their experience Jesus of Nazareth, the man fully possessed by the Spirit and thus united with God, meets them from the other side of death? Or must Spirit christology after all give way at this point to the concept of incarnation of the pre-existent divine being, the Logos/Son? [47]

Notes

1. Oscar Cullmann, *The Christology of the New Testament* (London, 1959), p. 3.
2. John Knox, *The Humility and Divinity of Christ* (Cambridge, 1967), pp. 56ff.
3. John Knox, *The Death of Christ* (London, 1959), p. 125.
4. Reginald Fuller, *The Foundations of New Testament Christology* (New York: Charles Scribner's Sons, 1965), pp. 247ff.
5. H. R. Mackintosh, *The Doctrine of the Person of Jesus Christ* (Edinburgh, 1920), pp. 294ff.
6. M. F. Wiles, "The Doctrine of Christ in the Patristic Age," in N. Pittenger, ed., *Christ For Us Today* (London, 1968), p. 85.
7. Wolfhart Pannenberg, *Jesus—God and Man* (Philadelphia: The Westminster Press, 1968), pp. 34-35.
8. See, for example, Gregory of Nazianzus, *Oration* XXIX, 20.
9. S. W. Sykes, "Christ and the Diversity of Humanity," *The Modern Churchman*, n.s. Vol. 14 (April, 1971), pp. 182-191.
10. Peter Hodgson, *Jesus—Word and Presence* (Philadelphia: Fortress Press, 1971), pp. 69-70.
11. *Ibid.*, p. 71.
12. Joachim Jeremias, *New Testament Theology*, vol. 1 (London, 1971), pp. 76-85.
13. *Ibid.*, pp. 51ff.
14. James Dunn, "Spirit and the Kingdom," *The Expository Times*, vol. 82 (Nov., 1970), p. 38.
15. Ingo Hermann, *Kyrios und Pneuma* (Munich, 1961), Passim.
16. Hermann, *ibid.*
17. See, for example, Irenaeus, *Adversus omnes Haerses* III. XVII.6 and IV. XXXIV.8 and F. D. Maurice, *The Patriarchs and Lawgivers of the Old Testament* (London, 1878), pp. 66ff.

18. James Dunn, "Jesus—Flesh and Spirit: An Exposition of Romans I.3-4," *Journal of Theological Studies,* n.s. vol. 24 (April, 1973), pp. 54ff.
19. *Ibid.,* p. 59.
20. Joachim Jeremias, *The Prayers of Jesus* (London, 1967), p. 57.
21. Norman Pittenger, *The Holy Spirit* (Philadelphia: United Church Press, 1974), p. 72.
22. H. Wheeler Robinson, *The Christian Experience of the Holy Spirit* (New York: Harper and Brothers, 1952), pp. 83ff.
23. Robert North, *In Search of the Human Jesus* (New York: Corpus Books, 1969), p. 38.
24. *Ibid.,* p. 51.
25. Karl Barth, *Church Dogmatics* (Naperville, Illinois: Allenson, 1958ff.), III/2, pp. 425-432.
26. George Hendry, *The Doctrine of the Holy Spirit* (Philadelphia: The Westminster Press, 1956), p. 107.
27. W. R. Matthews, *The Problem of Christ in the Twentieth Century* (Oxford, 1950), pp. 80f.
28. *Ibid.,* p. 83. In fairness to Matthews it should be noted that he does not hold that the meaning of the Incarnation is exhausted under the category of inspiration.
29. John Hick, "Christology at the Cross Roads," in F. G. Healey, ed., *Prospect for Theology* (London, 1966), p. 152.
30. *Ibid.,* p. 154.
31. Friedrick Schleiermacher, *The Christian Faith,* ed. by H. Mackintosh and J. Stewart (Edinburgh, 1928), pp. 392ff.
32. George Hendry, *The Gospel of the Incarnation* (Philadelphia: The Westminster Press, 1958), chapters 4 and 5.
33. John Hick, "Christology of D. M. Baillie," *Scottish Journal of Theology,* vol. 11 (March, 1958), pp. 1-12.
34. G. W. H. Lampe, "The Holy Spirit and the Person of Christ," in S. W. Sykes and J. P. Clayton, eds., *Christ, Faith and History* (Cambridge, 1972), pp. 118-119.
35. Norman Hook, "A Spirit Christology," *Theology,* vol. 75 (1972), p. 229.
36. W. R. Matthews, *op. cit.,* p. 82.
37. Pittenger, *The Holy Spirit,* p. 72.
38. Lampe, *op. cit.,* p. 124.
39. *Ibid.,* p. 128.
40. See Rusch, Chapt. 3, pp. 76ff.
41. "The First Apology of Justin the Martyr," in Cyril Richardson, ed., *Early Christian Fathers* (Philadelphia: The Westminster Press, 1953), p. 263.
42. G. L. Prestige, *God in Patristic Thought* (London, 1956), pp. 17-21.
43. Harry Austryn Wolfson, *The Philosophy of the Church Fathers,* second ed. rev. (Cambridge: Harvard University Press, 1956), pp. 183-191.

44. Regin Prenter, *Spiritus Creator* (Philadelphia: Muhlenberg Press, 1953), p. 92.
45. Cyril Richardson, *The Doctrine of the Trinity* (New York: Abingdon Press, 1958).
46. *Ibid.,* pp. 53-54.
47. Lampe, *op. cit.,* pp. 129-130.

Harold H. Ditmanson

The Significance of the Doctrine of the Holy Spirit for Contemporary Theology

This topic, "The Significance of the Doctrine of the Holy Spirit for Contemporary Theology," is to be seen within the context of other presentations in this volume which focus upon the biblical foundations and the history of this doctrine, and upon the church and the charismatic movement. In order to avoid undue overlapping, this topic will be delimited by understanding the word "significance" to mean "importance." The following three affirmations about the importance of the doctrine determine the order of this presentation:

First, a new concentration on the doctrine of the Holy Spirit is important for contemporary theology because a church that is continually being reformed needs a far deeper awareness of the fact that renewal is the work of the Spirit;

Second, the deeper awareness that is needed for an appreciation and appropriation of the full scope of the Spirit's renewing activity is hindered by a sterile antithesis between the restricted pneumatology of the theological tradition and the independent pneumatology of the enthusiasts of all ages, from Montanism to Pentecostalism;

Third, we should make an effort to reconceive the doctrine of the Holy Spirit in such a way that this antithesis can be overcome and a sound theological rationale be provided for the renewing work of the Spirit both within and beyond the sphere of the church.

I. Renewal: The Work of the Spirit

Any attempt to provide a panorama of the contemporary theological scene is bound to appear highly subjective and individualistic. The

204

materials and themes are too vast and diverse to permit complete or accurate analysis. Even the attempt to determine dominant trends is very difficult because it depends upon what church, what country, what theologians one holds before one's attention.

A rough description of the contemporary scene would have to include mention of the classical and ongoing themes of theology. It is often said that we have seen the disappearance of the great theological systems which until recently bore the major weight in articulating the faith of the church. Yet, many lesser works have contributed to the deepening and strengthening of long-continued emphases and concerns. George S. Hendry, for example, relates pneumatology to such central and inescapable tenets of both ancient and modern Christianity as Christ, God, the church, the Word, and the human spirit.[1]

But alongside the classical concerns, there are new accents which represent reversals of the dominant trend of the last thirty or forty years. The last generation produced what is often called a "theology of the Word." Karl Barth found it necessary for Christian faith to turn inward upon itself and to ask what is authentically and ultimately its own kind of truth.[2] Roger Hazelton has referred to this kind of theology as "an essay in self-discovery and self-definition."[3] More recent theology has found it imperative to move out into the world again, on the basis of this self-understanding, and to engage with the world in a movement of exploration. In the effort to resume conversations which had been carried on in other centuries, with good or bad results, the theology which displaced "neo-orthodoxy" has concerned itself with a variety of themes and approaches.

It can be said that contemporary theology "does not differ from the theology of the past in any essential way," but that "it is distinguished by a set of problems, and by proposals for their solution, not present in past theological work."[4] It is unavoidable that contemporary theology should be a response offered by Christian believers to the development of the modern world itself, under the influence of the rise of science and technology. In this cultural and intellectual situation, the ancient question of what we mean by God and how, if at all, God can be encountered and understood took on a new form. Closely allied to this question was that of how to speak about revelation in the absence of a "verbally inspired" Bible. Generated by these questions were the problems of the relation of faith to religion, the relation of Christianity to the religions of the world, and the relation of the Christ of faith to the Jesus of history.[5] The relationship of the church to society takes on a new form and urgency as we confront the problems of justice and peace in our political life. The relation of the church to the churches has been a central question for a long time, but has been given a new prominence by the ecumenical leap of Roman Catholicism out of its fortress into our midst. Some say that "one can now, and surely in the future, find and only speak of *Christian* theology, not of Protestant or Roman Catholic theology." [6] Religious ecumenism in the broadest sense has transformed the whole theological scene.

All of these themes, problems, and approaches give forceful expression to the widespread conviction of theologians that divine revelation has to do not only with the religious dimension of human life but with the entire process, personal and social, by which men enter into their humanity. This is to say that theology is becoming "secular." The line between sacred and secular is no longer as sharp or plain as it once seemed to be. Cultural change has tended to blur that line, but some reasons for the situation proceed from "the Christian faith's own understanding of itself as world-responsible and world-redeeming," [7] A secular theology is one that is fundamentally oriented to the secular world which for good or ill largely forms our sense of reality, truth, and value. Such a theology would be in contrast to any theology that moves us away from that world to another sacred realm or authority, a special section of life in which man encounters the divine. Gregory Baum, echoing leading ideas of Karl Rahner, remarks that recent Catholic theology and piety

> tend to think of God not as the supreme being, ruling human history from above, but rather as the transcendent mystery present in human history and alive in the relations between man and man that create the human world. God is looked upon not as the supreme "outsider" who rules from above, but as the supreme "insider" who frees men to create their own future. In this context, man is not regarded as facing two worlds, the earthly world of every day and the divine world toward which he must occasionally turn in his religious moments, but rather as facing a single world, the world of every

day, of which the transcendent mystery is the deepest dimension.[8]

It is obvious that such a secular theology has developed a new understanding of how divine transcendence and immanence are related "to one another. Today theologians wish to say that a vital theology must be fundamentally based on the creative current presence of God in all facets of our life—personal, cultural, and historical. Logically, therefore, the first attribute of God is his immanence—otherwise there is no relation and nothing to say." [9] Thus, God's Word is not only present in the history of Israel and the person of Jesus Christ, as recorded in Scripture and preached by the church. The Word of God is present in a more hidden and provisional way in the whole of human life. Gregory Baum contends that "the Christian who acknowledges God's Word incarnate in Christ should be able to detect this saving Word present as judgment and grace in the history, personal and social, of his generation." [10]

At an earlier point we saw that recent theology is not an effort at self-definition but a movement of exploration. Contemporary theology has for one of its major purposes the rediscovery and repossession, in Christ's name, of vast territories of human culture which have long been lost to the Christian intelligence. In order to achieve this purpose the Christian must come to the world with an affirmative attitude, not in the sense that he approves everything that happens in it but that he ceases to be threatened by it and courageously involves himself in it. Roger Hazelton asks: "What then is theology but probing the meaning of life-in-the-world by the standard of God's word and deed in Jesus Christ?" [11]

The aim of re-exploring and repossessing lost provinces informs all of the new accents and approaches in recent theology. But this aim cannot be realized except in terms of a theological imagination which sees that man's encounter with the divine does not take place in a special section of his life, in his religious moments, but in the entire process, personal and social, by which he comes to be. "In such a context, man would not turn away from what happens every day to face the divinity present elsewhere. It is rather by being in touch with what happens every day and by discerning its deepest dimension that a man opens himself to the divine." [12]

If renewal is indeed the work of the Spirit, then pneumatology is important for contemporary theology because a great deal of the church's weakness and lack of effective leadership in society springs from a failure to invigorate the thought, work, and worship of the church by recovering a deeper and wider vision of the workings of the Spirit. More than a hundred years ago, F. D. Maurice wrote: "I cannot but think that the reformation in our day, which I expect is to be more deep and searching than that of the sixteenth century, will turn upon the Spirit's presence and life." [13]

As we bear witness to our faith both to fellow-believers and to others, we will not be able to help any of them to identify in their own experience a source of truth and power which as yet they have never or only dimly associated with any idea of God, unless we make ourselves sensitive to what is happening in the whole range of human life, to the forces which are shaping history, and to the insights which are prompting intellectual advance, artistic creation, social reconstruction, and moral adventure.

F. A. Cockin writes:

> There is a famous passage in the Book of Wisdom in which it is said that "the Spirit of the Lord has filled the world." That is a truth too easily forgotten and ignored by those who would restrict his working to the sphere of the church. Nor is it enough to say that the study of his working within the church is the only safe clue to the discovery of his working in human life as a whole. Indeed the reverse may be true. [14]

Cockin's complaint points to a central theme of contemporary theology: just as the Word is the principle of particularity and God's self-definition, so the Spirit is the principle of universality and God's self-impartation and diffusion.

II. Ambiguities and Antitheses

The inability of the theological traditions, major and minor, to relate the theology of the Holy Spirit to the quest for renewal is due largely to what Albert Outler calls

> the strange reticence and ambiguity of the traditional teaching about the Spirit, both in the Scriptures and in the church

tradition. Despite heroic hermeneutical efforts by recent exegetes, the biblical notions of pneumatology are far from simple and clear. The creeds of the early church are almost cryptic. . . . The bibliography of important literature in pneumatology is downright skimpy; we have no "classics" here to compare with those in theology proper, in Christology or Christian ethics.[15]

When one considers that the Spirit is mentioned in the classical creeds in one sentence after many sentences about Christ, and when one notes the comparative importance that is popularly attached to the festivals of Christmas and Easter, on the one hand, and to Pentecost, on the other hand, then one may think it is little wonder if the average church member tends to regard the Spirit as an occasional, exceptional, even slightly abnormal element in the faith and life of the church.

Many reasons can be given for the lack of clarity and quantity in this area of theology. Some are theological and have to do with the New Testament presentation of the work of the Spirit as that of leading our attention away from himself to Jesus Christ. Some reasons are historical and have to do with the fact that the Montanists, and other enthusiasts through the centuries, emphasized the presence of the Spirit in such a way that the official churches were frightened and discouraged by what they saw as a "lessening of the ties between the Spirit and the historical Christ, or between the Spirit and the letter of the Scriptures, or between the Spirit and institutional church life." [16] Confronted by threats to the unity of the Godhead, by evasions of the fact of God's incarnation in Jesus Christ, and by a vague and unregulated spiritualism, the church fathers made a definite choice. They used ideas available from such sources as the Wisdom literature, which might have been employed in working out a theology of the Spirit, and applied them to the elaboration and enrichment of the doctrine of the Logos, the Second Person of the Trinity. The major theological tradition has tended to absorb pneumatology into Christology or to subordinate it to the doctrine of the church. The minor theological tradition has tended to give the Spirit an almost independent status which other Christians have found eccentric and even dangerous. In its opposition to liberalism, the dominant systematic and biblical theology of the last generation gave a new emphasis to Christology, largely at the cost of interest in the cosmic, ecclesiastical, historical, and eschatological aspects of the Spirit's working.

According to Hendrikus Berkhof, we live with an unhappy and sterile alternative.

> On the one hand we see the established larger churches which are unwilling to focus their attention on the action of the Holy Spirit; in their midst faith is in danger of becoming something intellectual, traditional, and institutional. On the other hand, we see the rapidly increasing Pentecostal movements, where the reality of the Spirit is often sought in the emotional, individualistic, and extravagant.[17]

The sterile antithesis works itself out into the restricted pneumatology of the major theological tradition and the independent pneumatology of the minor theological tradition. The Roman Catholic, Lutheran, and Reformed types of churchmanship subject the Spirit rather strictly to the historic Christ and see the work of the Spirit as that of applying the salvation accomplished by Christ to mankind. The work of the Spirit is merely instrumental. The Spirit is a second reality alongside Christ, but entirely subordinate to him, serving in the realization of justification and sanctification.

Enthusiasts from the second century Montanists to the Pentecostals of the twentieth century have protested against the lack of spiritual reality in official church life and have done so in the conviction that the Holy Spirit is "an independent reality with his own content." He is not only instrumental to Christ but is also "a center of new actions." His coming to us is a great new event in the series of God's saving acts. He creates a world of his own, "a world of conversion, experience, sanctification; of tongues, prophecy, and miracles; of mission, of upbuilding and guiding the church." [18] Just as the major tradition subordinates the Spirit to Christ and restricts his action to ecclesiastical structures, so the minor tradition fails to do justice to the intimate connection of the Spirit with Christ and runs the risk of letting Christ fade into the background as the historic founder of the church. On the one side there is the threat of institutional objectivity, and on the other the threat of individualistic subjectivity.[19]

An effort should be made to overcome this antithesis by the development of a rationale which will correct the mistakes of both traditions, without losing their central insights. We will give our attention mainly to the harmful effects of the restricted pneumatology of the major tradition. It can be argued that the church can never be truly "led by the Spirit" unless it looks for the workings of God's Spirit outside as well as inside the bounds of the church and

> is continually alive to the fact that the world is God's world, that he is always and everywhere present in creation and the shaping of history, and that signs of that presence are to be discerned, directly or indirectly, in movements which at first sight may often appear to be unrelated to, or even in direct opposition to, the religious setup of the time.[20]

III. The Spirit Within and Beyond the Church

How can the doctrine of the Holy Spirit be reconceived so as to overcome the debilitating historic antithesis and enable Christian people to discern and respond to the renewing work of the Spirit? The shape of an adequate pneumatology for our time rests upon two fundamental propositions. First, when we speak about the Holy Spirit, we must be clear that we are speaking about *God*. Second, when we speak about the work of the Holy Spirit, we must point to the *whole created order* as the field of his operation.

Is it really necessary to say the first thing, that the Holy Spirit is God? It is. Christians resist Unitarianism, but often themselves fall into a kind of tritheism. Since most Christians are not aware of the subtleties of the ancient word "person," they tend to think of Father, Son, and Spirit as three distinct and separate personalities, in the sense that Olson, Johnson, and Nelson are three separate and distinct persons. This leaves them with a mental picture of three kings trying to sit on the same throne, or of a divine committee of three. It is so easy to lapse into tritheism that church members cannot be blamed for doing so.

When tritheism prevails in popular religion, the Father and Son get most attention. The Father is associated with creation, providence, and the last judgment. The Son is associated with atonement and the church. By a division of labor, the Holy Spirit is relegated to third place and is restricted to the function of applying or reproducing the action of the Second Person in the primary areas of ecclesiastical and personal life. There is little in this conception to prevent the individualistic and institutionalistic introversion of the faith. Recognition of this danger can be found in the massive efforts to overcome introversion and to clarify the manner in which the church is "led by the Spirit" into the world that have been put forth by Vatican II in Schema 13 [21] and by the World Council of Churches in the Geneva Report of 1966 on Church and Society.[22]

The Holy Spirit can be seen in proper perspective if we stress three things: the unity, the action, and the grace of God. First, the *unity* of God. The doctrine of the Trinity is meant to affirm, not deny, the oneness of God. In the great movement of Father, Son, Spirit we have to do not with three entities, but with one and the same acting and saving God. The one God is not a bare mathematical unity, but a single reality characterized by inner richness and complexity. Perhaps the nearest we can get is to say that the nature of God is personal, existing and expressing itself in three eternal aspects and activities which together constitute the divine being.

Further emphasis on the unity of God is found in the formula which is known as the canon of trinitarian orthodoxy: "The works of the Trinity, directed outwards from itself, are undivided." This means that there can be no act of God that is not the act of all three persons. If we are to associate creation with the Father, redemption with the Son, and sanctification with the Spirit, it cannot be in any such way as to imply that creation, redemption, and sanctification have separate agents in the three persons of the Godhead.

Classical theology had some reason for identifying, if not subordinating, the Spirit to Christ, for the New Testament itself does identify the Spirit with Christ and says in many passages that the Spirit is the risen Christ himself acting in his congregation, or that the Spirit is Christ's new way of existence and action, his continued presence in another mode. But in responding to this witness, classical theology has tended to make the Spirit's work merely instrumental. Therefore it was natural that dissenters should underscore those themes in the New Testament which suggest that the Spirit's work is far more than instrumental. Hendrikus Berkhof contends that this antithesis can be overcome if we recognize a tension in the New Testament presentation of the relation between Christ and the Spirit.[23]

One line of thought describes Jesus as the *bearer* of the Spirit. This is dominant in the Synoptic Gospels which stress the prophecies that the Spirit will rest on the Messiah, and say that the Lord has anointed Jesus with his Spirit. Here the Spirit has divine priority over Jesus. But, mainly in Paul and John, there is another line of thought. Here Jesus is not so much the bearer as the *sender* of the Spirit. These two pictures are really complementary, for Jesus can be the sender of the Spirit only because he is first the receiver and bearer of the Spirit.[24] It is possible to understand the person and work of Christ as the result and starting-point of the work of the Spirit among men without denying the deity and centrality of Christ. To do this would recover the emphasis on Christ as the bearer of the Spirit, and in so doing would clarify the unity of the divine action and protect us from the danger of tritheism which restricts the Spirit by dividing up the work among the three persons. The conclusion we draw from this stress on the unity of God is this: the Spirit is not the third, and least important, member of a divine committee, with special tasks to perform. Whatever God does, the Spirit does. If God is active in the world at large, that is the work of the Spirit.

This conclusion is strengthened by a consideration of the relation between the Spirit and God's *action*. Recent biblical and theological studies agree in using the formula: "the Holy Spirit is God in action." The etymology of the biblical words for "spirit" provides a basis for saying this. The Hebrew and Greek words refer primarily to wind or storm. The meaning shifts to the movement of air caused by breathing, and from breath it is a short jump to principle of life or vitality. "Spirit" means that God is a living God who grants vitality to his creation. It is worth noting the kind of words that are associated in the New Testament with the Holy Spirit. They are words like life, love, liberty, power, unity, fellowship—all having reference to the practical effects of the presence of God in human life. The rich variety of the Spirit's work is further indicated by such words as vocation, cleansing, regeneration, election, illumination, conversion, justification, and sanctification. All of these terms come to a focus in "life," and are in harmony with the name given to the Spirit in the third article of the Nicene Creed: "I believe in the Holy Spirit, the Lord, the Life-giver." The concept of life goes from the creed back into the New Testament, and beyond that to the Old Testament where the Spirit had come to be regarded as the source of all life, the giver of physical, mental, emotional, artistic, and religious vitality. Perhaps we can say that this *is* the divine mission—to give life, to bestow being, and to exert steady pressure against all the forces that spoil and destroy life.

What God does, the Spirit does. The Spirit is God in action. Now we should relate the Holy Spirit to God's *grace*. Can we say that grace is essentially God's bestowal of his personal presence throughout the entire created order? To be in God's presence is to be alive, in a far deeper sense than the medical. To be in God's presence with and through Jesus Christ is to have "the life which is life indeed" (1 Timothy 6:19). It is to be alive in, through, and with God and one's fellow-creatures. For it is of the very essence of grace to be inclusive. Grace thus reflects the nature of God who is both complete and inclusive. God's being expresses without qualification or exclusiveness whatever is of value anywhere. The existence of God is the affirmation, the ruling in of all significant possibilities. To love God is to affirm the value of his being and also to love the world, and particularly our fellow-creatures because God himself affirms the whole. Thus, "If anyone says, 'I love God' and hates his brother, he is a liar" (1 John 4:20).

Grace or presence goes out from the One to the many, incorporating the parts into the whole. The Spirit is the expansion of the gracious divine presence over the earth. The aim of the movement or mission is incorporation. John Macquarrie insists that

> grace is to be understood as the overcoming of alienation and as the reconciling of what has been thrust apart. . . . We may say that grace is at work wherever that which has become isolated and fragmented is incorporated into a larger whole, but incorporated in personal terms, rather than being merely absorbed or annexed into the whole. . . . The work of grace is to build up wholes out of fragments, to overcome separations, to effect reconciliation.[25]

The line of thought we have followed in making the point that the Holy Spirit is God, fully God, and that in every act of God we have to do with one and the same God, is well summed up by Berkhof: "God is a living, acting God. In creation he transmits his life to a world outside of his being. In the act of creation, he therefore becomes a life-giving Spirit. As Spirit he sustains and develops his created world, he elects and protects Israel, he calls and governs her leaders. In the fullness of time, God himself becomes man. Incarnation is the highest act of his Spirit. From now on the world has the center of God's activity in its midst. Jesus Christ is the acting God present in our world. God's spirit from now on is Christ's spirit, without ceasing to be present in a more general way in the created world. God's action in Christ is his more specific operation, in the light of which his general operation is revealed in its ultimate meaning." [26]

In seeking to recover the biblical breadth of the understanding of the Holy Spirit as God's grace in action, we have emphasized the unity of God. To this should be added the declaration that the whole created order is the field of the Spirit's operation. It is necessary to say this because we have a history of restricting the work of the Spirit to the building of the church and the edifying of the faithful. If we are to think productively about the Spirit, we must go beyond the church and the believer without implying that they are unimportant.

In the early church, theologians pondered the relation of the closer and more intimate presence of God in the church to the widest perspectives of divine activity. Origen used the figure of three concentric circles to illustrate the respective spheres or ranges of activity belonging to the three persons of the Trinity. He confined the range of the Spirit to the "saints" or church members. But the apologists of the second century made no clear distinction between the Logos or Word of God and the Spirit of the pre-existent Christ. They boldly claimed for this Logos-Spirit, not only the inspiration of the Hebrew prophets, but any and all enlightenment of the human mind. One sees in their thinking an effort to extend the sense of the Spirit's work beyond the sphere to which classical theology has confined it.[27]

Hendrikus Berkhof, in his valuable study of the Holy Spirit, makes fascinating use of the image of concentric circles. He suggests that the relation between the Spirit and the whole range of created reality can be understood if one thinks in terms of three circles. After discussing the relation of the Spirit to Christ, to the mission of God, and to the church, Berkhof says that we should try to think of God the Spirit drawing "wider and wider circles around Christ." God in Christ is at the center. The church and the believer are "somewhere in the middle between Christ and the universe, as a partial realization of his goal and as representative of his deeds and purposes toward the world." [28]

Thus, one can think of the work of the Spirit as having a narrower and a wider circumference. Within the narrow circumference, the works of the Spirit are the church and the individual, the "first fruits" of the Spirit in the world. Within the wider circumference, the works of the Spirit are to be seen in the creation, in history, and in the consummation of the world. The works of the Spirit in this wider circumference are all more or less neglected in our traditional theology. It is at this point that Christian vision must be renewed.

Space does not permit any attempt to fill in the details of the work of the Spirit within the narrower circle constituted by the church and the individual. It is enough to say that one would start from God in Christ as life-giving Spirit engaged in a mission of grace. The mission itself is the first and most basic category. Christ points to the mission, the mission points to the church, and the church points to the individual. Thus, mission is not at the disposal of the church. Both mission and church, however, are at the disposal of the Spirit, who is the gracious movement of the One to the many. Perhaps the highest work of the Spirit is his dwelling in the lives of individuals, but this work presupposes the work in the church.

Nor does space permit full discussion of the work of the Spirit within the wider circle of physical creation, human personality, the structures of culture, the events of history, and the ultimate consummation. It is easily recognized, however, that it is in this wider circumference that some exceedingly important and creative theological work is being done today. One is reluctant to mention even a few names without giving an exhaustive bibliography. Yet, even a rather short list would have to include several prominent writers.[29]

Lutherans have traditionally found the idea of the "two kingdoms" to be a useful way of talking about God's action in the world and of distinguishing it from God's action in the gospel and in the church. Christians have always understood that there is a duality in God's activity. Since they also affirm that the one God is a triune God, they have wanted to relate God's action in the world to the Second Person of the Trinity as well as to the First Person. Some theologians tend to understand God's action in both nature and history in relation to the First Article of the Creed. God's "humanizing" action comes under the heading of his providential ordering of events. The action of Jesus Christ is then related to the church and the affirmation of the lordship of Christ becomes doxological and acknowledges the personal lordship of him who has come in Jesus of Nazareth. The tendency of Lutheran thought has been to think of God's action in the world in terms of the Father and of his action in the church in terms of Jesus Christ.

There are other theologies which tend to expand the scope of the lordship of Christ to the point where this idea replaces the doctrine of providence or is synonymous with it. It has been pointed out that Schema 13 of Vatican II, in seeking a theological basis for solidarity with the modern world, uses a generalized christology according to which Christ is in all things and in all men.[30] The incarnation is applied directly to all men in all situations.

Perhaps it is to be expected that talk about "the universal Christ," "the pre-incarnated Christ," and "cosmic christology" will seem vague. Talk about God the Father and Creator and Judge does not seem impossibly vague even though it is projected on a cosmic scale. But when we talk of Jesus Christ, who lived in Galilee and died and rose again in Jerusalem, as "a cosmic presence" we may lose the very concreteness that makes it possible to affirm that he is the criterion of true humanity. Do we really gain anything by talking about the "universal lordship of Christ" that we have not already achieved by talking about the overarching sovereignty of God, especially since for Christian understanding all divine action is concretized and personalized by the affirmation that Jesus Christ is the Second Person of the Trinity? By referring the lordship of Christ to the church, to the gospel, and to faith we at least prevent an unmanageable abstraction of the concept.

Lutherans may be satisfied with the idea of the "two kingdoms" as a way of distinguishing between God's action in the world and his action in the gospel, and may prefer this model to that of the cosmic lordship of Christ. Yet, they must ask whether it is not advisable that deeper study should now be given to ways of thinking about God's action in nature and history in connection with the Third Person of the Trinity. In past centuries, Christians have tended to develop extensive theologies of God the Father and God the Son. They have thought in terms of the polarity between nature and the Creator (the whole corpus of natural theology and the encounter between religion and science), or of the polarity between the soul and the Redeemer (the *ordo salutis,* controversies about grace, the sacraments, synergism-monergism). Have we now come into an age when the important polarity will be that between society and the Spirit?

Many signs can be construed as pointing in this direction. The obvious concentration of many churchmen on human fulfillment in this world, the relative silence about eternity in preaching, the uneasiness most of us feel with isolation or exclusivism of any kind, the desire to cooperate for human betterment with men of other faiths or of none, the growing dialogue between Catholic and Protestant, and between Christian and Jew, the assertion that God is at work everywhere and always, the awareness of the universality and priority of grace and the work of the Holy Spirit outside the confines of the institutional churches, the attempts to develop a theology of secularization, of revolution, of ecology, of technology, or bureaucracy—all these signs point to an era in which Christians will understand the divine action in terms of the Holy Spirit, who is present here and now, active in all realizations of freedom, integrity, compassion, competence, justice, brotherhood, reconciliation, and joy. Churchmen have long said that the doctrine of the Holy Spirit has been the most neglected of all doctrines. Perhaps this doctrine is now forcing itself upon us. Perhaps this aspect of faith has had to wait for an age of universal and instantaneous communication, of fantastic technical mastery over nature, of unlimited human aspirations to come into its own. An era in which Christian witness will increasingly take the form of ethics, in response to the Creator Spirit, may well see a truer balance in Christian faith than has been seen before.

Notes

1. See George S. Hendry, *The Holy Spirit in Christian Theology* (Philadelphia: Westminster, 1956), especially pp. 20 seq.
2. See, for example, Karl Barth, *The Humanity of God,* tr. Thomas and Wieser (London: Collin, 1961), p. 20; *Church Dogmatics* I/2, p. 347 and III/1, p. 3, eds. Bromiley and Torrance (Edinburgh, 1936 seq.).
3. Roger Hazelton, *New Accents in Contemporary Theology* (New York: Harper Brothers, 1960), p. 11.
4. William Nicholls, *The Pelican Guide to Modern Theology* (Harmondsworth: Penguin Books Ltd., 1969), p. 17.
5. *Ibid.,* p. 71.

6. Langdon Gilkey, "Theology in the Seventies," *Theology Today*, Vol. XXVII, No. 3 (October, 1970), p. 293.
7. Hazelton, *op. cit.*, p. 12.
8. Gregory Baum, "Where Is Theology Going?", *Theology Today*, Vol. XXVI, No. 3 (October, 1969), pp. 236-237.
9. Gilkey, *op. cit.*, p. 300.
10. Baum, *op. cit.*, pp. 237-238.
11. Hazelton, *op. cit.*, p. 138.
12. Baum, *op. cit.*, p. 237.
13. Quoted in Alec R. Vidler, *Christian Belief* (New York: Charles Scribner's Sons, 1950), p. 55.
14. F. A. Cockin, *God in Action* (Harmondsworth: Penguin Books Ltd., 1961), pp. 25-26.
15. Albert C. Outler, "The Doctrine of the Holy Spirit," in *New Theology No. 4*, ed. by Martin E. Marty and Dean G. Peerman (New York: The Macmillan Company, 1967), pp. 195-196.
16. Hendrikus Berkof, *The Doctrine of the Holy Spirit* (Richmond: The John Knox Press, 1964), p. 11.
17. *Loc. cit.*
18. *Ibid.*, pp. 23-24.
19. *Ibid.*, p. 24.
20. Cockin, *op. cit.*, p. 121.
21. *Lumen Gentium*, 13.
22. *Christians in the Technical and Social Revolutions of Our Time: World Conference on Church and Society* (Geneva, 1967).
23. Berkhof, *op. cit.*
24. Berkhof, *op. cit.*, pp. 17-18.
25. John Macquarrie, *Three Issues in Ethics* (New York: Harper & Row, 1970), pp. 125, 136.
26. Berkhof, *op. cit.*, pp. 115-116.
27. For further information, see Rusch, pp. 68-74 in this volume.
28. Berkhof, *op. cit.*, p. 94.
29. Ian Barbour, *Myths, Models and Paradigms: A Comparative Study in Science and Religion* (New York: Harper & Row, 1974).
Gregory Baum, *Man Becoming: God in Secular Experience* (New York: Seabury, 1970).
Hendrikus Berkhof, *Christ the Meaning of History* (Atlanta: John Knox, 1966).
John B. Cobb, Jr., *Is It Too Late: A Theology of Ecology* (New York: Bruce Publishing Co., 1971).
Arnold Come, *Human Spirit and Holy Spirit* (Philadelphia: Westminster, 1966).
Peter Fransen, *The New Life of Grace* (New York: Seabury, 1972).
Langdon Gilkey, *Naming the Whirlwind: The Renewal of God-Language* (Indianapolis: Bobbs-Merrill Co., Inc., 1969).

William F. Lynch, *Christ and Prometheus: A New Image of the Secular* (Notre Dame: University of Notre Dame Press, 1970).

John Macquarrie, *God and Secularity* (Philadelphia: Westminster, 1967).

Thomas Oden, *The Intensive Group Experience: The New Pietism* (Philadelphia: Westminster, 1972).

Albert Outler, *Who Trusts in God: Musings on the Meaning of Providence* (London, 1968).

Wolfhart Pannenberg, *What Is Man* (Philadelphia: Fortress Press, 1970).

Karl Rahner, *Spirit in the World* (New York: Seabury, 1968).

Ian T. Ramsey, *Religion and Science: Conflict and Synthesis* (Naperville, Illinois: Allenson, 1964).

Eric C. Rust, *Towards a Theological Understanding of History* (London, 1963).

Aarne Siirala, *Divine Humanness: Toward an Empirical Theology in the Light of the Controversy Between Luther and Erasmus* (Philadelphia: Fortress Press, 1970).

Joseph Sittler, *Nature and Grace* (Philadelphia: Fortress Press, 1972).

Daniel Day Williams, *The Spirit and the Forms of Love* (New York: Harper & Row, 1968).

30. *Lumen Gentium,* 13.

Appendix A

Preface to the Conference Report

The document which follows grew out of a series of four study conferences convened by the Division of Theological Studies of the Lutheran Council in the USA in 1974-76. The study began chiefly as an attempt to reexamine the doctrine of the Holy Spirit biblically, historically, and systematically. The group became increasingly convinced, however, that it had a unique opportunity to say something of value to our churches on a subject of timely importance: the charismatic movement and its relationship to the church today. This report document is an honest, albeit imperfect, accounting of the dialogue on the charismatic movement which took place at all four of the study conferences, but very particularly at the last two, following a procedural decision that any document produced should be dialogical in character.

The conference participants numbering 20-25 pastors and teachers from the three church bodies participating in the Lutheran Council, were aided significantly in their understanding of contemporary charismatic manifestations by the presence and participation of four Lutheran theologians identified with the movement, two of them seminary professors, one a university professor, and one a parish pastor.

Much was clarified in the course of these conversations, though admittedly some problems of communication persisted. The prevailing fraternal spirit, however, allowed differences in theological approach between "charismatics" and "non-charismatics" to be openly aired and constructively addressed.

Careful reading of this document will expose some of the ambiguities and struggles of the group as well as demonstrate an earnest underlying desire to achieve understanding and agreement among the participants.

To stimulate further study and dialogue for which this document might serve as a basis, it will be helpful to cite aspects of the discussion which ensued within the Standing Committee of the Division of Theological Studies as it received the material, reviewed it, and authorized its publication as an appendix to this volume of essays.

Section I was composed by one of the participants, then subjected—as were all sections—to group discussion, reworking, and final editing. (It will be helpful to read it against the background of the essay by Olaf Hansen, "Spirit-Christology: A Way Out of Our Dilemma?".)

Some have criticized this theological segment for imprecise terminology and have questioned portions of its exegetical work. "Spirit-Christology," they say, is an ambiguous construction as presented here. To cite a few examples: "Christ is experienced in the Spirit *and as Spirit*" (p. 224 below); "the Spirit is present *in the cosmic process and historical development not as an immanent, impersonal force, but as dynamic personal reality*" (p. 229). (italics added)

Section II was composed by the four "charismatics" in the group, summing up the concerns which they, desiring to be loyal to their Lutheran theological heritage, wanted to place before the church. Others who participated in this conversation, however, did not agree with the assertion by their "charismatic" brothers (p. 234) that "this special interest in the charismatic phenomenon in Scripture does not lead to a new set of doctrines or new methods of interpreting Scripture." Their judgment is that charismatics *have* developed particular methods of interpretation, or exhibit hermeneutical tendencies which lead, for example, to the strong prominence given hierarchical models for family life and church polity (p. 236). In connection with the assertion (p. 236) that "those involved in the charismatic movement do not fancy that they have some kind of unique experience in virtue of which they are to call the church into judgment," the experience of many in local congregations might justify denial.

The third section is a response by those participants in the group *not* identified with the movement.

Section IV, like Section I, is a product of this whole group. However, at the final meeting, time did not permit thorough discussion of its contents and it became necessary to circulate this segment by mail for final changes and approval. Some have noted here terminological unclarities connected, for example, with the usage of "charismatic movement" and "charismatic renewal" (e.g., pp. 241f.), with the former being more descriptive in nature and the latter tending to render a value judgment.

Clearly this document is not a "last word" on the matter. None of the participants would claim that. While the conferees exhibited a remarkable spirit of openness on all sides, the group did not emerge with unified opinions toward the charismatic movement. One person, for instance, declined to identify with the document solely because of the sentence (p. 242), "The movement should be allowed to develop."

Consideration was given to convening a fifth conference to work through remaining difficulties, but it was generally felt that even then the final word of consensus could not be spoken.

Yet the study process was valuable. The Division of Theological Studies has authorized inclusion of this document in the volume of published essays, not because it represents the consensus of the division (it does not), nor even of all the conference participants (several chose not to have their names attached), but because a useful purpose can be served by sharing it with a wider readership.

The document does represent a very serious attempt to speak a pastoral word to the church today. It has been forged in the context of an open, exceptionally frank exchange. It speaks pastorally to a number of practical concerns. On the one hand, it will point to a yet unfinished task which Lutherans have—to give more attention to the charismatic movement. On the other hand, it will also be of assistance to those members of the charismatic movement who wish to identify themselves as Lutheran.

PAUL D. OPSAHL

Section I:
The Doctrine of the Holy Spirit

There is a marked awareness of and openness to the Holy Spirit in today's church. New spiritual movements are attracting attention to doctrines and life-styles which are sometimes set forth as new and revolutionary. While the church has always affirmed that God, by his Spirit, is present in and manifests himself through believers, some of these movements intimate that either the presence or the power of the Holy Spirit has not been fully realized, individually or collectively.

The church would do well in her response to these movements to restate her doctrine of the Holy Spirit, refurbishing neglected and even forgotten themes in her understanding of the Spirit's activity. This essay is intended to contribute, therefore, to the church's own awareness of her spiritual resources and to an evaluation of contemporary spiritual movements which emphasize the Holy Spirit. For the sake of conciseness, this essay is presented from four perspectives.

A. *Christological Perspective*

1. Christ is experienced in the Spirit and as Spirit. The Spirit is therefore a Christological reality. The Spirit in the church is the same Spirit which was in Christ. To have the Spirit is not to have something other or more than Christ.

The Gospels make clear that from his birth to the resurrection Jesus was possessed by the Spirit in a unique manner in order to be the instrument by which God's kingly rule was to be established. At his baptism the Spirit authenticated his unique sonship and anointed, sealed, and equipped him for his calling as Messiah. At the resurrection Jesus was appointed Son of God in power by the Spirit (Romans 1:4) and "became a life-giving Spirit" (1 Corinthians 15:45).

Since Pentecost, the gift of the Spirit was as "another Counselor" (John 14:16); the Spirit is thus the continuation of the presence of Jesus on earth. He acts in relation to persons in the same way as Jesus had done. This accounts for the persisting identification of the work of the Spirit and Christ in the Epistles of Paul (1 Corinthians 6:11).

2. The Holy Spirit reveals Christ to us through Word and sacrament. "Through these as through means, he (God) gives the Holy Spirit, who works faith when and where he pleases in those who hear the Gospel." (Augsburg Confession, V.) The "distinctive" work of the Spirit is not something apart from or in contrast to Word and sacrament. In revealing Christ, the Spirit enables us to say that Jesus is Lord, gives us the new birth, seals us in Christ, and enables us to

become children of God who call God "Abba" in prayer (John 14:26, 1 Corinthians 12:3, John 3:5, Ephesians 1:13, Romans 8:15-17).

The Spirit guides into the apprehension of the One who is himself the truth, not creating new truths but illuminating the word concerning Christ, and working faith and obedience in him. Nor does the Spirit initiate or foster independent or autonomous revelations. Any teaching or religious experience that does not shed light on Jesus Christ or is not congruous with his life and ministry is not of the Spirit of God.

The work of the Spirit is not merely an identification with the redemption completed by Christ but a daily repetition of Christ's death and resurrection in us. The Spirit is not merely creative of faith, but sustains this faith by reaffirming to us the righteousness of the present and living Christ. But this faith and the new life are not as such the basis of justification. The only basis is the alien righteousness of Christ with which the Spirit acts always to identify us. The righteousness is of Christ who by his death made satisfaction for our sins (Augsburg Confession, IV) and by his resurrection sanctifies, purifies, strengthens, and comforts through the Holy Spirit all believers in Christ (Augsburg Confession, III).

B. *Ecclesiological Perspective*

1. The Spirit through the proclaimed Word is the power of that life which the church has in Christ. The church is therefore a pneumatological reality. The church does not exist of herself, nor of any essence given to her by God, but only in relation to Christ, the head of the body, through the Spirit. The relation of the Spirit to the church affirms her Christological character.

The people of God are inseparable from the Spirit. The Spirit's presence implies a community just as the love of God implies the love of neighbor. The Spirit promises to be among those gathered by Word and sacraments. The community that is created and the institution that is established are subject to the authority of the Spirit.

The church as witness to Christ in Word and sacrament is the locus of the action of the Holy Spirit. "Since in this life many hypocrites and evil persons are mingled with believers" (Augsburg Confession, VIII) it is incumbent upon the church to "test the spirits" (1 John

4:1). For she may be tempted to rely more on spiritual experiences, indeed on faith itself as the best "good work," rather than on Christ alone.

2. The Spirit establishes the Christological character of the church through the witness to Christ. The church comes into existence wherever the witness mediates Christ through the Spirit—whether it be written as in the Bible, spoken as in the sermon, or acted as in the sacraments. Word and sacraments are vehicles of the Spirit's action. The unity formed by preaching and the sacraments is to be safeguarded since without the sacraments the sermon may lose its character of witness to the gospel, as without the sermon the sacraments may be regarded as magical. The establishment and the edification of the church as a community of Christ is the work of the Spirit. The Spirit is "given" to the church and "poured out" upon her so that the community is united to Christ and her members to one another. The Spirit unifies the church in enabling her to live in solidarity with mankind by sacrificial service toward the neighbor and in deepening fellowship in prayer and worship. The twofold direction is not incompatible with the Spirit's working since without prayer and worship the church will be unable to serve the neighbor in a steadfast manner. Holiness is more than the cultivation of moral qualities; it is the depth of relationship with the Lord as the church serves in the world. The church is therefore a genuinely human community in which the Spirit works through human words and acts, fashioning her after the pattern of Christ.

The form of the church is envisaged as one of fellowship developed through the interaction of spiritual gifts and ministries. The body metaphor of 1 Corinthians 12 is that of mutual interdependence, with each gift exercised for the wholeness and well-being of the church. The gifts of the Spirit are not so much qualities as functions according to the listings in Romans 12 and 1 Corinthians 12. Spiritual gifts and functions are not to be concentrated on the few, since there are gifts for all members. The unity of the church given by the Spirit (Ephesians 4:1-6) makes possible the proper functioning of the diversity of the gifts. The charismatic structure provides opportunity for mutual growth and service. There is no aristocracy of those endowed with particular spiritual gifts since the Spirit gives gifts to all. The vision is neither chaos through abuse of more spontaneous gifts, nor stultifying uniformity through the exercise of certain ministries, but order in freedom in the body of Christ.

C. *Eschatological Perspective*

1. The Spirit not only prepares persons for the future Kingdom but also enables the Christian to experience the future Kingdom in the present. As such the Spirit is an eschatological reality. Christians live in the overlap of two ages, the present age and the age to come. In the power of the Spirit they share not only in the struggle against evil and darkness but also in the struggle within their own lives as they await the fulfillment of God's purpose for them. Thus the Christian lives by the Spirit not merely in remembrance of what God has done in Christ but also in expectation of what he will do. The church is what she is by reason of expectation of what God will accomplish in the end.

The Spirit is the down payment *(arrabon)* of the Kingdom. As *arrabon* the Spirit is not only the guarantee of the full inheritance (Ephesians 1:14) but also the beginning of that inheritance. The many descriptive terms for Kingdom,—i.e., justification, salvation, resurrection, redemption, sanctification—reflect the state of being and becoming. This present-future tension is not merely one of sequence, for the Christian *is* already what he or she will become. The Spirit is the Spirit of hope and the assurance that the Christian will grow up into Christ. The Christian is simultaneously righteous and sinner *(simul justus et peccator)*.

2. The Spirit thus sustains the church in the contrast between what her life is and what she is called and intended to be. The wholeness and cleansing which she does not yet possess are nevertheless present in her life, already grasped by hope. It is an "already" by faith and a "not yet" by sight. The church is at once assured of her justification and called to a life of holiness. In Luther's words: "For the forgiveness of sins would not be genuine if it did not spur you on to begin to drive out sin through the indwelling Holy Spirit." (See Regin Prenter, *The Word and the Spirit*, p. 100.) Thus the church lives in repentance in relation to what is really coming-to-be and, therefore, in justification.

"I believe that by my own reason or strength I cannot believe in Jesus Christ, my Lord, or come to him. But the Holy Spirit has called me through the Gospel, enlightened me with his gifts, and sanctified and preserved me in true faith, just as he calls, gathers, enlightens, and sanctifies the whole Christian church on earth and preserves it in union with Jesus Christ in the one true faith" (Small Catechism, Creed, Article III). The Holy Spirit is the sanctifier by whom the Christian is being transformed into the image of Christ (2 Corinthians 3:18), the active subject using the law to awaken to true repentance and the power of the gospel to create faith. Thus the Spirit continually leads the Christian to Christ and away from his own egocentricity and dependence on his own piety.

Increased growth means increased awareness of the disparity between the Christian's pious achievements and the life of Christ. Increased holiness of life means increased knowledge of sin. A theology of the Spirit is a theology of the cross, for the Word and Spirit conform us to Christ. The crucifixion of the sinful nature is repentance; the resurrection of the new nature is hope. The rhythm of growth is being crucified and raised with Christ, an experience not limited merely to something inward, to religious experience. The cross we bear involves the trials, temptations, and sufferings in ordinary earthly existence, just as the resurrection of the new nature also takes place there.

Consistent with the Reformation principle, "the church must always be reformed" *(ecclesia semper reformanda est)*, the Holy Spirit enables us to look in hope to the victory which is to come. We are vividly reminded of the Spirit's continual work—love (Romans 5:5), prayer (Romans 8:36), assurance of sonship (Romans 8:15), and moral transformation (1 Corinthians 6:9-11). But encouraging as these may be, they are merely the signs that point to the fullness of life in the kingdom in which all the gifts of the present will be transformed. The task of the church is to listen for the wind of the Spirit, to discover present manifestations, and to yield to the Spirit's many ways of presence.

D. *Cosmological Perspective*

In the Nicene Creed the Spirit is called "the Lord and Giver of Life." In Scripture "life" includes the idea of Spirit as its source in all its aspects—physical, mental, emotional, religious. At the same time, the Scriptures affirm an indispensable relation between Christ and the activity of the Spirit in the world. Thus we cannot hope easily to separate the activity of the Holy Spirit from that of the human spirit by drawing a sharp line between the natural and the supernatural. The following guidelines may assist in understanding the sovereign, universal, and gracious presence of God in the world.

1. The Spirit is present in the cosmic process and historical development not as an immanent, impersonal force but as dynamic personal reality. The Spirit is operative in the creation as God's providential activity (Genesis 1:2). Yet the Spirit is not identical with the world. Rather the Spirit works in and through the world. The Spirit also gives insight into the events of history by illuminating the minds of the prophets. These events become media of God's self-disclosure to mankind when they are seen as crises of judgment and grace. The Spirit is immanent in the world as the transcendent One who is Creator, Judge, and Redeemer.

2. Just as the Spirit is present in all process without being identical with or lost in process, so the Spirit is present in all times and places but in such a way that certain times and places are of unique significance. Pentecost means that the activity of the Spirit as the bringer of God's Kingdom is not synonymous with the history of man but is tied to the specific proclamation of Jesus as Lord. Since all evil has not yet been eradicated and creation not brought into unity with Christ, the Spirit brings the world into judgment (John 16:8-11). Yet the kingdom will come and the work of the Spirit is to lead the creation to its future (Romans 8:18-25).

3. It is fitting to consider the fulfillment of human life as the work of God which unites creation and redemption. Where the purposes of God are discerned—peace, reconciliation, justice, healing, integrity, openness—there we confess the presence of the Spirit in and with the creativity of humanity. Yet we must not assume that any particular human experience, movement, or achievement can easily be identified as the genuine work of the Spirit to the exclusion of other such movements. The Christian should not be deceived by utopianisms and other false hopes, for the Christian experience of the Spirit brings with it an awareness of the reality of sin and evil. The Spirit of God is not bound. He works when and where and how he pleases.

Section II:
Concerns the Charismatic Movement Among Lutherans Addresses to the Lutheran Church

A. *Introduction*

We live in an age of "consciousness expansion" of all sorts, some good, some bad. Questions about the nature of human existence and the possibility of transcending the normally accepted boundaries of human freedom and potential are being raised. The secular-spiritual milieu has formed the cultural setting in which the charismatic renewal has also occurred. Language of broadening, widening, and deepening of human experience is language common to the charismatic movement and to a host of contemporary humanistic movements. Individuals within the charismatic movement, for example, often testify to a range of phenomena which have widened their spiritual experience beyond their expectations. In searching for the meaning of these experiences they ask for their church's understanding, guidance, and counsel.

The word "charismatic" derives from the Greek word *charismata,* which means "gifts." The root word is *charis,* which is translated "grace." Two definitions for the word "charismatic" are currently in the religious scene.

The fundamental meaning of the word is illustrated in the phrase, "All Christians are charismatic." Here the word means that every Christian has the Holy Spirit, is called to follow Christ, and has the right and duty to manifest the Holy Spirit in his or her life.

Since 1960 the word "charismatic" has taken on a second meaning. It is now used to describe an historical movement which began at that time. A charismatic in this sense is a person who has chosen to identify himself with this movement, though the degree of involvement may vary. Not all Christians are charismatic in this sense. A Christian who is not charismatic in this second sense is not a lesser or a second-class Christian. Christians who are involved in the charismatic movement are not better Christians.

That which has happened to Christians involved in the charismatic movement is described by the Rev. Kilian McDonnell in *Theological and Pastoral Orientations on the Catholic Charismatic Renewal* (Malines, Belgium, May, 1974):

In the first place, this difference is to be found in a difference of awareness, expectation, and openness. By way of example, imagine for the moment that the full spectrum of how the Spirit comes to visibility in a charism extends from A to Z. This example has a built-in limitation. By saying that the Spirit will come to visibility along a spectrum which extends from A to Z, one has already limited the Spirit. Obviously what the Spirit has to offer is the unlimited expanse of his life and the unlimited possibilities of ministries and services. This weakness of the spectrum analogy is clearly recognized, but the analogy is nonetheless helpful in clarifying how early communities differ from contemporary parishes.

It is here supposed that in the section of the spectrum which extends from A to P are such charisms as generosity in giving alms and other acts of mercy (Rom. 12:8) and teaching activities of various kinds. Obviously the charisms in the A to P section of the spectrum are so numerous and varied as to be beyond the possibility of numbering and naming them. The section of the spectrum which extends from P to Z is supposed here to include such charisms as prophecy, gifts of healing, working of miracles, tongues, interpretation.

It is evident that in the life of the early Church the communities expected that the Spirit would manifest himself in ministries and services which might fall within the spectrum which extends from A to P, but they also expected the Spirit to manifest himself in other ministries and services within the section of the spectrum which extends from P to Z. They were aware that prophecy gifts of healing, working of miracles, tongues, and interpretation were real charisms, real possibilities for the life of the Church. The early Christian communities were aware that these gifts were gifts to the Church, they expected that they would be manifested in their communities, they were open to them, and these gifts were in fact operative among them. In this they differ from most contemporary communities. Communities in the Church today are not aware that the charisms in the section of the spectrum which extends from P to Z are possibilities for the life of the Church. These communities do not expect the charisms in this section to be operative and manifest in their midst. To that degree they are not really open to them, and in most communities these charisms are, as a matter of fact, not operative.

For a community to have a limited expectation as to how the Spirit will manifest himself in its midst can profoundly affect the life and experience of that community. . . .

Lutheran charismatics feel they have experienced a resurgence of charismata which have lain dormant in the life of the church for some time. Specific individual experiences suggest to many charismatics that this resurgence might include many of the following expectations:

- The experience and exercise of the charismata described by Paul in 1 Corinthians 12:4-10.
- A deepened appreciation and use of prayer.
- The possibility of an experience of God ("baptism in the Spirit") which makes one's Christian heritage (baptism) come alive in new modalities of Christian growth (sanctification).
- A greater love of the Bible and its message.
- An awareness of a dimension described biblically as "principalities and powers."

Many charismatics would attest to these phenomena and others as experiences of their "new walk" in the Spirit. They are concerned that all Christians see their experiences as ways in which the Spirit of God may work among his people. They are concerned that their church hear their testimony empathetically. In part, they desire a reemergence of the whole range of spiritual gifts in the body of Christ for its edification. It is, in other words, an ecclesiastical concern.

Does the Lutheran heritage have room for this testimony of possibly widened (or deepened, or broadened) spiritual horizons or are there fundamental motifs in the Lutheran tradition which would call some or all of these interpretations of religious experience into question?

B. *The Charismatic Movement and the Lutheran Congregation*

What is the charismatic movement saying to the Lutheran Church about its congregational life, about the quality of its fellowship in the Spirit?

What follows is a positive picture, based on a variety of contacts and firsthand experience. Its purpose is to highlight some of the questions and challenges which the charismatic movement is posing to the Lutheran Church.

1. Worship. The charismatic movement has vitalized worship. For many people, what had been routine has been transformed into a dynamic, joyful, Spirit-given encounter with God and with fellow believers.

The most typical expression has been the prayer meeting. Largely informal and spontaneous, it brings together such elements as singing (the movement has already produced a significant hymnody), testimony, prophecy, teaching, prayers for healing, prayers for personal needs (often accompanied by the laying-on-of-hands), and, of course, much free prayer, including speaking or singing in tongues.

In some Lutheran, Anglican, and Catholic circles the movement has influenced liturgical worship as well. The structure of the service may be opened up to allow for more spontaneous or participatory expressions. For instance, the reading of Scripture may be followed by a time of free prayer; the distribution of communion may be accompanied by words of prophecy; the sermon may make room for response and testimony from the congregation; verbal intercessions may be augmented by direct ministry with laying-on-of-hands.

Where the congregation has two services, one may be opened up for this kind of innovation, while the other retains a more familiar format, for members who prefer a more traditional mode of worship.

The form of charismatic worship is not as important as that which gives rise to it: a sense of *expectancy*. People expect God to speak and act among them—not only through the pastor or the formal worship structure but also through a many-membered, variously gifted body.

What is the state of the prayer life, private and corporate, in our Lutheran congregations? How vital is the worship service in a Lutheran congregation on a typical Sunday morning? Is the church ready to receive this impulse from the charismatic movement for a more vital experience of worship?

2. Bible. Renewed and deepened interest in the Bible is a basic ingredient of ᴛᴇe charismatic movement.

One aspect of this is broad and is not unique to the charismatic movement; it is, nevertheless, an important part of what is going on in the movement. This broad interest is not focused on any particular part of the Bible. At a charismatic prayer meeting or conference virtually any part of the Bible could turn up as subject for the Bible study. Charismatics have a great interest in studying the Bible. They recognize it as authoritative for Christian faith and life and are eager to increase their understanding of it.

Charismatics rarely have to be exhorted to read their Bibles. The raw material of enthusiasm is there. They are eager to be taught. Is the church prepared to capitalize on this readiness? Have the pastors and teachers of the Church made the necessary effort to gain their trust and confidence?

The charismatic movement has a second, more specialized interest in the Bible. Their experience of the Holy Spirit and his gifts is linked to Scripture in a twofold way. On the one hand charismatics find in the Bible the source of their expectations; they expect the gifts and power of the Spirit to be operative in their lives because these things are promised in Scripture. On the other hand, charismatic experience is very much subjected to the tests and norms of Scripture; it is not spiritual experiences and phenomena as such which gain a standing in the charismatic movement but rather that which is understood, on the basis of Scripture, to be a manifestation of the Holy Spirit. (A practical illustration of this would be seen in the suspicion with which charismatics regard such things as healings, visions, or revelations which are associated with the realm of the psychic or occult. Not that charismatics would dismiss the possibility of such phenomena, but they would judge them to be alien and opposed to valid Christian experience.)

This special interest in the charismatic phenomena in Scripture does not lead to a new set of doctrines or new methods of interpreting Scripture. What it does is open up possibilities of understanding the text in new ways. For example, because things like healings, visions, exorcisms, tongue speaking, and interpretation occur in their own midst, charismatics find little difficulty in accepting the biblical record of such happenings as historically accurate. This does not make them "wooden literalists" in their approach to Scripture. Charismatics with background and training in the interpretation of Scripture do not abandon the scholarly study of it when they become charismatic. Rather they bring new kinds of questions to the text.

This may be one of the ways in which the charismatic movement is offering a fresh impetus to biblical studies in the Lutheran Church.

3. Evaluating the Renewal. A careful reading of charismatic literature reveals that already in this young movement there are self-critical and evaluative forces at work. This is even more evident when one participates in charismatic conferences and consultations at the leadership level. Both the theology and practices taking place within the movement come in for searching evaluation. Is the Lutheran Church at this point being challenged to remember her task of "continual self-reformation?"

Beyond the self-critical task, "church" and "renewal movement" can be further helped as they submit to evaluation by one another.

The charismatic movement has brought people into certain kinds of experiences, for example: renewal of prayer, the exercise of certain spiritual gifts such as tongues, prophecy, vision, etc., ecumenical fellowships and communities. These need evaluation from points-of-view outside as well as within the movement. Lutheran charismatics would profit by testing the insights and the experience growing out of the renewal against the historic Lutheran norms of Scripture and the Lutheran Confessions.

Within traditional church structures people likewise are brought into a variety of experiences; for example, disciplined worship and church membership, systematic theological work, catechetical instruction, social involvement. These also need the kind of evaluation which could come from the charismatic movement.

The habits and practices of the church are brought under scrutiny by any renewal movement. Is the church ready to receive this kind of scrutiny from the charismatic movement?

4. Order and Authority. In the charismatic movement a fairly widespread emphasis on order and authority has emerged. Critics fault

charismatics for constructing a whole spirituality around private experience. Yet a cavalier spiritual individualism is challenged in the milieu of the charismatic renewal just as much as it is in the average Lutheran congregation. Charismatics see personal experience and behavior as subject to structures of authority.

In some areas of renewal, this has manifested itself through a serious examination of family and church order. When this examination of family and church order has taken place, hierarchical as opposed to egalitarian or democratic models have prevailed. These charismatics speak easily and without embarrassment of father-led families, elder-led communities.

Charismatics are doing more than theorizing about the structure of Christian community. They are putting their insights to hard tests of practice. They are shaping their understanding of words like "authority," "submission," "headship," "responsibility," "obedience," and "freedom" in the context of radically committed relationships. Where this kind of emphasis has taken root and had a chance to mature, forms of Christian fellowship and community have developed which can be instructive for a greater understanding of inter-personal relationships.

An age widely characterized by an anti-authority mood and militant individualism is being offered some serious counter-proposals by some individuals within the charismatic movement. These proposals speak both to the culture at large and to the church. They run counter to some popular currents of the day.

Is the church open to consider the proposals? Is she prepared to call into question her tendency to identify with that which is fashionable?

Those involved in the charismatic movement do not fancy that they have some kind of unique experience in virtue of which they are to call the church into judgment. Their experience may have helped them formulate the questions, but their right to speak them is the right of any believer to raise questions which the church should consider. And the questions are raised for the healing and upbuilding of the church.

C. *Lutheran Charismatics and the Lutheran Theological Heritage*

Charismatics who explicitly continue to identify themselves as Lutheran are eager to assume the responsibility of witnessing to charismatic experiences in a way consistent with their commitment to the Lutheran theological heritage. Many are convinced that the Lutheran "theology of the cross" is a crucial theological perspective. They desire to share with their Lutheran brothers and sisters, as well as other Christians, a theology of the cross which is ruled and normed by the Holy Scriptures in their evangelical interpretation. They also grieve over a cultural reinterpretation of that theology which appears to secularize the event of the cross by disallowing or discouraging certain manifestations of divine power, thus running the risk of reducing the expression of God's love to manifestations consistent with the limitations imposed by an autonomous humanity.

The biblical witness is replete with testimonies to the power and glory of God in "signs and wonders"—and this, apparently, without detracting from the central permeating perspective of a theology of the cross. Many involved in the charismatic movement give manifold testimony to contemporary "signs and wonders" in their own experience. Lutheran charismatics are concerned with the way in which these biblical data as well as contemporary charismatic experience can be interpreted without denying either the reality of their experience or the principle of the theology of the cross, and they solicit the help of fellow Lutherans in working through this task.

Section III:
Concerns Addressed to Lutheran Charismatics

The Bible speaks of God's saving work in Christ in a variety of ways. Lutherans comprehend this variety in terms of "justification by faith," as the "chief articles of the Christian faith" (Augsburg Confession, IV; Apology IV, 2,3; Formula of Concord, Solid Declaration III, 6). "Nothing in this article can be given up or compromised" [for] "on this article rests all that we teach and practice" (Smalcald Articles II, 1,5 f.). Thus Lutheran theologians are instructed to affirm and present this article clearly in every age. Here the church tests its witness, doctrine, life, and work. Where it is believed and confessed, Lutherans are also free and open to variety, and even prize it as an expression of the true freedom of the gospel which the article on justification affirms. Lutherans will be open to ways in which God the Spirit may be working in the charismatic movement. They will neither condemn nor reject charismatic Lutherans simply because of a variety of worship forms, forms of expression, or even life-styles (Augsburg Confession, VIII). Indeed such a variety may well be a mark of vitality in the church.

The following questions are asked in this spirit.

A. *What Is the Charismatic Experience?*

Lutherans affirm the experience of the gospel as God's unconditional promise of salvation. The comfort for the terrified conscience and the peace of the gospel as the new way of life are at the heart of the Lutheran confessional movement (Augsburg Confession, XX, 15-17). Through the gospel the Holy Spirit "calls, gathers, enlightens, and sanctifies the whole Christian Church on earth and keeps it with Jesus Christ in the one true faith" (Small Catechism, Creed, Article III).

In the Lutheran understanding of experience, so vividly portrayed in Luther himself, all experience, including the experience of faith itself, is ambiguous, and certainty cannot be achieved on the basis of experience alone. Lutherans therefore contrast "the certainty" of faith based on God's faithfulness to his promise with "security" based on faith itself. Lutherans affirm the "certainty" and question the "security." It is not clear to us whether and/or how Lutheran charismatics see charismatic experiences as always related to justification. Since no Christian experience is self-validating as a human experience, all experiences, be they ordinary or extraordinary ("gifts of the Spirit") are ambiguous. What then is the context of charismatic experiences and by what norm are they evaluated? If they are absolute and self-validating, by what principle are they exempted from the ambiguity of all human experience?

In the Lutheran understanding of sanctification and the Christian life this ambiguity is experienced as the simultaneous presence of original sin and the promise of grace. The Spirit is present as our new courage in the ongoing struggle of faith and despair. This experience is validated and normed by the Spirit's working through judgment and forgiveness (law and gospel).

How is this existential ambiguity in the Christian life expressed in the charismatic movement's description of charismatic experiences?

B. How Do Charismatics Use Scripture?

Lutherans cherish the fullness of Scripture as the manifold witness of God's covenant with humanity. The Bible, especially in its prophetic and apostolic witness to Christ, is the rule, norm and touchstone of the Lutheran confessional movement. (Formula of Concord, Epitome, Rule and Norm; Formula of Concord, Solid Declaration, Rule and Norm.) Lutherans use the dictum—Scripture interprets Scripture—as a basic principle of biblical interpretation, thus interpreting specific passages in the light of the whole. The consistent use of responsible and appropriate methods of biblical interpretation has always been an essential mark of Lutheranism. While we appreciate the seriousness with which charismatics approach Scripture, we are unable to see that these principles have been followed by them in instances such as the following:

1. Certain biblical phrases—baptized by the Spirit, "gifts of the Spirit," charismata, speaking in tongues—are sometimes used in ways which are not supported by the broader context, parallels elsewhere, or Scripture as a whole.

2. Certain early Christian practices are sometimes interpreted as preferable, or even normative, for the charismatic movement. This manner of interpretation is in danger of making normative what Scripture regards as descriptive.

3. The tendency is to highlight specific "charismata" (1 Corinthians 12:8-10) as normative for the renewal of the church. Why not also emphasize other charismata (Romans 12:6-21)?

4. The descriptive material in Acts and the writings of Paul are seen as more important for understanding the work of the Holy Spirit and his gifts than the clearly didactic sections of the New Testament.

C. Does the Charismatic Movement Renew the Church?

The church always needs to be renewed by the Holy Spirit. As the body of Christ on earth she participates in the fleshly character of her members while strengthening herself in the promise of forgiveness. The appointed means for her renewal are constantly with her—namely, Word and sacrament. It is in her diligent use of these means that the church is drawn closer to her Lord through the operation of the Holy Spirit. Therefore, what do charismatics understand by the Word of God and how do they understand the relation of the Spirit to the Word?

When charismatics seek the renewal of the church through "charismata" (1 Corinthians 12) they ask for gifts which Lutherans traditionally have not regarded as essential to the nature of the church. Specifically, we ask whether those spiritual gifts as explained in the schema "A-O," of Section II of this document are not more significant for the renewal of the church than the gifts of "P-Z."

Moreover, what is the relation of the exercise of gifts and growth in sanctification? The experience of the Corinthian church indicates that there is no direct correlation between the exercise of gifts, especially those in the "P-Z" category, and the spiritual maturation in commitment and life. This lack of direct correlation underlies the plea of Paul to "seek a more excellent way," that of love (1 Corinthians 13).

The special attention given to the exercise of charismatic gifts has tended to divide charismatic and non-charismatic Christians in the congregations. The charismatic movement occasionally has caused, or has been part of, tensions and divisions in congregations.

D. How Is the Charismatic Movement Related to the Ecumenical Tradition of the Church?

The Lutheran charismatic movement identifies itself with two historical manifestations: certain occurrences in the early church, and the current movement beginning circa 1960. Has not the Holy Spirit renewed the church in many times and places without "P-Z" elements? What is there in the present situation of the church requiring the reappearance of these gifts today? Is the gift of glossolalia included in the promise of the Holy Spirit? And is the church commanded to seek it?

Lutherans are open to charismatic experience in their midst, and they are concerned about the relation of this experience to the ecumenical experience of the church through the ages.

Section IV:

Pastoral Counsel

A. Reconsideration

1. *Reexamination.* Our study of the doctrine of the Holy Spirit has included a reexamination of the biblical roots, theological formulation, historical development, confessional exposition, and contemporary sig-

nificance of Christian belief in God the Holy Spirit. We do not pretend that the topic of pneumatology has been treated in any final way by our study. But we have sought to give this much-neglected doctrine the most reverent and careful attention. The importance of pneumatology has been urged upon us not only by the internal necessities and pressures of theology itself but also by the impact of events and movements within the Christian community and in the larger society.

The charismatic movement is among the events to which the church must respond when she reconsiders the doctrine of the Holy Spirit. In the preceding sections of our study, the origins, characteristics, and claims of the charismatic movement have been described.

2. *Openness.* We believe that openness to new knowledge, new circumstances, and new impulses in both thought and action is an essential part of Christian discipleship. The capacity to learn, to revise, and to build up larger and more inclusive structures of knowledge is a gift of God and therefore a Christian task. Willingness to learn and to receive extends to persons and relationships, as well as to information and skills. Such openness is essential to the ongoing health and periodic renewal of the life of the church.

3. *Evaluation.* We also believe that evaluation of new insights, circumstances, and movements is a normal and necessary part of human thinking and is therefore a necessary task of the church. Openness without discrimination is irresponsible and can lead to consequences just as harmful as those which follow upon a refusal to entertain new knowledge.

4. *Ambiguities.* In our discussions of the theological and practical aspects of the charismatic movement, we have observed the continual interplay of openness and evaluation. The charismatic movement, like all others, participates in the ambiguities of all things human. It contains elements which deserve commendation as well as elements which prompt words of caution.

5. *Renewal.* In acknowledging that God is powerful and endlessly creative in confronting his church with new initiatives, we acknowledge the testimony of Lutheran charismatics to a renewal of their spiritual lives. Many appear to have a new interest in prayer, Bible study, and witnessing. They give more freely of their time and money. They have found new strength and courage and new possibilities of giving and receiving love.

B. *Pastoral Counsel*

1. *Prejudice.* We urge that all Lutherans seek to overcome the prejudices and suspicions which arise when that which is new and unfamiliar appears on the scene. Lutheran charismatics are friends, neighbors, fellow-members of the body of Christ. All Lutherans should relate to them in a positive, pastoral way. Rejection and hostility cannot be the way of wisdom and love. The movement should be allowed to develop.

2. *Responsibility.* We commend the emphasis among Lutheran charismatics on the necessity of sound pastoral guidance. There are many ways in which Christian people are brought into contact with the charismatic renewal. The experience itself may be seen as powerful and unmistakable, but it may be tied to inadequate theology and undisciplined practice. At this point the influence of the clergy is of the greatest importance. They are called upon to shepherd their people in a responsible manner. Their ministry should be characterized neither by rejection nor by tolerance but by an effort to understand, to reassure and to lead the way, through example and advice, toward integration.

3. *Patience.* Lutheran charismatics understand that an atmosphere of acceptance and support, combined with sound pastoral guidance, implies a readiness to move with deliberation and with genuine respect for the convictions of other Lutherans and for the normative Lutheran tradition. When charismatic phenomena cause disagreement in a congregation, precipitous action should be avoided. Arrangements should be made to insure careful discussion of all the issues involved. If both sides in such a dispute rely upon prayer, patience, and an expectation that the Holy Spirit will bring enlightenment and unity, then the way is open to an increased appreciation of the variety of gifts which God has given his church. Lutheran charismatics hope that their testimony will help others to understand more fully how charismatic renewal can aid in building up the life of the church.

4. *Information.* We urge that Lutherans who are not involved in the charismatic movement seek to become informed. This is simply the other side of the avoidance of prejudice and suspicion. Those not involved should have accurate knowledge of what Lutheran charismatics are actually saying and should know what they are disclaiming. Lutheran charismatics say of themselves that they view the charismatic

movement as an effort to recall the church to certain things in its heritage which have been neglected. In a similar manner, the liturgical and social action movements aim at persuading the whole church to take more seriously the concerns felt by minorities within the church. The charismatic movement wants to tell the church that the third article of the Creed—the person, works, and gifts of the Holy Spirit— has been neglected. Lutheran charismatics do not contend that their message is "the whole counsel of God." They see it rather as a specific and valid concern and they wish to see it set in the context of the total Christian proclamation. Their goal is to see a separate "movement" fade out as its message is integrated into the ongoing life of the church.

5. *Concern.* The task of evaluation must include words of caution, concern, and even criticism as well as exhortations to openness, supportiveness, and patience. For the acceptance of a person and of his or her testimony about charismatic renewal does not necessarily imply that one will also accept that person's theological description of his or her experience. Lutheran charismatics have sometimes described their experiences in the categories of classical Pentecostalism. Such terms are often at variance with the central theological insights of the historic Lutheran tradition. Lutheran charismatics urge that an affirmative attitude toward the charismatic renewal does not involve the acceptance of a set of strange doctrines but rather the acceptance of a particular work of the Holy Spirit which is taking place in our time and the appropriation of that work at a new level of experience. Lutherans who are not involved in the "movement" show signs of uneasiness when the classical understandings of the Trinity, baptism, justification, the authority and interpretation of Scripture, the equality of all Christians under God, and the forms and procedures of the church appear to be challenged by some tendencies of the charismatic renewal.

C. Criteria

1. *Scripture.* Lutherans who are not charismatically involved but who affirm that they are "led by the Spirit" and have received his gifts will lay down certain basic criteria for their ongoing interaction with and evaluation of the charismatic movement. The work of evaluation is guided by the desire to maintain fidelity to Scripture and normative Lutheran doctrine based on the Book of Concord and to establish mutual respect and fair play among church members.

2. *Freedom.* In keeping with Paul's admonition, all Lutherans wish to be open to the freedom and glory of that which is new ("Now the Lord is the Spirit, and where the Spirit of the Lord is, there is freedom" (2 Corinthians 3:17). Those who have known God's forgiveness and patience will take a non-condemnatory attitude toward all people and toward their experiences and ideas. Lutherans ought to endorse and practice mutual instruction across the lines of divided opinion. Any form of worship that is genuinely doxological and edifying should be acknowledged. In matters of polity and terminology, we are not tied inflexibly to particular forms; rather, we expect that changing insights and circumstances will bring revision.

3. *Test the Spirits.* We are told to "test the spirits to see whether they are of God" (1 John 4:1). In fact, we are told to "test everything" so that we may "hold fast what is good" (1 Thessalonians 5:21). In the effort to maintain order and balance in dealing with the manifestation of charismatic gifts in the congregation, it is clear that no particular gifts should be either suppressed or given undue emphasis. Scriptural guidelines and wise pastoral direction can enable each gift of the Spirit to bring its distinctive blessing to the body of Christ.

4. *Edification.* No gift or set of gifts should be the ground of boasting, as though there are degrees of spiritual superiority within the church, nor should they be regarded as conditions for salvation. Such gifts should not be allowed to threaten or destroy the unity of the church or of any particular congregation. The gifts of the Spirit are given *to* the church and should be submitted to the church both in order that we might "maintain the unity of the Spirit in the bond of peace" and that we might realize *corporate* growth toward "mature manhood" in Christ (Ephesians 4:1-16).

The liturgical life of the church should be open to revision and improvement. Where charismatic worship experiences are clearly doxological and contribute to the edification of the church, there can be no ground for complaint. But whether a specific form of worship is in fact edifying should be determined by mutual agreement, not by coercion. A wise Christian pastor wrote in the second or third century: "The wish to save, to persuade, and not to coerce, inspired His mission. Coercion is incompatible with God. His mission was an invitation" (*Epistle to Diognetus*, vii).

5. *The Gospel.* The Spirit-given experience of mutual instruction

should focus on the heart of the gospel, namely, the cross of Christ and justification by grace through faith alone (Romans 3:21-28). Other passages of Scripture, the classical doctrines of our faith, and all new insights and experiences in the ongoing life of the church should be understood in the light of this central and abiding truth (Augsburg Confession, IV; Apology, IV, 2; Formula of Concord, Solid Declaration, III, 6). Our confessions allow that considerable diversity in "human traditions and ceremonies" is compatible with this soteriological criterion (Augsburg Confession, VII). The Lutheran tradition has acknowledged that the breadth of the church's life extends to polity, worship, and the moral life, with the understanding that pluriformity in organization is legitimate and necessary, that variety in worship must be consistent with a doxological norm, and that the moral life must be characterized by a commitment to the common good.

D. Summation

Lutheran charismatics assure other Lutherans that they wish to understand and experience charismatic renewal within the framework of our Lutheran heritage and tradition. The words of approval and warning contained in these pages are addressed to the end that the renewal will become so integrated into the total life of the church that it will be neither an isolated segment nor a cause of painful divisions. It is the hope of all Lutherans that a healthy development will mark the course of the charismatic renewal so that its major strengths will bear witness to the presence and power of the Spirit and contribute in a disciplined and coherent way to the vitality of Christian life.

Robert Bertram	*Richard Jensen*
Paul Bretscher	*Theodore Jungkuntz*
Larry Christenson	*Thomas Kraabel*
Harold Ditmanson	*Edgar Krentz*
Karlfried Froehlich	*Gerhard Krodel*
Eric Gritsch	*Paul Opsahl*
Olaf Hansen	*William Rusch*
Mark Hillmer	*Edwin Schick*
Bernard Holm	*Robert Schultz*
Horace Hummel	*Carl Volz*

Appendix B

The American Lutheran Church and Neo-Pentecostalism*
An Interpretive Resource for Pastors

The theological convictions expressed in this document have not been given official status by The American Lutheran Church in convention or by the Church Council. They were written in response to requests from the district presidents for assistance in dealing with the neo-Pentecostal phenomenon, and with encouragement from the president's cabinet.

The constitution of The American Lutheran Church requires the Division for Theological Education and Ministry to "develop and disseminate to this church information concerning significant developments in theological research and trends" (12.72.17), and to "develop resources to assist the pastors in their preaching, teaching, and other pastoral responsibilities" (12.72.18). Consonant with these directives, we offer this material for the purpose of building up the Body of Christ.

Walter R. Wietzke, Director
Division for Theological Education and Ministry
The American Lutheran Church

Some Things Neo-Pentecostals Emphasize That Are Important for The American Lutheran Church:

1. *Charismata*, i.e., the gifts of the Spirit. To call attention to the gracious gifts of God is no disfavor to the church. It is consistent with

---

* This document was issued in 1975 by the Division for Theological Education and Ministry of the American Lutheran Church. [Editor]

biblical testimony and acknowledges that the church, classically, has always been a charismatic community. "And his gifts were that some should be apostles, some prophets, some evangelists, some pastors and teachers, to equip the saints for the work of ministry, for building up the body of Christ" (Ephesians 4:11-12).

2. *Freedom in worship.* The easy, uninhibited style of worship observed in neo-Pentecostalism offers a constructive opportunity to review both the content and method of staid liturgical forms. In the Reformation tradition, the style of worship has never been canonized, and we would both plead for toleration as persons worship more freely and ask that the office for parish worship within the Division for Life and Mission in the Congregation make an earnest effort to see what facets might gainfully be used in the development of new worship forms.

3. *The reality of God and the reality of the faith relationship.* It is of ultimate significance that we understand Christianity not as our possession of religious truths but as the Lord's possession of us, and that we stand before him in a direct faith relationship. We have not always been aware of the subtle shift in our attention from God's person to the church's doctrine.

4. *Insistence on prayer.* A hallmark of neo-Pentecostalism is a rigorous life of prayer. Most surely this points to a neglected portion of the church's life and calls us to a renewed exercise of that which characterized the life of our Lord and the apostolic church, viz., prayer.

5. *An emphasis on the ministry of healing.* While we should be very cautious about trying to manipulate God for our purposes, we should accept in good grace the challenge of neo-Pentecostal friends to review and reconsider the whole ministry of healing.

Some Things The American Lutheran Church Emphasizes That Are Important for Its Neo-Pentecostals:

1. *A reminder of the historical context.* No one concerned with the Spirit can ignore the relationship of Spirit to Word and Spirit and Word to church. What happened to Montanism or what happened to Luther in his struggle with Münzer is not unimportant, but it is even more important that we explore the meaning of the nineteenth and twentieth century contexts in which the neo-Pentecostal phenomenon

arises.[1] The strength and weakness of movements in that time must be dealt with most incisively.

2. Theological insights.

a) *The unity of God.* Christians have always struggled with the definition of God. Their descriptive efforts have sought to keep a creative tension between divinity and humanity, immanence and transcendence, mutability and immutability, wrath and love. Such language, however, is never totally adequate.

Our doctrine of the Trinity, e.g., has inherent in it the possibility of understanding God tritheistically. Individuals continue to deduce that Father, Son, and Holy Spirit are disjointed entities, that is, three Gods. On the contrary, the Athanasian Creed insists that ". . . we worship one God in three persons and three persons in one God without confusing the persons or dividing the divine substance . . . . (it further insists that) there are not three who are almighty but there is one who is almighty . . . . not three Gods but one God . . . . not three Lords but one Lord . . . (and) one Holy Spirit and not three Holy Spirits."

Nonetheless, some deal with God in tripartite or bipartite fashion. There is truth in the contention that "We sometimes divide Christ from God," and that "Lutherans are dominated by a Second Article mentality."

It must also be recognized that we can be dominated by a First Article mentality or by a Third Article mentality. If, for example, we think of the Holy Spirit as a third entity, separate from Father and Son, we again distort the unity of God, and must be called back to that which the church has repeatedly affirmed, one God in Trinity, and Trinity in unity.

b) *Baptism.* St. Paul's great statement (Ephesians 4:4ff.) also points us to unity in other areas. One of vital importance is baptism. He says, "There is one body and one Spirit . . . . one Lord, one faith, *one baptism,* one God and Father of us all, who is above all and through all and in all." Baptism is the sacramental act of God whereby a person is incorporated into the community of faith. To be "baptized in the Spirit" or "with the Holy Spirit" (Luke 3:16) means, in rudimentary terms, to be brought into the life *(zoa)* of God—but that is not a second or superior kind of baptism.

To understand water baptism as having only symbolic significance,

and spirit baptism as having actual (i.e., real, experiential) significance, is to revert to Manichean categories.[2] It is to deny the unity in
baptism and the unity in God who gives it.

c) *Church.* Another great concern, inspired by Christ and Paul, is
the unity of the church. The word the apostle uses is *henotes,* meaning "oneness."

The church consists of those who know and believe "one hope . . .
one Lord, one faith, one baptism, one God and Father of us all." At a
time when men ponder the significance of denominations and live
with the illusion that unity is an achievement of men, the New Testament reminds us that it is an act of God. Unity is something already
created by God in Jesus Christ. We either witness to it or detract
from it, but we cannot create it. It does not come by everyone being
in the same ecclesiastical organization, by having the same conviction
regarding every statement from the Bible (or the confessions of the
church), or by having the same emotional experience and response.

Unity is realized when we know *(oidō)* the one Lord, faith, baptism,
etc. But the unity of the church is a unity *in* it, not outside of it or
against it. It would be the grossest of distortions to say, "There is
Egypt and Israel. Israel is the 'spirit people,' Egypt is the church.
We've got to get Israel out of Egypt." Such "spiritual" elitism is foreign
to the New Testament.

c) *The acknowledgment of faith's intellectual, moral, and mystical
content.* These components should neither be absolutized nor eliminated. The challenge is to keep them in dynamic tension. Neo-Pentecostals should be dealt with no differently than those whose emphases
incline toward the rational or moral. While the church must confess to
the charge of "intellectual preoccupation," it must also insist that faith
(i.e., trust, response of the whole man to God) not become supersti-
tion, and that it is not the irrational part of man that connects him
with God.

3. *Ecclesiastical authority.* Within our church, authority is not by
episcopal right. Our synodical confraternity signifies that we freely
enter into relationships with other congregations and voluntarily give
a portion of our freedom to the church at large. Our pastors, district
presidents, and congregations are a support system. That doesn't mean
giving approbation to everything; it does mean treatment as peers and
allies, not inferiors and enemies.

Some Things Neo-Pentecostal Lutherans and Traditional Lutherans
Should Be Conscious of in the Pursuit of Working Relationships:

1. *Allowance for diversity.* There never was a time when the church was truly monolithic. Heterogeneity contributes to strength.

2. *The New Testament preeminence of love.* Passion for truth notwithstanding, the mark of the Master is love. "By this all men will know that you are my disciples, if you have love for one another" (John 13:35).

3. *Perspective on essentials.* Peripheral matters, e.g., speaking in tongues, should not be made essential by neo-Pentecostals as a sign of superior spirituality nor should traditionalists make glossolalia the chief target of their reactions.

4. *Subtle temptations to pride.* Some may say, "We have the pure doctrine." Others may say, "We have the true experience." Both can become occasions of pride.

5. *The necessity of honoring canonical and noncanonical documents.* We are people rooted in the biblical tradition, people with an evangelical, confessional history. Therefore we must take seriously:

> The Holy Scriptures
>
> The Lutheran Confessions
>
> The Constitution of The American Lutheran Church

6. *The avoidance of scandal to Christ by unwarranted division and/or divorce within congregations and homes.*

7. *Commonality of faith in the same Lord under whom all spirits are tested.*

8. *Awareness that growth comes through challenge.* We are in a circumstance where, together, we can existentially reflect anew on the relationship between Spirit, Word, and community.

Notes

1. Friedrich Schleiermacher, who stands at the fountainhead of this period, said, "You reject the dogmas and propositions of religion. Very well. Reject them. They are not in any case the essence of religion itself. Religion does not need them. It is only a human reflection on the content of our religious feelings which requires anything of the kind. The religion to which I will lead you demands no blind faith, no negation of physics and psychology; it is wholly natural and yet again, as the immediate product of the universe, it is full of grace. . . . The nature of religion

has been misapprehended. It is not a science, it is not morality, its seat is not in reason, conscience or will. Since religion is the direct touch of the soul with the Divine, its home, its seat can be found nowhere but in feeling."

Addresses on Religion to Its Cultured Despisers, as quoted in *Types of Modern Theology,* H. R. Mackintosh, pp. 43-44, a summation of Schleiermacher's view of religion. In America, "religion as emotion" was popularized by Liebman, Peale, and Fosdick. Now, at a time in human history when outer absolutes have been eroded, men have sought certainty by "turning inward." Discerning pastors and congregations will explore all the ramifications of this.

2. Manicheism suggested two orders of reality: the material, which is base and confining, and the spiritual which is above, apart from, and superior to that which belongs to earthly experience.

The Charismatic Movement in the Lutheran Church in America

A Pastoral Perspective*

In the decade past, increasing numbers of people in the Lutheran church have had religious experiences of the kind formerly associated with Pentecostalist groups. It has happened among Lutherans in Europe as well as in North America. It has happened in the Episcopal church, the Presbyterian churches, and the Roman Catholic church. However the phenomenon is labeled, the life in the Spirit is being experienced by many in a new and different way; their lives have been manifestly changed by their experience.

These phenomena in the so-called mainline Western churches come at a time when Pentecostalism is sweeping Asia, Africa, and South America. Walter Hollenweger, a prominent researcher of the Pentecostal movement, predicts that the day is not far off when Christians with a Pentecostalist orientation will outnumber those of the historic churches of the West.

It is not the purpose of this paper to comment upon the spread of Pentecostalism in other continents nor is it to study the Pentecostal churches. We shall be focusing on "Pentecostal manifestations" in the Lutheran Church in America and, to some extent, in other mainline churches. In so doing, we hope to offer a pastoral perspective which will be useful both to church leaders and to those involved in the

---

* This document was approved by the Division for Parish Services for report to the Seventh Biennial Convention of the Lutheran Church in America in 1974. It (was) "submitted to the convention as information, with the intention that it be used by the Division to provide guidance for congregations and other church-wide agencies." [Editor]

growing movement. Much work remains to be done; this statement is only a first step.

Pentecostal or Charismatic?

The name one calls this movement is significant. Those American groups called Pentecostalist trace their origins to a revival in 1906 held in the Azusa Street Mission, Los Angeles. Prominent among the many groups are the Assemblies of God, the Churches of God, the Pentecostal Holiness church and the Full Gospel Business Men's Fellowship International. The Full Gospel Business Men have often bridged the gap between the Pentecostalist groups and the mainline churches. The label *Pentecostal* emphasizes what for many outside the movement is the typical characteristic of the adherents: the gift of tongues. Most Pentecostalist groups teach a two-stage way of salvation. The first step is conversion or regeneration; the second and distinct step is baptism in the Holy Spirit evidenced by speaking in tongues. This teaching allows Pentecostalists to distinguish between two groups of Christians: those who have received the baptism in the Holy Spirit and those who have not.

Recently it has become common to distinguish between the Pentecostalist groups themselves and the later neo-pentecostals—those who share the experience called baptism in the Holy Spirit but are members of the mainline churches. It is this latter group which is our major concern. Roman Catholics have preferred the designation *charismatic* rather than neo-pentecostal for the movement among them. Lutherans also prefer that designation because neo-pentecostal suggests a closer tie with the theology of the Pentecostalist groups and with certain Pentecostalist stereotypes than they wish to have. For this reason we shall refer to the charismatic movement among Lutherans.

The charismatic movement in the mainline churches is usually traced back to the emergence in 1960 of speaking in tongues at St. Mark's Episcopal Church, Van Nuys, California. It should not, however, be seen as without precedent in the Lutheran church. It has points of contact with earlier evangelistic forms of pietism and, perhaps, with an even earlier type of mysticism.

Some have objected to the designation *charismatic* claiming that, on the grounds of Lutheran theology, all Christians are charismatics (*charismatic* derives from the Greek word *charisma* which is used in the New Testament for the gifts [graces] of the Holy Spirit). While that is true, one may still agree to a somewhat arbitrary use of the term for the sake of convenience. A better term than neo-pentecostal is needed; charismatic is in common use. *To avoid misunderstanding what follows, it is important to distinguish between Pentecostalist and charismatics.*

Renewal

Charismatics understand themselves as a power for renewal. Their purpose is to revitalize Christian community and thus to revitalize the mission of the church. That goal is similar to goals of other renewal enterprises—the ecumenical and liturgical movements for example. Since it has implications both for Christian fellowship across denominational lines and, at least potentially, for the quality of congregational worship, the charismatic movement could become an ally of the ecumenical and liturgical movements.

Among the various thrusts for renewal, however, the charismatic movement is unique in being overwhelmingly a lay movement. (This is true of the charismatic movement as a whole. In the Lutheran churches, interestingly, the leadership has tended to rest with the clergy.) Therefore, its proponents have often had little or no professional training in biblical or systematic theology and may not articulate their experience in language harmonious with the confessional stance of the church.

It is important to distinguish between the experience itself and the verbalization of it. It is one thing to question the validity of the description; it is quite another to question the validity of the experience. The most important contribution for pastors and theologians is helping charismatics understand their experience in harmony with the Scriptures and the confessional position of the Lutheran church. Not enough has been done in this area.

The charismatic movement among Lutherans has grown and matured since its earliest manifestations. Its leaders have begun to take seriously the task of bringing it theologically and exegetically into harmony with Lutheran tradition. This work has the potential of giving the charismatics a new solidarity and the Lutheran church new zeal. Because of it, one ought not judge the present movement by earlier expressions of it.

Baptism in the Holy Spirit

No Christian is without gifts of the Holy Spirit—that we have affirmed. The Lutheran church teaches unequivocally that one receives the Holy Spirit in one's baptism (Augsburg Confession 2; Apology 2; *Large Catechism*, Part 4). That is why Lutheran theologians have problems with the usual answer to "Who is a charismatic?" which is "A charismatic is one who has received the baptism in the Holy Spirit." Such an answer seems to imply that baptism in the Holy Spirit is something separate from baptism with water and that those baptized with water have not yet received the Holy Spirit.

The Pentecostalist two-baptism concept corresponds to the two-stage way of salvation taught by most groups. It is the source of the condescending attitude Christians sometimes experience from their "Spirit baptized" colleagues. Pentecostalist theology implies that persons who have not received the baptism in the Holy Spirit are less fortunate members of the Christian community.

The Pentecostalist teaching of a separate baptism in the Holy Spirit has a long and complex history. It has points of contact with such New Testament passages as Luke 3:16 (and parallels) and Acts 10:44-48. Given the lineage of the Pentecostalist groups and their general lack of theological and biblical scholarship, it is not surprising that they should use *baptism in the Holy Spirit* to describe their experience.

Since Lutheran charismatics have often had their initial experience in company with Pentecostals, and since the Lutheran church has not given them much guidance, it is not surprising if they have accepted the Pentecostal explanation. The charismatic movement among Lutherans has been marked from the beginning by little theological engagement. Charismatics have therefore often taken a theological stance in conflict with the teaching of the Lutheran church. On the one hand, they cannot deny their experience, but on the other they are caught between irreconcilable theologies, each claiming biblical support.

Because of this conflict, other expressions have been suggested for baptism in the Holy Spirit. Larry Christenson, a Lutheran charismatic leader, points out that St. Peter used four terms in Acts 10 and 11:

"received the Holy Spirit, the Holy Spirit fell on them, baptizing with the Holy Spirit, the same gift." [1] To these should be added "filled with" (Acts 2:4, 7:55, 9:17), "poured out" (Acts 10:45), and "came on" (Acts 19:6). Kilian McDonnell, a Roman Catholic researcher of the movement, lists extra-biblical alternatives: "release of the Spirit, renewal of the sacraments of initiation, a release of the power to witness to the faith, actualization of gifts already received in potency, manifestation of baptism whereby the hidden grace given in baptism breaks through into conscious experience, revivescence of the sacraments of initiation." [2]

What is this charismatic experience usually called the baptism in the Holy Spirit? It is indicated in the alternative terms listed above; it is described below:

> . . . The Holy Spirit comes to him in a way that he can know it. As a result of this coming of the Holy Spirit, he experiences a new contact with God . . . the Holy Spirit not only comes to that person in a new way, but he also makes a change in him. His life is different because his relationship with God has been changed. . . . Being baptized in the Spirit is an introduction to the life of the Spirit. [3]

> The essence of a charismatic experience is the experience of encountering Jesus Christ as the Head of His Body, which is the church. [4]

> . . . The most commonly accepted interpretation [among Roman Catholics] of that ambiguous phrase "baptism in the Holy Spirit" is that it represents a saying yes, with expanded expectations, to what was received in Christian initiation. [5]

> The baptism in the Holy Spirit . . . is simply the full reception of the Holy Spirit. [6]

In the Pentecostalist tradition, baptism in the Holy Spirit, then, is an experience marking the threshold into a life of heightened awareness of God's Spirit in one's life and a consequent joy and zeal not present before. It may be dramatic and intense; more often it is a growing awareness. (Lutherans should note the similarity between this description of awareness of the presence of the Holy Spirit in one's life with that which would be offered by a Lutheran pietist in answer to questions about conversion.)

The best New Testament scholarship and the mainline traditions of theology insist that such an experience of the Holy Spirit is always to be understood in relationship with the sacrament of Holy Baptism. Scholars insist that passages such as Luke 3:16 and Acts 10:44-48 be taken in the context of the whole New Testament witness.

The Lutheran zeal to preserve sacramental objectivity (baptism is God's act) may have led to an undue focusing on the rite itself with a corresponding neglect of the paradigmatic function of baptism (a pattern for the Christian life). " . . . The old Adam . . . should be drowned by *daily* sorrow and repentance and be put to death, and that the new man should come forth *daily* and rise up . . ." *(Small Catechism,* Part IV, 4.) It has certainly produced a mistrust of emotional or highly experiential manifestations of the life in the Spirit. Where this truncation of the vitality and scope of Luther's own teaching on baptism is encountered, the proper remedy is not a Pentecostalist separation of water and Spirit. It is rather to restore the fulness and reality of a total New Testament theology and practice of baptism (see Guideline 7 below).

For baptism to accomplish its function in God's economy there must be a response of will and style of life. This response is a lifelong task; it is not a mechanical reaction. God's act (traditionally called justification) and the life it initiates (traditionally called sanctification) must be separated for purposes of theological clarity, but they are not so neatly separable in a person's life. The Lutheran emphasis on the doctrine of justification can lead to a neglect of the doctrine of sanctification. The charismatic emphasis on the power of the Holy Spirit in the whole Christian life can challenge what has often become a severely minimalistic view of baptism among Lutherans.

Lutheran theologians are encouraged to study this area carefully to provide help for charismatics in understanding their experience in consonance with a full Lutheran concept of baptism. We must neither cast doubt on the authenticity of "baptism in the Holy Spirit" nor accept a Pentecostalist explanation of it.

Glossolalia

Glossolalia is the biblical term for speaking in/with tongues. Most classical Pentecostalists insist that one must speak in tongues as a validation of having received the baptism in the Holy Spirit. Outsiders are prone to spotlight this activity seeing it as the center of the charismatic movement; insiders tend to have a more balanced, less exotic view. LCA pastors who are intimately associated with the charismatic movement state that glossolalia should not be overemphasized. A balanced view is reflected in this statement:

> Many outside of the renewal attribute a centrality to tongues which is not reflected in most sectors of the renewal. On the other hand, persons involved in the renewal rightly point out that the charism was quite common in the New Testament communities. Those who stand outside the renewal and attempt to evaluate the charism of tongues will fail if it is not understood in the framework of prayer. It is essentially a prayer gift enabling many using it to pray at a deeper level.[7]

Glossolalia has a prominent place in the account of Pentecost (Acts 2:4). It is one of the charismata or gifts of the Spirit (1 Corinthians 12:10). It results from Peter's preaching in the household of Cornelius where it follows the falling-upon-them of the Holy Spirit and precedes baptism (Acts 10:46), and, in Ephesus, from the laying-on-of-hands and the coming of the Holy Spirit following baptism (Acts 19:6). It is part of the problem in Corinth (1 Corinthians 12:30; 14).

Debate among scholars on how the speaking in tongues by the apostles on Pentecost is to be understood and how that relates to glossolalia as reported elsewhere in Acts and 1 Corinthians is of little immediate concern here, because in the charismatic movement, glossolalia is primarily used in personal prayer and in prayer group meetings. It seldom, if ever, becomes part of the liturgical worship of the entire congregation. If it does, St. Paul's words about interpretation should apply (1 Corinthians 14:26-28).

Praying in tongues is supra-rational prayer (1 Corinthians 14:14), prayer which is expressive of depths of being words cannot express (Romans 8.26). "It seems as though every gift and every blessing I have already experienced in the Lord is refreshed and revitalized.[8] Once the gift of tongues has been received, a person can exercise it at will as one can engage in other forms of prayer at will. Glossolalia is not confined to speaking; there is also singing in tongues (1 Corinthians 14:15).

To the Christian conditioned by the piety of mainline churches, glossolalia may seem threatening because it is supra-rational and may be emotional. He may, therefore, try to discredit it by noting St. Paul's evaluation of it in Corinth or even by linking it with psychological instability. St. Paul does put glossolalia at the end of the list (1 Corinthians 12:26), but he still encourages its use (1 Corinthians 14:5). The temptation to generalize on the basis of the Corinthian situation must be resisted; St. Paul is speaking against the abuse of the gift. The remedy, as Larry Christenson reminds us, "is not disuse but proper use." [9] As for psychological instability:

> The glossolalists represented a cross-section of all the usual personality types; they employed the full range of personality mechanisms and character defenses. This came to us as a surprise.[10]

There is nothing specifically Christian or even religious about speaking in tongues. It is a phenomenon which has been characteristic of various kinds of behavior. John Kildahl, a Lutheran psychotherapist, maintains that it is learned either directly or indirectly, and that glossolalists tend to be submissive to authority figures (their models for glossolalia). He states that if one can be hypnotized, under proper conditions one is able to speak in tongues—the two phenomena root in similar relationships between subject and authority figure. He notes that a situation of personal stress or crisis generally precipitates the charismatic experience. This latter is testified to by Lutheran respondents.

(Kildahl's work is cited because it is known among Lutherans. It does not, however, represent a consensus of psychological studies. Vivier, for example, found that Pentecostalists scored *lower* in suggestibility [the issue in the hypnosis comparison] than the non-Pentecostalist control group.[11] Vivier appears in Kildahl's bibliography, though his work is not mentioned within the book.)

Whether or not one agrees with each of these psychological observations is, for our purposes, beside the point. All religious behavior is open to psychological analysis, and such studies should be pursued.

But their proper function should be kept clear. For example, to demonstrate that certain types of people are attracted to the ordained ministry does not preclude the theological concept of divine call. Or, the fact that most of the liturgical acts which shape Christian worship can be found in other religions as well does not make them inauthentic for Christians.

The crucial question is how glossolalia is used, in what spirit and to what end. Addressing the situation in Corinth, St. Paul saw the possibility of the wrong use of tongues. This possibility puts a burden upon the church to guide and evaluate the use of the gift.

If one's use of glossolalia enriches and deepens prayer, if it leads to greater joy and service, if it strengthens one's sense of fellowship with God and the Christian community—if it is an expression of *agape* (love, charity), it is beneficial and should not be condemned. If one's use of glossolalia is divisive, if it leads to arrogance, if it makes one judgmental of fellow Christians, if it results in histrionic display—if it lacks agape, it is detrimental and should be condemned. Kilian McDonnell has observed:

> A certain healthy skepticism with regard to religious experience is very much in place . . . but a deep fear of religious experience, with the consequent complete rejection of all religious experience as hysteria can lead to another kind of religious superficiality.[12]

"The tree is known by its fruit," said Jesus. St. Paul gave us the standard: "If I speak in the tongues of men and of angels, but have not love, I am a noisy gong or a clanging cymbal" (1 Corinthians 13:1).

It is important to emphasize that the evaluation of the gifts must also exhibit love and a true understanding of the Christian fellowship. Where glossolalia has polarized congregations, the fault does not necessarily lie only with the charismatics. Kildahl observes:

> Since many of the churchgoers we interviewed thought of their institution as a private club, new opinion and new practice was looked upon with suspicion.[13]

Christian love requires an openness to the Spirit's leading and, on all sides, a climate of mutuality.

This section began with the statement that glossolalia should not be overemphasized. Yet more space is given it than any of the other gifts. That seemed necessary since so much debate has centered upon it.

Prophecy

Just as the concept of priest is expanded from the Old Testament to the New, so the concept of prophet is broadened from the few to the many. St. Paul writes to Corinth, ". . . Earnestly desire the spiritual gifts, especially that you may prophesy" (1 Corinthians 14:1). St. Paul makes a sharper distinction between glossolalia and prophecy (*prophecy* is speaking rationally to others; *glossolalia* is speaking supra-rationally to God) than does Luke-Acts (compare Acts 2:4 and 17). In both writings, however, *prophecy* is obviously understood as speaking to other people.

Scholars are concerned with the difference just cited and also with the difference between St. Paul and St. John the Divine where the element of ecstasy is more prominent. As it is reflected in the New Testament generally, prophecy is authoritative proclamation of the will and purposes of God with appropriate exhortation to action on the part of the Christian community. (It is prophecy in this sense that is implied when speaking of the great prophetic tradition of the Bible.) It is authoritative because it is a gift of the Spirit; in terms of edification, St. Paul says it is the most important gift. The prophet is not generally a seer but a recipient and preacher of the Word. He is not possessed by God in such a way that he has no control and therefore becomes a mere mouthpiece; he is full of self-awareness. There is also, however, the picture of the prophet as ecstatic seer.

Formerly, among Pentecostalist groups prophecy in the sense of foretelling the future played an important role. It was seen as more than inspired utterance; it was the actual voice of the Spirit himself. Prophecy was *the speaking Spirit*. Where Pentecostalism has become more structured, spontaneous prophecy which is more than edification seems to retreat into the background. One finds only slight emphasis on prophecy in much of the literature in the charismatic movement.

Prophecy is obviously hazardous and the church always has the duty to test it against the clear testimony of the Scriptures. Gullible acceptance can lead to great difficulty. In St. Paul's congregations, just as the glossolalist had an interpreter, so the prophet had his examiners who assessed what he said (1 Corinthians 14:29). Prophecy requires the checks and norms operative within the Christian community. Special pastoral vigilance is required vis-a-vis a naive view of prophecy which has an almost magical belief that one's life in every detail is infallibly guided by the Holy Spirit. It is on this level that mischief or sometimes even tragedy most frequently occurs.

Healing

Charismatics believe that divine miracles still occur, and testify to miraculous healings in answer to prayer. Other Christians in the mainline churches are often either skeptical about miracles or deny them altogether. As one becomes aware of the "psychosomatic" dimensions of illness, however, one becomes at least more tolerant of accounts of spiritual healing. There are numerous accounts of healings at places such as Lourdes or by such charismatics as Oral Roberts. A combination of the personal magnetism of healers and the suggestive atmosphere of the gathered congregation can be explained psychologically, but they can also be seen as God's gift. That a phenomenon has a psychological explanation does not prevent it from being a gift of the Spirit. As with other charismata, everything depends upon how the gift of healing is used.

But prayer for healing can also be much less dramatic and not centered in the personality of a healer. Prayer for healing also need not be set against medical procedures. Healing services have been held in Lutheran churches for some time by people who have not identified with the charismatic movement at all. In recent decades pastors have given high priority to their ministry to those disabled by illness.

Healing as an emphasis of the charismatic movement is rooted in the conviction that salvation is for the whole man, and is related to the expectancy with which prayer is offered. When charismatics pray, they expect something to happen, also when the prayer is for healing. Surely that attitude can only be affirmed. Lutheran respondents testify to healings in response to their prayers.

What happens, however, when healing does not follow? Many Pentecostalists would say that the patient himself is the problem, that he hasn't enough faith. Many Lutheran charismatics as well as Lutherans in general reject such a view not only because of the untold despair it can foster, but also because of the concept of faith which is operative. Pentecostalist theology is always in danger of transforming faith into the greatest of human works, seeing it as a prerequisite for God's action. When prayers for healing result in no healing, the Christian can neither regard it as God's will that the person should not recover nor as the fault of a weak faith in the patient. The Christian can only bow in humility before a mystery not revealed and continue to pray and offer comfort. Jesus did not promise his followers a life free from suffering—quite the contrary!

Good pastoral care requires that people be shielded from the cruelty which can result when, having been led to think that a miracle will surely occur, nothing happens. Prayer of the community rather than the impassioned prayer of a healer is less of a problem along these lines. Pastoral concern requires that an emphasis on healing be free of any anti-medical bias. The capacity to heal medically must also be regarded as part of God's preserving care.

Worship

The characteristic form of the charismatic movement is the prayer meeting. Even where clergy are involved, the leader of the meeting can be a lay person. The content and form of these sessions varies and will likely reflect the backgrounds of most of the people. Usually, however, they consist of reading from the Bible, much prayer, perhaps singing in tongues, perhaps speaking in tongues, perhaps prophecy, perhaps healing. If someone is present who desires the "baptism in the Holy Spirit," people will pray over him and lay hands upon him in the expectation that the Spirit will respond. Where a number of charismatics are present in a congregation, the prayer meeting may consist only of people from one denomination. More often, however, the group contains a mixture of Pentecostalists and charismatics from mainline churches. One finds in this mixture an indication of the ecumenical thrust of the movement.

The prayer meeting can be divisive or it can enrich a congregation's life. Where the meetings exist harmoniously within the congregation, it is usually because of the involvement and guidance of the pastor who may or may not be a charismatic. A few LCA prayer groups have succeeded in blending charismatics and non-charismatics together. Lutherans influenced by the pietistic tradition should find groups for prayer and Bible study unremarkable.

Where there has been no effort to integrate the charismatics into parish life, they often exist on its edges—having, for all practical purposes, become Pentecostalists. But a few Lutheran situations indicate and the Catholic charismatic movement demonstrates dramatically that this need not happen.

Rather than turning their backs upon the traditional worship and the forms of Lutheran congregational life, charismatics often find new depth and significance in them. They testify that the liturgy and the celebration of the Lord's Supper have more meaning for them than ever before. Charismatics have much to offer the rest of the congregation in the sense of expectancy and joy with which they participate in liturgical worship. Our historic liturgy does not have to be used with the stiff formalism and lack of joy and humanity it often is. The spirit of celebration is in the words waiting to be released. Clothed in a ceremonial of color and movement and involvement, the liturgy can be exciting; allowed to be naturally flexible rather than narrowly rubricistic, it can accommodate spontaneity within its structure.

Social Concern

Adherents of the charismatic movement are often accused of having no social vision, of being concerned only with the quality of individual piety. Whether this is true of Pentecostalists is not for us to say, but a few observations are in order about charismatics in mainline churches.

The charismatic experience can be so overwhelming and so filled with joy that the period immediately following it may be compared with a honeymoon. One must have time to come to terms with the new experience and may be excused an overenthusiastic buttonholing of everyone in sight to share it. Charismatics must be helped to a more mature understanding of their experience which recognizes the implications of the life in the Spirit for serving others. The Holy Spirit is not given only for our enjoyment, but to make us more effective servants of those who need us. The church must hold that truth before the charismatics. The charismatics, on the other hand, by demonstrating the joy of the Spirit-life are a sign to the church to keep this power-for-others view from becoming a grim duty ethic.

Charismatics have reacted against what they have seen to be a concept of social action which had little time for prayer, worship, or biblical preaching. Their emphasis upon these basics is at the root of their call for renewal, and can be a witness within the church toward keeping its priorities in proper balance.

The orientation of charismatics to Christianity and the Scriptures prompts them to interpret responsibility toward others in individualistic terms. The social posture of mainline churches, however, is that because of the complexities of modern society Christians must go beyond person to person service to affect the social structures themselves. This stance has developed out of an ethical viewpoint informed by the clear thrust of biblical theology, though it cannot merely be proof-passaged from the New Testament.

Some charismatics reject this position outright. More often, however, they are sympathetic to it, questioning only whether Christians should respond to a social need just because it is there. Rather, they say, the community must be certain that the Spirit is leading them to deal with a specific situation. That leading will be related to the community's having the necessary gifts to be of service. The social posture of the charismatics, then, tends to be selective. While it is true that without the needed capability one can hardly serve, it is also true that the selective posture could easily become an excuse for noninvolvement. At this point, too, the ultimate test is what love requires.

The Christian community is to be a servant within the larger human community. That means that the Christian life is lived for others, not for one's own pleasure or gain. The gifts of the Spirit are given the *community* to enable its mission both by building up the Christian fellowship and by making its service more effective. All gifts used in this way, not just tongues and healing, are gifts of the Spirit. The church needs the "non-remarkable" as well as the "remarkable" gifts. It has been pointed out that a gift is "not a *what* but a *how*." [14] The lists of charismata in the New Testament are not inclusive lists. In fact, it is probable that gifts are needed by today's church which were unknown in Bible times or were irrelevant to the mission of the primitive church. Keeping the understanding of gifts related to the community context and the church's mission is an antidote for an undue emphasis upon one's own spirituality. It should also illumine the social implications of the church's mission.

Just as it must help the charismatics to deal with their experience on a level deeper than that of Pentecostalist exegesis and theology, so the Lutheran church must help to sharpen and deepen their vision of social concern. In return, the charismatics can spread some of their cheerful trust in God among Christians who may have become tired or cynical in their efforts at social reform.

Guidelines

On the basis of what has been discussed, some guidelines are offered the Lutheran Church in America for its relationship to the charismatic movement within its congregations:

1. Where it is authentic—that is, where it bears good fruit—the charismatic experience must be understood *within* the scope of the church's life. There is no cause for Lutheran pastors or people to suggest either explicitly or implicitly that one cannot be charismatic and remain a Lutheran in good standing.

2. The church on all levels should make every effort to help those who are charismatics understand the "baptism in the Holy Spirit" in a manner consonant with the Scriptures and traditional Lutheran theology (including the legitimacy of baptizing infants born within the Christian fellowship). Where this effort has not been made, many Lutherans and a few Lutheran congregations have, to all intents and purposes, become Pentecostalist.

3. As a renewal movement, the charismatic movement should be welcomed as a judgment against mechanical worship, non-biblical preaching, preoccupation with church structure and congregational success, lukewarm faith which expects nothing, compromise with the life-style of the world, etc., wherever these exist. Willingness to benefit from the movement does not require uncritical acceptance of its answers and remedies. Other groups and movements are also dealing with renewal; the charismatic movement does not have the only answer.

4. Congregations and pastors should endeavor to deal with the charismatic movement naturally and objectively, divesting themselves of stereotypes built through hearsay or experience with the more radical forms of Pentecostalism. The image of Pentecostalists which many mainline church people have is one of the greatest barriers to acceptance of the movement. Lutheran people need help to put such issues as "baptism in the Holy Spirit" in the context of the whole biblical witness so they can deal effectively with the questions of proof-passage quoting Pentecostalists. They need to become informed through study and mutual discussion with charismatics.

5. While the church should recognize the validity of charismatic piety, adherents of the charismatic movement must be helped to see that the form or style of their piety is one of several within the Christian community:

> The difference between a devout Christian who is not particularly drawn to the Charismatic spirituality on the one hand and a charismatic Christian on the other is a matter of focus. The charismatic Christian's focus is on fulness of life in the Spirit, the exercise of the gifts of the Spirit directed toward the proclamation that Jesus is Lord to the glory of the Father. The devout Christian who is not drawn to the charismatic spirituality in no way excludes those elements of the charismatic spirituality, but they are not where he focuses his spiritual attention. Further, his own personal sanctity may far exceed that of his charismatic brother.[15]

6. A distinction must be made between the renewal aspect of the charismatic movement *within* the church and the evangelistic outreach which charismatics share with all others in the church. Zeal for charismatic experience must not lead charismatics to regard fellow church members as proper objects of evangelization. Charismatics share the responsibility to proclaim the gospel to those outside the people of God.

7. Lutheran charismatics should resist any understanding of the Spirit's indwelling which deemphasizes or renders superfluous the proclamation of the Word, the sacraments, or the Christian fellowship. A narrow concept of the activity of the Holy Spirit is unacceptable and open to all Luther's criticism of the Enthusiasts. An individual's experience of the Holy Spirit is not immediate; the Spirit's work cannot be separated from the mission of Jesus of Nazareth. God works through means: the Word and sacraments. (It must be understood that this is a theological assertion, not a description of a given person's experience. In an experiential sequence the Spirit and the means of grace seem disconnected; the theological statement should not be understood as implying an immediate cause-immediate effect sequence.) To deny that is eventually to fly in the face of the incarnate Word, for the Holy Spirit is the Spirit of the incarnate Son. The teaching of the Spirit's sovereignty must not be separated from the teaching of the means of grace (see the Augsburg Confession 5 and 18). God, of course, cannot

be bound to our perceptions of him, but *we* are bound to his self-revelation in Jesus Christ, the incarnate Word.

8. As persons who have pledged to minister to the whole congregation, pastors should involve themselves in counseling with charismatics in their parishes and with prayer groups. Pastors should not accept all manifestations of what seem to be the Spirit's gifts uncritically, but neither should they be intolerant or judgmental vis-a-vis a form of piety they do not share. If pastors feel unable to deal adequately with the situation, especially at first, they should seek the counsel and help of a fellow pastor who is involved in the movement or who has had experience with it.

9. Pastors who are themselves part of the charismatic movement should not use their office to pressure their members into the movement, nor should they give preferential pastoral care to those members who are adherents. They are pastors of the whole congregation and must also respect the integrity of other styles of piety.

10. Since it is normal for charismatics to attend a prayer group, such groups could be established in Lutheran congregations, especially those with several charismatics. Prayer groups need not be exclusively for charismatics; they should be open to all members. A Lutheran prayer group better enables the pastor to offer guidance and support to charismatic members, and it allows natural interaction among charismatics and other members. In some instances several Lutheran congregations together might establish prayer groups.

11. The Lutheran Church in America should, through its synod presidents and district deans, give assistance to congregations and pastors caught in the tensions which usually arise when the charismatic movement first appears. It should be a network through which experience and information may be shared and counsel given.

12. The Lutheran Church in America should, through its various divisions and agencies, recognize the charismatic movement as a part of its life and provide educational materials and opportunities both for pastors and lay people to increase understanding of the movement and to help adherents toward a deeper and more authentic understanding of their experience.

13. Seminaries and programs of continuing education should assist pastors in gaining knowledge about the charismatic movement and developing skills in ministering to Lutherans who are adherents.

14. Theologians should be encouraged to undertake a sympathetic but critical study of the charismatic movement in general and many particular issues which cannot be covered in this kind of paper. In addition to the problem of interpreting the "baptism in the Holy Spirit," issues such as these should be addressed: the relationship between the periodic emergence of the charismatic phenomena and the cultural and/or ecclesial context; justification and sanctification in the light of the charismatic experience; baptism and the Holy Spirit; and so on.

Afterword

Church history is punctuated with accounts of individuals and groups who have testified to uncommon religious experiences. It also records that such people generally left the parish churches to become hermits or monastics, or to form sects. In their initial resistance to organizational structures, this has also been true of Pentecostalist groups from the turn of the century until now. What is different about the charismatic movement, as the noted historian Jaroslav Pelikan has pointed out, is the disposition of its adherents to remain in the established churches. It remains to be seen, he said, whether the attempt to blend charismatic piety with sacraments and ecclesial structures will be successful.

Certainly one element in that possible success is the attitude in which charismatics and others within the Lutheran Church in America deal with each other, and the climate created by pastors and church officials for that interaction. The charismatic movement has a contribution to make to the quality of the life of the LCA. The LCA has a rich tradition of knowledge and experience to contribute to the charismatic movement. Neither group has cause to be arrogant or exclusivist toward the other. As St. Paul taught the Corinthians, the hallmark of all authentic Christian behavior is the kind of love which is not arrogant, rude, imperious, irritable, resentful or gloating, but rather which is patient, kind, affirming—a love which bears all things believes all things, hopes all things, endures all things.

Notes

1. Larry Christenson, *A Message to the Charismatic Movement* (Minneapolis: Dimension Books, 1972), p. 66.
2. Kilian McDonnell, "Statement of the Theological Basis of the Catholic Charismatic Renewal," *Worship* 47 (1973), p. 617.
3. Stephen B. Clark, *Baptized in the Spirit* (Pecos, New Mexico: Dove, 1970), pp. 15-16.
4. Arnold Bittlinger, "Baptized in Water and in Spirit," *The Baptism in the Holy Spirit as an Ecumenical Problem* (Notre Dame: Charismatic Renewal Services, n.d.), p. 14.
5. McDonnell, "Statement," p. 610.
6. Frederick Dale Brunner, *A Theology of the Holy Spirit* (Grand Rapids: Eerdmans, 1970), p. 60.
7. McDonnell, "Statement," p. 616. On the commonness of tongues in New Testament times, see Krister Stendahl, "Glossolalia in the New Testament," *The Charismatic Movement, Confusion or Blessing,* ed. Michael Hamilton (Grand Rapids: Eerdmans, 1974).
8. Larry Christenson, *The Gift of Tongues* (Minneapolis: Bethany Fellowship, 1963), p. 16.
9. *Ibid.,* p. 11.
10. John P. Kildahl, *The Psychology of Speaking in Tongues* (New York: Harper & Row, 1972), p. 49.
11. *Glossolalia* (Microfilm, American Theological Library Association, 1963).
12. Kilian McDonnell, *Catholic Pentecostalism: Problems in Evaluation* (Pecos, New Mexico: Dove, 1970), p. 8.
13. Kildahl, p. 68.
14. Kilian McDonnell, *Baptism in the Holy Spirit as an Ecumenical Problem* (Notre Dame: Charismatic Renewal Services, n.d.), p. 50.
15. *Ibid.,* p. 48.

The Lutheran Church and the Charismatic Movement

Guidelines for Congregations and Pastors*

Preface

As the charismatic movement continues to grow, questions are arising regarding the validity of experiences being reported within the church today such as miracles of healing, speaking in tongues, exorcism, and prophecy. Members of the charismatic movement are convinced that the nine spiritual gifts referred to in 1 Corinthians 12 are present among Christians of the 20th century even as they were in apostolic times and that they are in fact being manifested among God's people in our times. Other Christians are equally certain that the extraordinary gifts such as tongues, divine healing, and prophecy were given by the Spirit to His church in apostolic times but that they have since disappeared from the church. They therefore doubt the validity of the experiences being claimed by charismatics today. Such differences of opinion have frequently caused tension to arise among Christians.

Charismatics hold that "baptism with the Holy Spirit" meets a need within the Christian church as well as in their own personal lives. Their primary objective is to produce a spiritual renewal within Christendom. Like many other Christians they are deeply concerned over conditions within the institutional church. They see a lack of commitment on the part of many who claim church membership. They sense

---

* This document was adopted by the Commission on Theology and Church Relations of The Lutheran Church—Missouri Synod in early 1977 and distributed to all of the Synod's pastors, teachers, and congregations. [Editor]

that many Christians do not find in their faith the joy, peace, and certainty which members of the apostolic church evidently experienced, that many Christians do not demonstrate the love for one another that they should, that in many congregations there is a lack of emphasis on the work of the Holy Spirit, and that church services are often too impersonal and formal.

While charismatics contend that "baptism with the Holy Spirit" is the cure for these ills within Christendom, it is apparent that some of the practices and theological tenets of this movement conflict with biblical doctrine, thereby causing divisions within various congregations. Perhaps the most serious doctrinal problem of this movement is its tendency to claim direct spiritual illumination apart from the Word, a malady that may have its origin in a loss of confidence in the divine efficacy of the bare Word. To counteract such a flight from the Word itself, confessional Lutheranism emphasizes that *solo verbo* (by the Word alone) is as basic to biblical and Lutheran theology as the great Reformation emphases on grace alone, faith alone, and Scripture alone. Anything that leads people away from the Word for the assurance of the Spirit's presence and power in their lives is a soul-destroying, satanic delusion.

> We should not and cannot pass judgment on the Holy Spirit's presence, operations, and gifts merely on the basis of our feeling, how and when we pereceive it in our hearts. On the contrary, because the Holy Spirit's activity often is hidden, and happens under cover of great weakness, we should be certain, because of and on the basis of his promise, that the Word which is heard and preached is an office and work of the Holy Spirit, whereby he assuredly is potent and active in our hearts (11 Cor. 2:14ff.). (FC SD II, 56)

Christian love suggests that the church must endeavor to give counsel and guidance to congregations and individuals in this area. It was in this spirit that the Commission on Theology and Church Relations released a report in 1972 bearing the title "The Charismatic Movement and Lutheran Theology." This document provided a detailed study of the relevant sections of the Scriptures. For the same reason and in the same spirit the Commission is now offering congregations a second document in which it will briefly restate the Synod's doctrinal stance with respect to the charismatic movement and offer pastoral guide-lines for ministering to the spiritual needs of those who are affected by the current tensions.

In this document we shall employ popular terminology and use it in the commonly accepted sense. Words such as "charismatic move-ment" or "charismatic renewal" will be used to refer to that religious movement which sprang up within many mainline churches in the 1960s and was characterized by the emphasis it placed on the experi-ence called "baptism with the Holy Spirit." Because its basic beliefs resembled those of Pentecostalism, it became known in some circles as neo-Pentecostalism. The movement within The Lutheran Church-Missouri Synod gradually and increasingly came to assume the name "charismatic" rather than "neo-Pentecostal."

In this document a person will be designated "a charismatic" pro-vided he has chosen to identify himself with the charismatic move-ment, shares in the experiences and socialization which characterize it, reads its literature, goes to its meetings, and becomes engaged with elements of the theology and life-style emerging from the movement.[1]

Abbreviations

All citations of the Lutheran Confessions are taken from *The Book of Concord*, ed. T. G. Tappert (Philadelphia: Fortress Press, 1959).

The following abbreviations have been used:

AC—Augsburg Confession
Ap—Apology of the Augsburg Confession
Ep—Epitome of the Formula of Concord
FC—Formula of Concord
LC—Large Catechism
SA—Smalcald Articles
SD—Solid Declaration of the Formula of Concord

Scriptural quotations are taken from the Revised Standard Version.

I. The Theological Basis

In view of present world conditions Christians welcome the greater emphasis that has been placed on the work of the Holy Spirit in recent years. They yearn for a spiritual renewal in the church, for less apathy in carrying on the Lord's work, and for greater zeal and commitment in proclaiming the Gospel of Jesus Christ to the nations. Christians in general are agreed that there is great need for a deeper appreciation of the work of the Spirit in the church today.

However, the Commission on Theology and Church Relations reiterates some of the concerns which it set forth in its first document.

A. *Spiritual Gifts Are Not to Be Considered Means of Grace*

The church will remember that the Holy Spirit and His gifts are offered only where God has promised them, in the Word and sacraments. The Scriptures and the Lutheran Confessions frequently emphasize that the Holy Spirit builds the church solely through the means of grace. Only through the witness of the Gospel and the sacraments does the believer come to faith, receive the assurance of God's love and forgiveness, witness to others, live in accord with God's will, and remain steadfast in the faith. Through the means of grace the Holy Spirit bestows on the church *all* the blessings that are ours in Christ as well as every spiritual gift that is needed to carry out the mission of the church in a sinful world. (Cf. Matt. 28:19; Luke 16:29; Rom. 10:17; 1 Cor. 11:26; AC V, 4; Ap XIII, 13; XXIV, 70; LC II, 52-59, 61-62)[2]

The church will accept with joy and gratitude any gift which the Spirit in His grace may choose to bestow on us for the purpose of edifying the body of Christ. It will recognize that the Lord does not forsake His church but promises the abiding presence of His Spirit. The church, therefore, will not reject out of hand the possibility that God may in His grace and wisdom endow some in Christendom with the same abilities and powers He gave His church in past centuries. It will take care lest it quench the Spirit by failing to expect or pray for God's presence and power in building His church. But it will also take seriously the admonition of the apostle to "test the spirits to see whether they are of God; for many false prophets have gone out into the world" (1 John 4:1; cf. also 1 Cor. 12:10). Above all, the church will not employ such gifts as though they were means of grace.[3]

In examining teachings and emphases of the various individuals and groups who espouse the charismatic movement, we find reason to express anxious concern. Our concern is, first of all, that the doctrines of Holy Scripture be taught in their purity. We note that such vital doctrines as justification by grace through faith, Baptism, the means of grace, and other major articles of the Christian faith are involved. Second, we are concerned for the spiritual welfare of those who are engaged in charismatic teaching and activity and for those who are under their spiritual care. The "concerns" expressed below indicate the doctrines which are at issue in the charismatic movement. They are directed toward a common concern for Scripture as the norm of Christian belief and practice. They do not intend to call into question the goodwill and sincerity of those who espouse one or more of the charismatic emphases. The issue is not personality or new kinds of worship forms, but the teachings of God's Word.

Lutherans are deeply concerned, therefore, when "baptism with the Holy Spirit" is considered to be a second experience beyond the sacrament of Baptism and when it is said to grant powers and blessings that are not given through the Word and sacraments. Such a view denies the full benefits of Baptism. Only Baptism, the Lord's Supper, and the use of God's Word are external means. By these alone the Holy Spirit has chosen to work among us in grace. Prayer, for example, is not a means of grace but a proper response to God's grace as offered in the sacrament of Baptism. Our Lutheran Confessions state that Baptism grants to the believer "the grace, Spirit, and power to suppress the old man so that the new may come forth and grow strong." (LC IV, 76) [4]

Lutherans are also concerned when speaking in tongues is described as a spiritual gift which imparts to the one using it a keener realization of his sins, a deeper and more constant awareness of the Spirit's indwelling presence, a stronger faith, the ability to pray at a deeper level, an awakened interest and a deeper hunger to study the Bible, and a new freedom to witness to others what Jesus means to him. Such a view raises the experience of speaking in tongues to the level of a means of grace and attributes to it functions which can be performed only by the Gospel and the sacraments.

We are deeply concerned also when the experience of "baptism with the Holy Spirit" is treated as a means by which God equips the church for its mission in the world, particularly when the "baptism with the Spirit" is regarded (in practice, if not in theory) as a supplement to the means of grace. Beyond the Word and the sacraments nothing is needed to equip the church for its task, for through them the Spirit gives life, power, and growth to the church. Christians will therefore continue to seek power and renewal for the church in the Word and sacraments, not in special signs and miracles.[5]

B. *God Has Not Promised to Reveal His Will to Us Directly and Immediately (Without Means), as for Example Through Visions and Dreams*

God has revealed His will directly and immediately to the prophets, the apostles, and other holy men of God, and through them He has made His will known also to us. However, the Lutheran Confessions describe as "enthusiasm" the view that God reveals Himself and bestows His spiritual gifts to us apart from the objective and external Word and sacraments. Luther warns in the Smalcald Articles:

> In short, enthusiasm clings to Adam and his descendants from the beginning to the end of the world. It is a poison implanted and inoculated in man by the old dragon, and it is the source, strength, and power of all heresy, including that of the papacy and Mohammedanism. Accordingly, we should and must constantly maintain that God will not deal with us except through the external Word and sacrament. Whatever is attributed to the Spirit apart from such Word and sacrament is of the devil. (SA III, viii, 9-10)

The Biblical teaching of the external Word as the instrument of the Holy Spirit, emphasized in our Lutheran heritage, rejects the subjectivism that seeks divine comfort and strength through "a personal experience" instead of in the objective word of the Gospel. To make the former rather than the latter the basis of Christian certainty leads either to pride or despair instead of humble trust in the Gospel promises.[6] (AC V; FC Ep II, 13)

Since Scripture nowhere promises that God reveals His will to us as He did to the apostles and prophets, directly and immediately or through visions and dreams, Christians are urged to learn and respond to God's will by means of a diligent study of the Holy Scriptures and a proper use of the sacraments.

C. *Special Signs and Wonders Are Not Indispensable Guarantees That the Spirit of God Dwells Within an Individual*

To be sure, Scripture relates numerous examples of miraculous healings in both the Old and New Testaments. It is clear from the Gospels that healing the sick was an important and integral part of the ministry of Jesus; and when the Savior sent forth His 12 apostles into the cities of Galilee, He gave them specific instructions that they were "to preach the kingdom of God and to heal" (Luke 9:2). Soon thereafter when He appointed 70 others and sent them ahead of Him, He told them also to "heal the sick . . . and say to them, 'The kingdom of God has come near to you'" (Luke 10:8-9). According to the Book of Acts the miracles of healing in the early church continued at least for a time after the Savior's ascension into heaven.[7]

God can choose to perform such mighty works in and through His church today. Lutherans affirm the supernatural and the possibility that God can and does intervene in the course of natural things. However, Scripture warns repeatedly against the type of miracle-mindedness which places undue emphasis on the performance of supernatural deeds rather than on the proclamation of the Gospel: "Jesus therefore said to him, 'Unless you see signs and wonders you will not believe'" (John 4:48). Jesus warns the church against being deceived by signs and wonders which will appear in the last days to lead Christians astray: "For false Christs and false prophets will arise and show great signs and wonders, so as to lead astray, if possible, even the elect" (Matt. 24:24). Scripture warns the world against demanding miracles from the church to prove its faith: "'An evil and adulterous generation seeks for a sign, but no sign shall be given to it except the sign of Jonah.' So he left them and departed" (Matt. 16:4). The Bible states that even such signs as casting out devils, prophesying, and other mighty works, though they be done in Jesus' name, do not in themselves guarantee that they are God-pleasing: "Not everyone who says to me, 'Lord, Lord,' shall enter the kingdom of heaven, but he who does the will of my Father who is in heaven. On that day many will say to me, 'Lord, Lord, did we not prophesy in your name, and cast out demons in your name, and do many mighty works in your name?' And then will I declare to them, 'I never knew you; depart from me, you evildoers'" (Matt. 7:21-23). Luke reports: "The seventy returned with joy saying, 'Lord, even the demons are subject to us in your name!' And he said to them, 'I saw Satan fall like lightning from heaven. Behold, I have given you authority to tread upon serpents and scorpions, and over all the power of the enemy; and nothing shall hurt you. Nevertheless do not rejoice in this, that the spirits are subject to you; but rejoice that your names are written in heaven.'" (Luke 10:17-20) [8]

D. Faith in Christ Does Not Necessarily Eliminate Illness and Affliction from the Life of a Christian

Lutherans believe that illness, pain, affliction, and death have come into the world as a result of man's fall into sin. We believe also that Christ has redeemed us from our sickness: "This was to fulfil what was spoken by the prophet Isaiah, 'He took our infirmities and bore our diseases'" (Matt. 8:17). However, this does not mean that God has removed sickness from the life of the child of God and that, if he has sufficient faith, he can be free of an illness by the power of the Spirit. Nor does it imply that sickness is an unmixed evil and a sign of a weak faith (Heb. 12; 2 Cor. 12:7). Afflictions are often works of God which are intended for our good. Therefore, while Christians pray for healing in the full confidence that their prayers are heard and answered and while they earnestly hope for recovery, they nevertheless submit patiently to the will of God since they know that all things work together for good to them that love God. The Christian does not expect to manipulate or control God, even with his prayers. He would hesitate to have in his own hands the power of life and death. In both joy and sorrow the Christian knows that God does not abdicate. The child of God therefore prays confidently and persistently but with the provision "Lord, if it is Thy will." [9]

E. Christian Certainty Is Not Based on "Feeling" But on the Objective Promises of the Gospel

While Lutherans appreciate and fully value the importance of spiritual experience, the Lutheran Confessions always point us to the objective promise of the Gospel as the unfailing basis of hope and certainty both in this life and in the life to come. As Dr. Francis Pieper has written: ". . . saving faith is always faith in the Word of Christ, faith in the external Word of the Gospel, which Christ commanded His Church to preach and to teach (Mark 16:15-16; Rom. 1:1-2). This external Word is both the object of faith ('Believe the Gospel,' Mark 1:15) and the means by which faith is created ('Faith cometh by hearing.' Rom. 10:17). A belief whose object is not the Word of Christ as we have it in the Word of His Apostles (John 17:20) . . . is according to the Scriptures a delusion, ignorance, and a human fabrication (1 Tim. 6:3-4; 1 Cor. 2:1-5: 'faith in the wisdom of men')." Dr. Pieper continues: "The modern theologians . . . substitute . . . 'the Person of Christ,' 'the living Christ,' etc . . . But he who bypasses Christ's words also misses the 'living Christ' " [10]

F. *"Baptism with the Spirit" Is Not a Basis for Church Fellowship*

Lutherans believe that Christians should pray earnestly for and work diligently toward a God-pleasing harmony among Christian churches. The Confessions frequently demonstrate this attitude (Ap Preface, 19, 16; FC Ep XI, 22; AC Preface, 10; FC SD XI, 96). However, the Lutheran Confessions do not countenance a view which would find a basis for church fellowship in a common experience of "baptism with the Holy Spirit." Before practicing altar and pulpit fellowship The Lutheran Church-Missouri Synod seeks agreement in the doctrine of the Gospel, in all its articles, and in the right use of the sacraments. Unionistic worship with those who deny doctrines of the Holy Scriptures dishonors the Holy Spirit and fails to give proper witness to the erring brother.[11]

G. *The Gift of the Holy Spirit Does Not Necessarily Include Extraordinary Spiritual Gifts*

While Lutherans rejoice in the gracious promise that the gift of the Holy Spirit will be given to all generations of believers (Acts 2:39), neither the Scriptures nor the Lutheran Confessions support the view that this gift of the Spirit necessarily includes such extraordinary spiritual gifts as tongues, miracles, miraculous healings, and prophecy (1 Cor. 12). According to the pattern revealed in the Bible, God does not necessarily give His church in all ages the same special gifts. He bestows His blessings according to His good pleasure. (1 Cor. 12:11)

Summary and Conclusion

When someone who is troubled because of his sins is told that he can find certainty and rest for his troubled conscience in some inner experience such as "baptism with the Spirit," he is directed away from

Christ to his own inner spiritual estate. Such teaching directs the troubled sinner to his own experience as the basis for his certainty and the joy of his salvation and places him once again under the bondage of the Law. This leads either to a self-righteous confidence in one's own inner experience or to spiritual despair for the person who has had no such experience. Confidence in human experience is carnal security, not the inner testimony of the Holy Spirit, who always directs us to Jesus Christ and God's promise in the preaching (teaching) of the Gospel, Holy Baptism, Holy Absolution, and Holy Communion.

The Gospel is the gracious promise of the remission of sins for the sake of Jesus Christ. The forgiveness of sins is apprehended by faith in the promise, and only by faith. The teaching that an inner experience such as "baptism with the Spirit" is a part of the Gospel promise and that without the promise of such an experience we do not have the "full Gospel" adds human works to the Gospel and stands under the apostolic curse: "But even if we, or an angel from heaven, should preach to you a gospel contrary to that which we preached to you, let him be accursed." (Gal. 1:8)

It is important that Christian people be warned against doctrine or teaching which is presented as the Word and will of God, when in fact the Sacred Scriptures do not clearly teach such doctrine. The Holy Scriptures forbid the teaching of pious personal opinions and private interpretation of Scripture as God's Word and will: "Behold, I am against the prophets, says the Lord, who use their tongues and say, 'Says the Lord.'" (Jer. 23:31; cf. also 2 Peter 1:20)

In order to provide guidance in determining whether or not doctrine and teaching in this matter is in accordance with the Sacred Scriptures, we offer the following summary of the biblical doctrine.

The Holy Scriptures Teach:

1. That we are justified alone by the atoning work of Jesus Christ.
2. That the forgiveness of our sins on account of Christ, promised and offered in the Gospel, is our righteousness before God.
3. That it is by faith alone that we accept God's promised offer of forgiveness and are justified.
4. That the faith by which we accept God's forgiveness on account of

Christ is the work of God's Spirit through the external means of grace, namely, the preaching (teaching) of the Gospel, Holy Baptism, Holy Absolution, and the Lord's Supper. Through these external means the Holy Spirit works faith in the heart when and where it pleases God. Through these external means of grace the Holy Spirit, together with all that is necessary for life and salvation, is given to those who believe.

5. That faith, which is the work of God's Spirit, is the confident assurance that for Christ's sake we are forgiven and accepted by God as righteous. Through this confident faith in the promise of God the accusing voice of conscience is quieted and the troubled heart finds rest.

It is Contrary to the Holy Scriptures, and Therefore Dangerous to the Salvation of Men, to Teach:

1. That God desires every Christian, following Baptism, to have a "second experience" such as the "baptism with the Spirit."
2. That the so-called "gifts of the Spirit" are external signs by which we can assure ourselves that we have faith, are living in God's grace, or have the Spirit of God.
3. That God promises every Christian such gifts as speaking in tongues, healing, discerning of spirits, and prophesy and that God has given such a promise as a part of the "full" or "complete Gospel."
4. That a "conversion experience," "baptism with the Spirit," or other inner religious experience is necessary for, or should be urged upon, Christians in order that they may be certain either of having faith and salvation or of the indwelling of God's Spirit.
5. That a Christian who has not had such an experience either has an incomplete faith, is unconverted and is still living under the rule of sin, or has only accepted Christ as his Savior but not as his Lord.
6. That the sanctification of a Christian is incomplete unless he possesses the gift of speaking in tongues.
7. That God promises healing and health to every Christian in this life and that, if such healing does not occur, it is due to a lack of faith.
8. That God gives guidance and leadership to the church today through visions and dreams or direct prophecy.

II. Guidelines for Congregations and Pastors

A. *Some Suggestions for Pastors Who Are Concerned About the Charismatic Movement in the Lutheran Church*

1. Study the spiritual needs of your congregation. Emphasize that it is the Holy Spirit who both brings us to faith and also gives us the joy, the assurance, the peace, and the love for one another which are marks of the believer. In addition, the Holy Spirit often strengthens God's children by leading them through great struggle and anguish, as He did with Jacob, Job, and Paul. The Spirit bestows these blessings upon us only through the means of grace. Neither tongues, nor miracles of healing, nor any of the other charismatic gifts referred to in 1 Corinthians 12 were given for the purpose of making God more real to man, to assure him of God's love, to give power for witnessing, or to bring about a renewal in the church. These were all *signs* that Christ had sent His Spirit.

2. Place more emphasis on the benefits of Baptism. Pastors should constantly remind their congregations that Baptism as Gospel is a means of grace which, as a covenant between God and His children, conveys great blessings not only in our childhood but throughout our life.

The Sacrament of Baptism not only grants us the forgiveness of sins throughout our life, but it also assures us of God's presence and His love. It produces in us the fruit of the Spirit: "love, joy, peace, patience, kindness, goodness, faithfulness, gentleness, self-control" (Gal. 5:22-23). Paul calls these the gifts of the Spirit in Romans 12:6-8. Baptism gives Christians the desire and the strength to live as children of God.

In short Baptism grants to us the Holy Spirit with His gifts. Therefore, we Lutherans believe that we have no need of praying for a special "baptism with the Spirit."

3. Emphasize the Lord's Supper and its blessings. Pastors should repeatedly emphasize in their congregations that Holy Communion as Gospel grants to the Christian the spiritual blessings which not only charismatics but all Christians are seeking: the guarantee of God's presence, the assurance of His grace and love, the power to live as children of God, love and appreciation for His Word, and power to witness to Christ.

4. In order to bring these important facts to the attention of the people committed to their care, pastors should study with their congregations the work of the Holy Spirit as described in such books of the Bible as the Gospel of John, the Epistle to the Romans, the Epistle to the Galatians, and the Epistle to the Ephesians. Pentecostal literature operates with Pentecostal presuppositions. It appeals to the spectacular. It often gives the impression that growth in the church is produced by the signs of the Spirit, such as divine healing and speaking in tongues.

5. Encourage members of the congregation to exercise more fully their right and responsibility to participate in the spiritual work of the church. Emphasize evangelism. In this connection it may be helpful to recall that God-pleasing opportunities for ministry include not only such activities as mutual exhortation and instruction but also service to one's neighbor by way of sick-visitations, calling on senior citizens, and helping out in homes where there may be illness. All of these are included in the list of charismatic gifts found in Romans 12:6-8. Encourage the laity to take a more meaningful part in the program of the church. They are asking for increased opportunities to serve their Savior with the gifts God has given them.

6. Look again at the orders of worship. Within the rich liturgical tradition of Lutheranism there are ways to insure warmth and fellowship in worship.

However, changes should not be thrust upon a church. Changes that occur too rapidly often offend. Moreover, other opportunities for fellowship may be provided.

7. In offering guidance proceed in a positive, evangelical manner. Christian admonition and discipline are to be administered in such a way as not to give the impression that the church is persecuting the charismatics. Statistics indicate that such an attitude frequently tends to drive charismatics into the Pentecostal churches.

B. Some Suggestions for Ministering to Pastors Who Are Charismatics

Pastors are key figures either in leading a congregation into the charismatic movement or in teaching the doctrine of the Holy Spirit as believed in our church on the basis of the Scriptures and the Lutheran Confessions. How then shall we minister evangelically to pastors involved in the charismatic movement?

1. Do not make the mistake of classifying all charismatics in the same category. There are many differences among them.

2. In conversations with charistmatics discuss the basic issues. (See Section I of this document.)

3. Do not treat charismatics as emotionally unstable or religious fanatics. If one reads the testimonials of many charismatics, it becomes apparent that some become interested in the movement because of concerns over such things as indifference in the church, lack of assurance regarding their own salvation, inability to sense the nearness of God in times of crisis, a sense of personal failure, illness, and drugs. Frequently they are deeply troubled by problems in their personal lives, problems in Synod, and problems in their family.

4. Therefore, in dealing with a charismatic, whether pastor or layman, try to discover his needs.

5. Apply Law and Gospel properly. If one needs assurance of his acceptance by God or of his value in the eyes of his Savior, he needs to be reminded that looking to such extraordinary gifts as speaking in tongues and healing as signs of assurance tends to erode the only saving faith there is, namely, that all people have already been fully accepted in God's grace by the crucifixion and resurrection of Jesus Christ. These special signs were not given for purposes of validating faith but in the interest of serving others in their need. The Gospel also gives us the power we need to live a life of commitment to the Savior. We need no other power either to build the church or to give purpose to our lives.

6. Advise strongly that the charismatic pastor read Lutheran commentaries as he studies the Scriptures and that he examine the Lutheran Confessions. A steady diet of Pentecostal literature frequently turns Lutherans into Pentecostals.

7. Lutheran pastors who are involved in the charismatic movement should be allowed time to wrestle with their consciences and think the matter through with prayer and the study of Holy Scripture. They should be encouraged to bring their concerns to their brethren at pastoral conferences. Such discussions can be mutually beneficial.

8. Pastors who propagate neo-Pentecostal doctrine in Lutheran congregations often divide the church and thereby give offense to their flocks. Therefore, they must take seriously the possibility of coming under church discipline.

9. Pastors should be shown the danger in practicing fellowship with other charismatics who do not share their views especially regarding the Gospel and the sacraments.

C. Suggestions to Pastors Who Are Sympathetic Toward the Charismatic Movement

1. Discuss with Lutheran brethren your views concerning the charismatic movement.

2. Take seriously the concerns expressed by your brethren. Keep an open mind. It is not without significance that leading theologians in all three major Lutheran bodies have expressed deep concern over the non-Lutheran direction in which the charismatic movement is going.

3. Consider carefully and seriously how the Pentecostal doctrine of "baptism with the Spirit" reduces the significance of the sacrament of Holy Baptism within the charismatic movement. Look carefully at the meaning which Baptism and the Lord's Supper have in Pentecostal churches.

4. Remember that the Lutheran Confessions warn against all forms of subjectivism which imply that the Holy Spirit deals directly with a person apart from Word and sacraments.

5. Read prayerfully and with an open mind what Lutheran commentaries have to say regarding passages such as Mark 16:17-20; Acts 2:1-14, 37-39; Acts 8:14-17; Acts 10:44-48; Acts 11:1-18; Acts 19:1-6; 1 Corinthians 12-14. Pentecostal literature approaches these passages with Pentecostal presuppositions. Also read carefully the Lutheran Confessions and note how they stress the centrality of the Gospel.

6. Give serious consideration to the fact that spectacular signs such as tongues, divine healing, and prophecy (in the neo-Pentecostal sense) may actually tend to draw attention away from the Gospel of forgiveness and center it instead on physical healings, on unintelligible language, or on foretelling future events in one's life.

7. Consider seriously the error of placing too much emphasis on signs and miracles. Jesus warns against asking for signs and relying on them for one's faith. (Cf. Matt. 7:21-23; 24:24; Mark 13:22; Luke 10:17-20; John 4:48).

8. Consider the seriousness of disturbing a congregation with doctrine contrary to that which the church confesses on the basis of the

Scriptures and the Lutheran Confessions or by unduly appealing to personal experience and pious opinion.

9. Try to realize the formative influence which Pentecostals and other non-Lutheran leaders (e.g., Dennis Bennett, Edward O'Connor, David DuPlessis) are having on Lutherans in the charismatic movement.

10. Avoid an attitude of spiritual superiority which makes the members of your congregation who are not charismatic feel they are inferior Christians.

11. Keep the Lutheran emphasis on the centrality of the doctrine of justification by grace through faith. This not only implies preaching that Jesus died for the sins of the world, but it also includes the emphasis that the Holy Spirit builds the church through the means of grace rather than through signs and miracles.

A Concluding Word

The Lutheran Church has a rich heritage of Spirit theology in its confessional writings, in its exegetical studies, and in its hymns and prayers. As the church seeks to fulfill its mission in the world, we are grateful to God for the renewed interest which many Christians in all generations take in the work of the Holy Spirit. May this same Spirit lead us into all truth as he has promised.

May we continue to implore our gracious Lord for an ever-increasing measure of His Holy Spirit. May we confidently trust that He will breathe new life into his church everywhere, calling sinners to repentance, creating in them through the Word a saving knowledge of the Lord Jesus Christ, working in them the desire and the strength to serve their Savior in newness of life, and sustaining them in this faith as we and all Christians everywhere wait for the coming of our Lord Jesus Christ. Through him we have spiritual life and strength, assurance and hope, for the Savior has promised: "I will pray the Father, and he will give you another Counselor, to be with you for ever." (John 14:16)

Notes

1. Larry Christenson, "A Theological and Pastoral Perspective on the Charismatic Renewal in the Lutheran Church," unpublished essay presented to the LCUSA Conference on the Holy Spirit at Dubuque, Iowa, 1976, p. 3.
2. "The Charismatic Movement and Lutheran Theology," A Report of the Commission on Theology and Church Relations of The Lutheran Church—Missouri Synod, 1972, p. 29. In 1969 The Lutheran Church—Missouri Synod was so deeply concerned about the tension and division that had arisen in certain areas of the church over such neo-Pentecostal practices as speaking in tongues, miraculous healings, prophecy, and the claimed possession of a special "baptism with the Holy Spirit" that it directed its Commission on Theology and Church Relations "to make a comprehensive study of the charismatic movement with special emphasis on its exegetical aspects and theological implications." After much study and consultation the Commission on Theology and Church Relations published its report in 1972 under the title "The Charismatic Movement and Lutheran Theology." Specific references to this report have been noted in this document, and readers will continue to find a study of this earlier report helpful. Since this booklet was not intended to provide detailed guidelines for dealing with pastors and laymen sympathetic to the charismatic movement, a supplementary report is now being offered to the members of Synod.
3. *Ibid.*, p. 25.
4. *Ibid.*, p. 29.
5. *Ibid.*
6. *Ibid.*
7. *Ibid.*, p. 31.
8. *Ibid.*
9. *Ibid.*, p. 32.
10. Francis Pieper, *Christian Dogmatics*, I, trans. W. F. Albrecht and others (St. Louis: Concordia Publishing House, 1951), p. 84.
11. "The Charismatic Movement and Lutheran Theology," p. 30.

Bibliography

1. "The Charismatic Movement and Lutheran Theology," a Report of the Commission on Theology and Church Relations of The Lutheran Church–Missouri Synod, 1972.

2. "Church Studies on the Holy Spirit," documents from the Presbyterian Church in the U.S., United Presbyterian Church in the U.S.A., Church of Scotland, and Presbyterian Church in Canada (Atlanta: Council on Theology and Culture, 1978).

3. "Glossolalia in the New Testament," by Lowell J. Satre, "Report of the Committee on Spiritual Gifts," and "Statement with Regard to Speaking in Tongues," in *Reports and Actions of the Second General Convention of The American Lutheran Church*, 1964, pp. 132-133, 148-164.

4. *Theological and Pastoral Orientations on the Catholic Charismatic Renewal*, prepared at Malines, Belgium, May 21-26, 1974. Available from the Communication Center, Notre Dame, Indiana.

Additional documents from within various churches